Philip Godsal, aged fifty-five, from a miniature by the actor and artist
Alexander Pope

COACHMAKER

The Life and Times of Philip Godsal
1747-1826

JOHN FORD

Quiller Press

First published in the UK in 2005
by Quiller Press, an imprint of Quiller Publishing Ltd

British Library Cataloguing-in-Publication Data
   A catalogue record for this book
   is available from the British Library

ISBN 1 904057 79 9

Printed in China

Quiller Press
An imprint of Quiller Publishing Ltd
Wykey House, Wykey, Shrewsbury, SY4 1JA
Tel: 01939 261616 Fax: 01939 261606
E-mail: info@quillerbooks.com
Website: www.swanhillbooks.com

Contents

Acknowledgements

Philip Godsal of Iscoyd Park commissioned the research into his family archives which forms the basis for this book. To him therefore I owe the most immediate debt, but much beyond that I am indebted to him for sharing his comprehensive knowledge of his family's history, his faithful curatorship of the collections of his ancestor the coachmaker and his encouragement and enthusiasm. His constructive suggestions on changes and additions to early drafts of the text have been of the greatest help. I would also like to record my thanks to him and his wife, Selina, for the warm and generous hospitality I have enjoyed at Iscoyd .

I am grateful also to other members of the family, to Alan Godsal and to the late Ian Buchanan, whose mother was a Godsal, and who was himself the historian of the Colleton branch of the family. Ian gave me his friendship and support from the beginning of the project and his son, Hugh Buchanan, the celebrated artist, has very generously designed the delightful book jacket.

Much of the research was carried out in the Flintshire County Record Office in Hawarden, and to Elizabeth Pettitt, the Archivist, I give my warmest thanks for her guidance, knowledge, interest and informed assistance over a period of three years. Her colleagues have been equally friendly and helpful.

I owe much to Rudolph Wackernagel of Munich for the stimulus of our many e-mail conversations and for sharing with me his unrivalled knowledge of English eighteenth century carriages and furniture design. I have also benefited greatly from my conversations with Tom Ryder, one of the great figures in the modern carriage driving world, and feel honoured by his friendship and hospitality. Mrs Clare Lloyd Jacob too has been generous in sharing with me her wide researches in eighteenth century newspapers.

My friends Peter Dale, James Sandwith, Steven Blake, Bill Walker and Keith Pettit have been particularly kind and generous in their help and I would also like to thank Chris Nicholson, carriage maker and advisor to the National Trust, and Lucy Wood of the Victoria and Albert Museum. I am especially grateful to Lord Egremont for permission to quote from the Petworth House Archives.

John Minoprio proved to be not only a skilful and creative photographer but also a delightful companion and Glyn Griffin a gifted and patient designer. I thank them warmly.

My wife Jill Ford has prepared the splendid comprehensive index and, as always, has made invaluable suggestions for improvements in the text. It is with love that I put on record my deepest gratitude.

Illustrations

I am most grateful to the following institutions for permission to publish illustrations of items in their collections

Bibliothèque Nationale, Paris, page 29 [1 & 2]
Cheltenham Art Gallery & Museum, Pages 180, 181, 184
Flintshire County Record Office. Hawarden, pages 8, 19, 23, 43, 95, 129, 130, 161
Fritz Lugt Collection, Paris, page 52
Huntington Library. Art Collections and Botanical Collections, San Marino, pages 17, 59, 107
The Lady Lever Art Gallery, page 50
National Museum of Ireland. Dublin. pages 45, 46 [2], 47
National Portrait Gallery, London pages 46 [1], 62, 114
The Winterthur Library: Joseph Downs Collection of Manuscripts and Printed Ephemera page 38

Other illustrations are from the author's collection and from those of private collectors to whom the author owes a very great debt of gratitude.

Currency Equivalents

One of the most striking and interesting aspects of the Godsal archive is that it provides a uniquely detailed record of the expenses of domestic and social life in the period 1789 to 1826 and the reader of this book is provided with many such fascinating details.

Except in the case of assessing Philip Godsal's **relative** wealth, the temptation has been resisted to offer the reader from time to time in the text an equivalent present day value.

To calculate **relative wealth** it seems to me that the most useful formula is that of Professor Bill Rubinstein of the University of Wales in which he compares the Gross National Product (G.N.P.) or Net National Income (N.N.I.) between the years 1800 and 2000 and divides by the relative populations. This calculation gives a figure of £21.40 per head for 1800 (£300 million divided by 14 million) and £8,016 per head for 2000 (£465 billion divided by 58 million). The relative wealth between the two eras therefore calculates as to-day being 375 times greater. An annual income of £7,000 (which Philip Godsal was enjoying) would therefore equal an annual income to-day of just over £2½ million.

For **equivalent values** Robert Twigger of the Economic Policy and Statistics Section of the House of Commons Library suggests a multiplier of fifty-five times. This is based upon an average price index (in this case between the years 1820–1830) divided into the 1998 figure. This gives the sum of £55.35 as representing roughly the purchasing power of £1 in the earlier period.

Both these formulas are helpful but it must also be noted that most of the factors influencing costs of living have risen at different rates. For example, between the years 1800 and 2000 property and wages have risen disproportionately more than most standard items of food and drink. Many salaries and wages to-day are over 200 times higher than their equivalents in 1800; housing in London has increased by at least 300 times yet the cost of a return ticket by diesel coach from London to Cheltenham has increased by only some four times against the stage coach fare of 1800. It will become evident to the reader that some things were cheap in 1800 and others were expensive.

It may be the most helpful way for the reader who wishes to get an idea of the relative cost of living in 1800 to remember the average unskilled/semi-skilled labourer (the majority of the population) rarely earned more than £1 a week (and that there were of course twenty shillings in the pound and 240 pennies). If this simple figure of a £1 weekly wage is compared to prices recorded in Philip Godsal's papers it may help the reader put prices into context.

Some of the thirty-seven volumes of Philip Godsal's diaries

Introduction

The personal papers of the coachmaker Philip Godsal (1747–1826) have been preserved in a remarkable archive which includes a Diary which he maintained for thirty-seven years with every item of his personal expenditure. The papers also contain his Memorandum Books, Bank Accounts, Property Registers and Leases, Investment Portfolio, business and private letters and coachmaking and domestic bills.[1]

Previously unpublished, they allow the first extensive modern study of the 'mystery' of coachmaking, and they provide an intimate portrait of a man and his business, his family and friends and the world in which they lived. His circle of acquaintances ranged from the Prince of Wales, to whose Masonic lodge he belonged, the Prime Minister, William Pitt who was his customer, the actress Mrs Abington, from whom he bought a house, his friend from boyhood, Jonathan Buttall, Gainsborough's 'Blue Boy', to Henry Fauntleroy, whom he sponsored as a freemason and who was hanged for forgery.

In December 1818 Philip Godsal faced the terrifying prospect of an operation (there were as yet no anaesthetics) for the removal of a stone in his bladder. At the age of seventy-one he did not expect to survive, and he prepared a detailed summary of his assets for the information of his executors.[2] In the event the operation was successful.

The summary showed the capital value of his assets to be £98,130, and he also listed the settlements he had made on his three children in the past fifteen years amounting to a further £51,442. In 1818 the Net National Income was a mere £300 million of which Godsal's aggregated wealth represented .05 per cent. This percentage of today's Gross National Product would equate his wealth at an astonishing £430 million. An analysis of the estates probated in 1818 indicate that he was probably amongst the richest thousand men in a population of fourteen million.[3]

The son of a coachmaker, Philip Godsal was educated at the Soho Academy before succeeding his widowed mother in the running of the family business in Long Acre at the age of twenty-one in 1768. It was a time of political instability. There were no fewer than eight government administrations in the next thirteen years. The very year in which he took over was marked by serious rioting and deaths in London when the government imprisoned the outlawed John Wilkes who had been elected as M.P. for Middlesex. High food prices caused civil riots throughout the country. The expensive Revolutionary war with America followed, to be succeeded in its turn by the even more costly French wars beginning in 1793. For some years either side of 1800 England was in danger of invasion (Philip Godsal joined a Volunteer Regiment formed to fight the invaders) and continental trade was closed down. The French wars had still not ended when Godsal retired in 1810 after forty-two years as a Master Coachmaker.

Despite political uncertainties these years had witnessed unprecedented economic growth. The great factories of the Industrial Revolution made England manufacturer to the world. The imagination and demands of the new merchant princes, of Arkwright, Boulton, Crawshay, Wedgwood and their like, drove improvements in technology based on scientific enquiry. A new, if imperfect, system of lending money was gradually put in place to advance capital to new commercial developments. Philip Godsal was both borrower and lender. Transportation was transformed by the building of canals and the dramatic improvement of the principal trunk roads by the turnpike trusts, itself part cause and effect of improvements in the trade of coachmaking.

The political and social influence of the old landed aristocracy did not diminish, but they now shared their spending power with a greater proportion of their fellow countrymen whose new money did not derive from land. There were still many 'have-nots' but there were a great many more 'haves', and for the first time, shops and shopping for items other than basic necessities, became a national pre-occupation.

The same period had seen a flowering in the arts. The influential Royal Academy, whose Annual Exhibitions Philip Godsal was to attend, received its charter in 1768, the same year that he took over the family business. The London theatre flourished and Godsal invested in both the Theatres Royal of Drury Lane and Covent Garden. The genius of the

Adam brothers, of Nash and Soane, of Sheraton and Hepplewhite, of Josiah Wedgwood and the taste of the Prince of Wales, later Regent and then King, influenced design and production. England at last had the will and confidence, spurred on by necessity, to challenge the dominance of France and the continent in the decorative arts, in furniture making, in the manufacture of china, and not least, in carriage making.

This was the England of the years 1768 to 1810 in which Philip Godsal built up his business to become one of the triumvirate of carriage manufacturers who supplied the fashionable world with the essential and practical means of transportation, and also the most visible and expensive of fashion accessories. He had also become the most discreet of bankers, advancing money to the aristocracy and gentry for the development of their estates and the payment of their debts.

Godsal's customers included William Beckford and Beckford's former catamite, Viscount 'Kitty' Courtenay; the Prime Minister William Pitt and his brother, the 2nd Earl of Chatham; the 1st Viscount Melbourne, the 5th Duke of Marlborough and the 12th Duke of Norfolk. He made the State Coach for Ireland's Lord Chancellor and carriages for the Spanish Ambassador, for the Austrian Ambassador, Prince Esterhazy, and, improbably, for the Emperor Napoleon's mother, 'Madame Mère'.

He had customers in India and the West Indies but his principal business was making private carriages for the aristocracy and gentry living in the fashionable squares and terraces of London and in the country estates where they lived the other half of their lives. No fewer than seventy-two members of the two Houses of Parliament and thirty members of the Irish aristocracy were his customers, and to many of them he also lent money.

His personal investment portfolio included Government funds, property in London and Cheltenham, and shares in insurance companies. He also bought shares in a variety of joint stock ventures including canals, bridges, mines, harbours, fisheries and the Sierra Leone Company.

Like his fellow coachmakers, John Hatchett and John Wright, he was a merchant prince and he lived like one. At various times he owned properties on Enfield Chase and in Hampstead and Cheltenham. He had grand town houses on Piccadilly, next to Devonshire House, and on Oxford Street, overlooking Hyde Park. They were decorated and furnished by the craftsmen employed by the Prince of Wales at Carlton House and, as Regent, at the Royal Pavilion in Brighton. Philip Godsal's houses were painted by the Craces, wall-papered by Robson and Hale, with plate glass

mirrors by Ashlin and Colling, and carving and gilding by Fricker and Henderson.

He bought his furniture from Gillow, Whitby and Hepplewhite. His armorial china was made in Canton; much of his silver came from Makepeace and Thomas Hamlet; his glassware from Blades; and his clocks, a particular passion, were made by Tompion, Vulliamy, Tregent and Earnshaw.

He commissioned paintings from Francis Wheatley R.A, John Hoppner R.A., Isaac Pocock R.A., Robert Freebairn, William Burgess and Thomas Luny. He bought a number of paintings by members of the Dutch and the French Schools and had an extensive collection of proof prints. He built up a large library, and his extensive cellars were replenished on a very regular basis by the London wine merchants.

Philip Godsal was well connected. He was a leading freemason, Grand Steward in the Prince of Wales's Somerset House Lodge. He held a Captain's commission in one Volunteer Regiment, was a mess member of another, and was an active member of several clubs and learned societies in London and Hampstead. His son was a member of the Court of King George III and married the daughter of Serjeant Best (later Lord Wynford), at that time Attorney to the Prince Regent and later Chief Justice of the Court of Common Pleas. One son-in-law was a Member of Parliament and the other was the Attorney to Admiral Lord Nelson.

Godsal certainly had excellent connections and he was significantly wealthy. Without doubt he was recognised as a gentleman. His membership of the Masonic Lodges, the Light Horse Volunteers and the Hampstead Clubs and his appointment as a Justice of the Peace and as a Governor of the Foundling Hospital all testified to that. In the press he was given the title of 'Esq' behind his name rather than the suffix of 'Mr' before it. The old *canard* that no one engaged in trade can be recognised as a gentleman was never true. Significant wealth has always enabled a man to find social acceptance; wealth speaks to wealth. Godsal was significantly wealthy and was recognised, by his inferiors, his equals, his superiors and by himself, as a gentleman.[4] But none would have regarded him as a member of the gentry.

Wealth and connections and indeed education, intellect, character and taste were not the sole determinants as to what made a man a member of the gentry. Godsal had all of these and they made him recognised as a gentleman, but they did not take him that further step to being a member of the gentry. There has been much modern research into the 'gentrification' of the entrepreneurial class to which Philip Godsal most evidently belonged.[5] Economic and social historians use the term 'gentrification' about individuals and families rather than neighbourhoods, about how newly wealthy individuals acquire for themselves and their descendants the characteristics of an older élite.

The gentry shared many secondary identifying characteristics including an education based on the classics, fashionable dress, domestic arrangements based on a significant house, well furnished and decorated, with servants and horses and carriages, the provision of generous hospitality and entertainment for friends and neighbours. Add to this, worship according to the practise of the Established Church of England, support of the Church financially and service to their community, (and to their own interests), as local magistrates. Godsal readily identified himself with, and was recognised as possessing, all these particular secondary characteristics of the gentry.

With other aspects of a culture, sufficiently widely shared to be seen as characteristic of the gentry, Godsal had more or less interest. The leisure to pursue personal pleasures and the means to indulge them are aspects of the aristocratic culture which were embraced by the gentry and in particular the pursuit of country sports, the patronage of the arts, and the predisposition to travel.

Philip Godsal took no part in field sports. He never hunted, shot or fished and attended no more than two or three race meetings in his life. But against this non identification with the 'hearty' heritage of aristocratic wealth, was balanced Godsal's interest in the cultural heritage of the aristocratic tradition, in the commissioning of works of art, patronage of the theatre and in his enthusiasm for travel and sight-seeing.

First generation wealth was undoubtedly something of a handicap in the gentrification process. Philip Godsal made the first 'serious' money in his family and remained in business for the whole of his working life. The evidence seems to be that he did not aspire to join the landed gentry, for the primary defining characteristic of that older élite, the hereditary aristocracy and the hereditary gentry is, and indeed always was, that both groups were significant landowners, either as individuals or as members of families which owned land. Philip Godsal clearly excluded himself from the ranks of the landed gentry by not buying a landed estate. At various times he owned fine town houses, on Piccadilly and Oxford Street and large properties in Enfield (with ten acres), Hampstead (with twenty acres) and Cheltenham (with six acres). He had the financial means to buy land but he did not choose to.

He knew his place in the still ordered society of the late eighteenth and early nineteenth century and he was content to accept it. He was a gentleman, but a lifetime in trade and first generation wealth would make transition to the role of landed gentry more difficult. He was not ambitious for himself to make this step after his retirement but he was fiercely ambitious for his only son Philip Lake Godsal.

The calculated and successful steps he took to prepare his son to join the ranks of the landed gentry are detailed in a later chapter. They included the early decision that the son should not engage in trade, to have him educated at Harrow and Oxford, to finance his membership of the Middle Temple, to buy him a position at Court, to marry him into a gentrified family and to hand on to him the inherited possession of considerable wealth to fund the purchase of a large estate.

This last consideration explains why Godsal left everything to his son and nothing to his daughters. It also explains why he himself continued in his trade as a coachmaker until the age of sixty-three, why he sold the business on his retirement and why , towards the end of his life he invested, not in land but in more profitable investments.

There was a time in 1821 when he enquired about the possibility of buying his son a landed estate in Gloucestershire with 2,000 acres. A suitable property was not found at that time and it was after his father's death that the son completed the second generation apotheosis from gentleman to landed gentry by buying a large estate on the borders of Shropshire, Cheshire and Flintshire.

It was the son and not his father, who joined the landed gentry, but it was the wealth created by Philip Godsal's coachmaking business which enabled him to do so.

'The Godsal-Lake coat of arms'

CHAPTER ONE
Family and Friends

Philip Godsal was born at seven o'clock in the evening of 5 November 1747.[1] No fireworks greeted the birth, for this element of Guy Fawkes' night was not yet widely employed.[2] But the parents, Thomas Godsal and Susannah, née Lake, had much to celebrate, for Philip was their first child. He was christened a fortnight later in the Church of St Martin in the Fields in London and he proved to be an only child.[3]

Philip's father, Thomas Godsal (1716–1763) was the second and only surviving son of Philip Godsal (1689–1762), a gentleman of property in Tewkesbury, Gloucestershire,[4] whose younger brother William (1694–1747), a tanner, served twice as Bailiff of the town of Tewkesbury.[5] The new baby's paternal grandmother was Frances, née Webb (1687–1754), whose father had been a Fellow of All Souls, Oxford, before becoming Rector of Bredon in Worcestershire.[6]

Philip's grandfather had moved to London and it was there that he apprenticed his elder son to a haberdasher and his younger son, Thomas to a coachmaker, Thomas Basnet, for the sum of £35 in 1747. Having completed his apprenticeship Thomas married Susannah Lake (1723–1786), the only child of Master Coachmaker Henry Lake (16 ?–1766), 'a very religious, good man'[7] in Long Acre. As Thomas Godsal's elder brother had died without issue, Thomas and Susannah Godsal christened their first son Philip in the established Godsal family tradition.[8]

At the age of two in 1749 the young Philip Godsal was sent to a nursery at Tilehill House, Primrose Hill[9] and about the age of twelve he was a pupil at the Soho Academy, described as the finest school in London and with a strong tradition in the teaching of art and drama. Philip was still at school in 1763 when his father, Thomas, died at the early age of forty-seven. Philip was later to describe him, 'as noble minded a man as ever lived'. There was no will and Susannah was granted letters of Administration.[10] She took over the control of the family coachmaking business until young Philip succeeded in the year 1768 at the age of twenty-one.

Susannah Godsal survived until 1786 and Philip was to remain devoted to her memory, 'a kind, sensible, good woman to whom I owe every comfort and prosperity in this life'.[11] She was buried in a vault in Wokingham Church, home of the Lakes. In 1798, twelve years after her death, Philip commissioned an elaborate memorial from the sculptor Richard Westmacott at the cost of £120.[12]

Philip, the only child of an only surviving son and an only daughter, nevertheless had seven cousins. The Webbs were the children of his father's sister Anne (17 ?–1795) who had married John Webb (1719–1766), a Tewkesbury ironmonger, who was her first cousin, the nephew of Frances Godsal, née Webb. Like his uncle, William Godsal, John Webb had served as a Bailiff of Tewkesbury before he died in 1766 as a result of breaking his back in a fall from a horse.[13] John Webb and Anne, née Godsal, had seven children. There was one boy, Samuel, who died young in 1753 and was buried in a vault with his Godsal grandparents.[14] There were six girls, four of whom married. The third sister Ann (1749–1834) married her first cousin, Philip Godsal.

When first cousins marry there is, of course, a common grandparent. In the case of Philip Godsal and Ann Webb the grandparent in common was Frances Godsal, née Webb (1687–1754) and she was therefore a stong genetic influence on the children of Philip and Ann. The significance of this link is reinforced by the fact that Ann's parents were themselves first cousins, so that Frances was also Ann's great aunt, her brother's son was Ann's father. As mentioned above, Frances was the daughter of a former Fellow of All Souls, Oxford, before he became the Rector of Bredon. Her mother's father was chaplain to King Charles II, and his father had been Bishop of Worcester before being driven out by Oliver Cromwell.[15] Philip Godsal was well aware of this distinguished ancestry and of the significance of the blood link. His Diary mentions having copies made of 'our grandmother's portrait'[16] and of having repairs done to 'our grandmother's picture'.[17] The portrait, however, has not been traced.

As to Philip's wife, Ann, little is known about her. There are portraits of Philip and of each of the three children but none of Ann. Throughout Philip's Diary and letters she is referred to as 'Mrs G', or very occasionally as 'my wife', but never as 'Ann'. Even then, there are few entries about her. We learn more about Philip's children, relations, friends, tradesmen and servants than we do about his wife. Even in the correspondence with her sisters, it always seems to be Philip who wrote and to whom the replies were addressed.

In the family lists which he put in his Commonplace Book and Diaries there is no mention of the date of his marriage to Ann. Indeed, throughout all the Diaries and letters there seem to be only three records of the intimacy of married life. In one, Philip records that during an overnight stay in Reigate on the way to Brighton, 'walked with Mrs G down the hill at ½ past seven o'clock'.[18] In another he writes of a February evening 'it was so warm that Mrs G & self went out towards Harrow with the landaulet hood down'.[19] In the third he records enjoying the view from Shooters Hill with Mrs G. Indeed, after his kidney stone kept him and his wife confined to the house, he wrote to Ann's sister, Susannah, 'never did we leave a place with more pleasure. We have become so long immured in peaceful quietude that we have become absolutely stupid – it is all very well having what is termed a comfortable tête-a-tête, but I tell you it will not do. Society is as necessary to the health of the mind as food is to the body.'[20]

Only in his will, made in 1818,[21] and in a letter to William Haslewood written in 1807, ('my dear wife who deserves everything of me')[22] does he refer to her in warm terms and it has to be observed that in the letter Philip was giving a reason for not lending Haslewood any money.

Mrs G went on many, although not all, of Philip's extended holidays, but rarely on the countless small excursions he took with children or friends. In a period of fifteen years Mrs G accompanied him only to Richmond, Hemel Hempstead, Windsor and Harrow. Philip made many other little overnight jaunts with his children or his male friends, Edward, Buttall, Devenish, Jeynes and Tubbs.

Ann certainly accompanied Philip to dine with their children and the other members of the family, including the Bests, and with their friends, the Edwards and the Tubbs. But many times Philip went alone to dine with his male friends while Ann stayed at home. She may indeed have had her own circle of ladies to whose homes she was invited, but if so, such occasions are never mentioned by Philip.

It may be imagined that she would often have entertained their guests at home, although her name is mentioned only twice in thirty years when Philip records,

'Mrs G's Rout'. Much of Philip's entertaining at home was of all male groups, and it seems likely that Philip planned the food and wine, with the cook and footman providing the necessary help. Naturally, she would not expect to join him at his many clubs except on Ladies Nights, and she was not as enthusiastic about the theatre, the opera or the Russell Concert Rooms where, the Diary records, Philip often escorted his elder daughter, Susannah Saxon.[23]

As a mother, Ann must have felt the early absence of both of her younger children at boarding school. Philip Lake was five when he was first sent to boarding school and for the next sixteen years he spent only a part of the holidays with his mother. Little Maria was only four when she was sent away from home.[24] When she was six she was sent to board with Miss Semple in Calais, so that even occasional visits from Mama were not possible.[25] Such an arrangement was not, and indeed, is not unknown. Philip was an ambitious man and his long term plans for his children can be seen to have been effective in that all received a good education and made good marriages. But there can be an emotional cost which is more often paid by the mother than the father.

Philip recorded many gifts to his children, but few to his wife, only a hair necklace, some jewellery and a Prayer Book (which remains, with her signature, in the family) are mentioned. Ann does not seem to have received a regular allowance, although the income from a property in the Strand appears to have been part of her marriage agreement. Only once, or at most twice, a year is there an entry 'Mrs G for herself'. In twenty years her husband gave her thirteen sums amounting to £185, while in the same period Maria, their daughter, was given £420.

Ann appears to have run the household only in respect of the supervision of the three female servants. Until 1814 the weekly housekeeping is recorded in the Diary as a round sum, usually £10.0s.0d or £10.10s.0d per week, and it is recorded as 'Mrs G housekeeping £10.0s.0d'. Presumably Mrs G was allowed to keep any part of that fixed sum not spent. From 1814, however, the weekly housekeeping is always recorded as an exact sum and there is no more mention of 'Mrs G'. It seems likely that Philip himself, in his retirement, took over the entire direction of the servants .

What is lacking in the Diary is evidence of any real warmth towards Ann, but it is perhaps necessary to guard against judging the expectations of a wife and her husband two hundred years ago against those of a modern married couple. And the evidence on which any suppositions about Ann are based are the records of her husband. If Ann's diaries and letters were to be found, it is possible the

Philip Lake Godsal, Philip Godsal's son, by an unknown artist

picture might appear very different. Certainly we know she lived a life of great ease and comfort, with splendid houses and furnishings and servants. We learn of her membership of the subscription libraries and the Spas.

There are many records of payments to doctors and apothecaries 'for Mrs G' and it is possible that she was a valetudinarian.[26] If so, she might well have found her husband's evident energetic pursuit of society and travel to be exhausting and have welcomed the comfort and tranquility of her elegant homes and gardens, the company of her pug dog and her green parrot.

Philip and Ann had seven children, three of whom survived infancy. Susannah (1772–1852) married Nathaniel Saxon (?1766–1844) a solicitor, and later for a short time an M.P. They had no children.[27]

Philip Lake (1784–1858) married Grace Ann Best (1797–1868), the daughter of the then Serjeant Best, later Lord Wynford, Deputy Speaker of the House of Lords. Philip Lake and Grace had one son and three daughters.[28]

Philip and Ann's third surviving child was Maria

(1785–1868) who married William Haslewood (17 ?–18 ?), at that time the Attorney to Admiral Lord Nelson. They had two sons and two surviving daughters.[29]

On his marriage to Ann, the Webb cousins became also Philip's sisters-in-law and he maintained close relations with all of them. The eldest sister, Elizabeth (1746–1806), three years older than Ann, married Charles Cole (1739–1803) and he and Philip remained close friends and occasional business associates. Charles acted as joint security on a bond for £2,000 which Philip took out with E.G. Lind in 1787 and it was Charles who persuaded Philip to invest in Polbreen Mine in Cornwall.[30] There are records of a number of short term loans between the two, as there were with others of Philip's friends. Philip described Cole as 'my most worthy friend and brother' and sponsored his son when he was balloted for and elected as a freemason in 1804, shortly after his father's death.[31]

In their later years the Coles lived in Park Lane and in Southgate and they were regular guests of the Godsals in Hampstead and Piccadilly. Elizabeth died two years after her husband, and was buried with him in the family vault in the Chapel on the Uxbridge Road belonging to the Church of St George's in Hanover Square.[32]

After the funeral, the four Cole children dined with the Godsals at 243 Oxford Street and Philip acted as executor in Elizabeth's will in which she left £600 to her two unmarried sisters.[33] One son, Philip Cole, had predeceased his parents, having been killed in action in India in 1802.[34] There were three other sons, Charles, George and Webb, and one daughter, Elizabeth who married Brownlow Bourdillon.[35] The Godsals remained in regular touch with all the children.

Ann's second sister Frances Webb (1747– ?), who was two years older than Ann, married Thomas Brown (1752–1811), a mercer who became a freeman of Tewkesbury in 1790 and in that year also served as Bailiff, as he did again in 1792. Philip noted in his Diary for 28 November 1789 'Agreed to let Mr Brown of Tewkesbury have my freehold house in the Lane for £20'. It was Brown who administered the Market House in Tewkesbury in which all the sisters appeared to have an interest. The Godsals visited the Browns in Tewkesbury from time to time, but they do not seem to have been as close as to the other sisters. Thomas Brown died on 1 January 1811, seven months before his daughter, Ann Elizabeth, and both have memorials in Tewkesbury Abbey. Frances Brown is last mentioned in the Diary in 1813; her date of death is not known. The Edward Brown who made the arrangements with the Abbey for Philip Godsal's vault was almost certainly her son.[36]

The other married sister, Mary (1757–1833) was eight years younger than Ann, and a favourite of both Philip and Ann. She married first Michael Procter (1743–1807), a maltster of Tewkesbury, who, like so many members of the extended family, was a freeman of the town and served as Bailiff four times. He was prosperous enough to order a coach from his brother-in-law which cost £216 in 1806.[37] The Godsals stayed with the Procters several times until Procter died in 1807 at the age of sixty-four. Thirteen months later, Mary married John Martin, another freeman, who served as Bailiff in 1811. In 1816 he too died (he has a memorial tablet in the Abbey), leaving the twice widowed Mary living in Tewkesbury with Miss Procter, a sister-in-law from her first marriage, as her companion.

After the Godsals retired to Cheltenham in 1814 they paid many return visits to Mary who also sent them frequent gifts of game. In 1820 she arranged with Philip to take out a large insurance on her life, presumably to benefit the two sons of her first marriage, Michael and William Procter. In the last year of his life Philip was obliging her by dealing with a mortgage she had granted on a property in Sherborne Street, Cheltenham.[38]

The two unmarried sisters, Sarah Webb (1758–1808) and Susannah Webb (1763–184 ?) were always in close touch with the Godsals. They shared a home in the fashionable North Parade in Bath until Sarah died in 1808 at the age of fifty (she was buried in Tewkesbury Abbey) when Susannah continued to live there alone until 1822 when her extravagances created a family crisis. Philip believed he had safely secured the financial futures of the two maiden ladies when, in 1806, he converted a debt from John Foster, at that time Chancellor of the Irish Exchequer in the English Parliament, into an annuity, which had devolved on to Susannah alone after Sarah's death.[39]

Poor Susannah, the very acme of the dizzy maiden aunt, seemed quite unable to live within her means, with a weakness for ribbons and gee-gaws. A friendship with a melancholy old invalid had the effect of reducing her own spirits. When the problem became a crisis in 1822, Philip enlisted sister Mary Martin to go to Bath to sort the whole thing out. Susannah Webb's story is told on pages 167–171.

Philip Godsal was a very sociable man with a great capacity for friendship. He had a number of close friends with some of whom he maintained relations over many years. His oldest friend was Jonathan Buttall (1752–1805), the model for Thomas Gainsborough's 'Blue Boy'. Buttall was the son of an ironmonger with a business on the corner of Greek Street and King Street, Soho, near Long Acre, who had also been a pupil at the Soho Academy. He was five years younger than Philip who nevertheless referred to him as 'my school friend'.[40] It seems likely that their fathers had done business together and they were near neighbours.

The 'Blue Boy' is believed to have been painted around 1770 when Buttall would have been eighteen, although he looks younger than that in the picture. The Buttalls had property in Ipswich and it has been suggested that the connection between Gainsborough and Buttall could have begun in East Anglia, although it is possible that it was made through the Soho Academy which had a strong tradition of teaching art and where a number of well known artists were teachers and pupils. Philip Godsal would have been twenty-three in 1770 and may be presumed to have taken a great interest in the project of his closest friend, although his archive has no records dating from that period.

Gainsborough died in 1788 and had expressed in his will the wish that his funeral at Kew Church be private, attended only by his family and fifteen named pall bearers and mourners, one of whom was Jonathan Buttall, now aged thirty-six. He was in exalted company, for his fellow mourners included Sir Josuah Reynolds, President of the Royal Academy; Benjamin West, a future P.R.A.; Sir William Chambers, architect of Somerset House; Richard Brinsley Sheridan, playwright and politican; John Hunter, the celebrated surgeon; Paul Sandby, the artist; Francesco Bartolozzi the engraver; and Thomas Linley, the composer.[41] Philip Godsal knew a social lion when he saw one and his friend had mingled with a positive pride.

Philip and Buttall were close. They shared excursions together, at Woburn Abbey in 1803. Philip recorded his friend's weight, still a trim 10 stone 5lb at the age of fifty-one. They took holidays together to the West country, shared lottery tickets, went to the theatre together and Jonathan was a guest at Philip's clubs and masonic lodges. When Buttall died in 1805 Philip wrote '...my most esteemed friend . . . another heartstring burst'.[42]

Philip attended the funeral in St Ann's, Soho and acted as the executor of Buttall's will in which he and Ann were both left a gold ring. Philip helped the widow invest in gilt-edged securities and kept in contact with her for many years. In 1811 there is a record of him escorting her to the Bank of England and to India House to collect her dividends and afterwards Philip took her to dine at Dolly's Chophouse in Paternoster Row.[43]

George Edward was a neighbour at Enfield Chase when Philip bought his estate there in 1791 and the two remained close friends until Edward's death in 1822. Edward and his

Jonathan Buttall, Godsal's oldest friend, had been the model for Gainsborough's Blue Boy

wife became regular visitors to the Godsal households in Piccadilly, Hampstead and Oxford Street. Edward became a trustee of the marriage settlement of Philip's daughter, Susannah Godsal, in 1802 and hosted the wedding breakfast at his town house in Park Lane. The following year the Edwards were the only non-family guests to dine with the Godsals and the Haslewoods after Maria Godsal's wedding.

Philip dined out more often with Edward than with anyone – at Greenwich, at the Greyhound in Enfield, at Spaniards in Hampstead and elsewhere. They went together to Epsom Races and the Epping Hunt and Edward accompanied Philip when he was made a freeman of Gloucester in 1803. The Godsals and the Edwards went to the theatre together and exchanged regular visits, often staying overnight, even when in London. They played cards, and the men, at least, had a good deal to drink, which may explain their overnight stays.

The Edwards also accompanied the Godsals on holidays to Margate, to East Anglia and to Bath, where in 1804 they shared a house in Queen's Square.[44] The men made excursions to South Wales and to Cheddar Gorge. In 1808 the two couples took a holiday in Teignmouth in Devon where the men became friendly with the artist Thomas Luny. Edward liked the area so well he decided to leave Bath where he had lived for three years and he moved to Bishopsteignton. From that time the two families saw little of each other.

Thomas Courtenay Devenish was an auctioneer with a business in Villiers Street off the Strand, near the present day Charing Cross Station. On one occasion Philip bought some bankrupt stock wine from him at auction but their relationship was a social rather than a business one. Philip accompanied Devenish to Essex to look at a country living in which Devenish appeared to have some family interest.[45] When he died in 1802 Philip wrote in his Diary of 'my most esteemed and dearest Friend'. He was the same age as Philip and his death at the age of fifty-five in 1802 was the result of a dreadful accident Philip's Diary recorded the details

The last time I saw Mr Devenish was in Villiers' Street at 12 o'clock when he left Town on horseback. Four days later, when two miles from Loughborough, he was thrown from his horse and broke three ribs. He was taken to the Bell Inn at Loughborough but was so bruised that he died of a mortification...our mutual friend Mr Wingfield went by mail coach to Loughborough and the Mail overturned killing a woman who was an outside passenger.[46]

Philip attended the funeral in Harrow Church, just four days before his daughter Susannah's marriage and when the will was opened later found that he had been appointed as an executor. In the event there was a most unfortunate misunderstanding with the widow Devenish. Shortly before the accident Philip had agreed to discount a bill for Devenish at two months date which had not been paid at the time of death. As executor Philip therefore paid himself the amount owed from the estate. The widowed Mrs Devenish, who was also an executor, took exception to this, perhaps not knowing of the debt, or perhaps feeling she should have been consulted as a fellow executor. Philip was furious at having his propriety questioned and forthwith resigned as executor, writing indignantly in his Diary 'I do not, and will not administer the will of the late Mr Thomas Courtenay Devenish'.[47] It was a sad end to a long friendship.

Sir Edwin Jeynes, who was elected Lord Mayor of Gloucester in 1800 and knighted the same year, had been a friend of Philip for some years. He joined the Godsals and the Edwards on holidays to East Anglia in 1799 and Margate in 1800. He sponsored Philip for his freedom of Gloucester and the Godsals paid him a number of visits until his death in 1810. His daughters were friends of the Godsal girls, and when Miss Jeynes married Vice-Admiral Thornborough in 1802 he too became a friend of the Godsal family. By the time of his marriage at the age of forty-eight, Thornborough had already had a long career at sea, distinguishing himself in a number of actions against the French. For a long period shore based, he was made a full Admiral in 1812. Sadly his younger wife died the following year.

The Tubbs were other family friends whom the Godsals saw often. Mr and Mrs Tubbs lived at Tew, near Beaconsfield and the Misses Tubbs lived at Friars Place in Acton, which Philip liked to call 'the Nunnery'.[48] The Godsals exchanged regular visits with the two Tubbs households, on one occasion being given a green parrot by Mrs Tubbs. Philip once bought a cow from Mr Tubbs with whom he went on occasional jaunts to view country estates. When Mr Tubbs senior ('my worthy old friend') died in 1810, his son, and indeed his grandsons, continued the agreeable practice of visiting country houses with Philip and on one occasion, visited the Tower of London and, a contemporary spectacle, the London Docks. The widow Tubbs and her two maiden sisters-in-law continued to visit and receive Philip and Ann.

It is the fate of old men to outlive many of their friends but Philip had younger friends. Charles Hatchett (1765–1847) was the son of the coachmaker John Hatchett,

Charles Hatchett, the distinguished chemist, was the son of a coachmaker and the friend of Philip Godsal

who with John Wright and Philip Godsal, made up the triumvirate of London coachmakers who dominated the London market. None of the three intended their sons to follow them in trade. Charles Hatchett, like Philip Lake Godsal, was educated to become a gentleman and he became a celebrated chemist, elected a fellow of the Royal Society in 1797 and a member of the Literary Club founded by Doctor Johnson, Sir Josuah Reynolds and their friends.[49] In 1814 Hatchett was appointed its treasurer and it is probable that it was he who secured the election of Philip Godsal.

Charles Hatchett was mid-way in age between Philip and Philip Lake and was a friend to both. He and his wife exchanged visits with the Godsals when the Hatchetts lived, first in Hammersmith and then at Belle Vue House, Chelsea and it was Mrs Hatchett who gave Mrs Godsal her first pug dog. In 1818 Philip asked Hatchett to agree to serve as the executor when he first drew up his will and the Hatchetts continued to visit the Godsals in Cheltenham and shared a holiday with them in Worcester and Malvern.[50]

Another younger friend was Charles Holford (1774–1838), a Hampstead solicitor, and friend of the artist John Constable. Philip had met him first as a member of the Hampstead Society and the Union Club, and kept in touch with him throughout the rest of his life, even in retirement when Holford came to Cheltenham. Philip often sent him gifts of game. Holford had been second in command of the Hampstead Volunteers in succession to Philip and they both shared an interest in astronomy. Serendipitously Holford had inherited Philip's former home at Grove House, Hampstead and both Philip and Philip Lake returned to Hampstead to dine with him. He was a trustee of Philip Lake's marriage settlement and an executor of Philip's will.[51]

In a long lifetime Philip had many other friends including Mr Winfield, the apothecary of St Martin's Lane. Philip stood godfather to Winfield's son, Philip, who, sadly, was killed while with his regiment in India in 1813. George Bogg of Doctor's Commons was a close friend with whom he dined regularly for some years. In his will Bogg left Philip five guineas to buy a mourning ring. Philip chose an amethyst. Another friend who left him money for a mourning ring was his solicitor, Evan Foulkes, senior partner in the law firm that was to become Farrer's, the royal solicitors.

Friends were important to Philip throughout a long life. A letter he wrote in May 1791, and the caring thoroughness it reveals, may go some way to explaining why his many friends would have appreciated his character and personality. John Parsons was an old friend from Tewkesbury who had written to Philip asking advice on accommodation. Philip replied

> I have made the necessary enquiries and you can have very genteel apartments at the Adelphi Osborne Hotel, that is two beds in different rooms for yourself & your niece, a good bed room for Mrs P's maid & room for your manservant at 13s 6d a night but if you have a mind to give 15s 6d you can be accommodated at the Royal Hotel in Pall Mall. This is what I should prefer, the difference being only 2s a night & it is in so much better a part of Town, more airey & where you continually see all the best people. If you will send me word which you would prefer & the day you mean to be in Town I will see you have the apartments in good order – your post chaise may be at my house – if you want to be near the City or any of the Inns of Court, most certainly the Adelphi is the more centrical [sic].[52]

A crane-neck Town Coach, with highly-worked iron and brass decorative features, designed by Ackermann

CHAPTER TWO
The Coachmaking Business

In 1787 *The Times* newspaper noted

The number of two and four wheel carriages in England which paid duty last year were near 16,000. A certain proof of the prosperity of the Nation and a very material branch of revenue.[1]

Carriages, the generic term for all manner of wheeled vehicles from state and ceremonial coaches, to stage and mail coaches, chariots, phaetons, landaulets, barouches, curricles, whiskeys, gigs, chairs or chaises and post chaises, were the products of the great manufacturing business of coachmaking.

It is surprising that economic and political historians have been so little interested in the details of such a major industry[2] which, as *The Times* remarked, made a significant contribution to the country's economy, through tax revenue of course, but also by its role in speeding up communications, a vital part of the framework which allowed the Industrial Revolution to develop so rapidly from the mid eighteenth century. It also transformed social life and the national provincial psyche by shrinking distances within England, Wales and Scotland, and making the ports to Ireland more immediately accessible.

Perhaps the relative neglect of a major industry has been a consequence of the too readily perceived lightweight association of stage and mail coaches with the sporting print, and of phaetons and post chaises with the heroes and heroines of novels. The fact that no film or television costume drama is complete without its stage coach or barouche perhaps reinforces the view of the carriage as being part of the sort of decorative anecdotal history which does not involve the study of original sources. Or perhaps it is because the documentary details of this complex manufacturing industry have been so hard to come by. Whatever the reasons, this neglect has been felt by students of transportation, of design and fashion who have pursued their tangential subjects without having an extended study of the coachmaking industry available to them. Coachmaking needs to be freed from the condescension of posterity.

Philip Godsal's was one of the great coachmaking manufactories in the last quarter of the eighteenth century and the first decade of the nineteenth. It was located at 103 Long Acre, on the north side of a street which had been the centre of the coachmaking industry in London since the early seventeenth century. During the Restoration when Charles II first granted a Charter to the Worshipful Company of Coachmakers and Loriners/Lorimers (harness makers) Samuel Pepys records visits there to buy a carriage and to have it serviced.

It was, however, during the second half of the eighteenth century, with the improvement of roads, both in towns and between towns, and the wider distribution of wealth, presenting an incentive and a market, that the coachmaking industry developed rapidly. By 1790 there were no fewer than twenty-one coachmakers listed in the directories as having their businesses in Long Acre itself with as many more in the surrounding streets.[3] At this date three of these were pre-eminent, John Hatchett, appointed in this same year as Coachmaker to the King, and Wright & Lukin, next door neighbours of the third in the triumvirate, Philip Godsal.[4] What these men sold was fashion and luxury united with utility. Their carriages were the Rolls-Royces, Daimlers and Jaguars of their day.

The other trades represented in Long Acre were those with close areas of overlap with coachmaking in terms of related craft skills, principally the furniture makers, with joiners and cabinet makers (Chippendale, Hallett and Vile all had their workshops there) and the sign writers with line and herald painters, upholsterers, lacemen and saddlers. Other luxury trades were represented in the street. In the year in which Philip Godsal took command of the family business Josiah Wedgwood was selling his newly named 'Queen's Ware' from a warehouse in Long Acre.

Long Acre runs between Drury Lane and St Martin's Lane parallel to the Strand just above Covent Garden market. In the day time the area was the focus of great industrial and commercial activity. In the evenings the area took on a quite different character as it became a haunt of pleasure with the two Theatres Royal of Drury Lane and

Covent Garden as the main focus attracting crowds of all classes. Its public houses and coffee houses were amongst the liveliest in London. That it became, after dark, a notable haunt of prostitutes, is graphically recorded in the testimony of James Boswell, William Hickey and others.

This then was the area where Philip Godsal, the son and grandson of coachmakers, inherited his business at the age of only twenty-one in 1768/9. By 1792 he had extended the factory, as he called it, from the original 103 Long Acre to include workshops and stores across the road at 48 Long Acre and in Cross Street and Castle Street, which formed the west and northern boundaries of 103 Long Acre. He also had business premises in nearby Charles Street, Nottingham Court, and Shorts Gardens. Long Acre has changed more than most streets in central London as many of the side streets have disappeared as Long Acre had developed into larger units. A plan of how it was in Godsal's day, based on Horwood's map of 1792, is on the endpapers.

Most of Godsal's premises were taken out on long leases from the Mercers' Company who owned much of Long Acre and the streets to the north. Details are given in the chapter 'Landlord and Tenant'. Godsal undertook many extensions, repairs and improvements and in 1804, when he renewed his partnership with Messrs Baxter and Macklew, he described his premises in Long Acre as

> containing two dwelling houses in Long Acre, the two tenements in Cross Lane – habitable – & one Workshop – also large & spacious workshops reaching from Long Acre through to Castle Street with Warehouse for timber & standing for carriages. A large & commodious yard with a gate way into Cross Lane – a large & spacious Smith's shop with five forges, filing loft & access to Cross Lane with large cellaring for coals – two pumps and every convenience fitted and properly adapted for residence & for carrying on to any extent the Coach Building business in all its various branches, as likewise the Harness Making.[5]

Since 1782 he had engaged in a continuous building and maintenance programme and he noted that most of the buildings had been built or re-built in the years 1792/3 and 1803/4. He had paid a bricklayer, Joseph Stutely £1,050 for work in the years 1782–1788, £349.11s.9d for new craft shops in 1792/3, a further £302.17s.6d plus £13.6s.6d costs after having been taken to Court for non-payment of the work in 1803/4.[6]

Fascinating detail of the layout and contents of his workshops can be found in a note to his solicitor in 1812 in which he sought his advice on what and how he should insure now that he was letting out the premises to his successors Baxter and Macklew

In respect of Fixtures

Coachmakers' benches with their screws and all that belongs to them
Wooden racks that are suspended over almost all the benches
Chopping Blocks & Body horses belonging to the Coachmakers
Sundry vices in the different lofts exclusive of those in the Smiths' Shop
All Desks – Horses for [coach] Bodies – Stools to sitt on for Painters – Grinding Stones – Potts, Brushes & all Implements for Painters' use in those lofts where they are employed.
All Pegs or conveniences of hanging up the Harness in the different Lofts or Store Rooms.
All Cutting Boards, Knives, Chairs & every other article used in the harness Department.
All fixtures used as Cupboards in the different Trimming Lofts – Cutting Boards – Body Horses
In the Smiths' Shop – Iron Water Troughs – Bellows & fixing – Anvils –

How is the Forges, are they considered as fixtures and not to be valued?[7]

He insured the Long Acre/Cross Street/Castle Street premises for £10,200 and his landlords, the Mercers' Company, insured them for another £7,950.[8] This was exclusive of stock in trade which is discussed below.

More details of Godsal's coachmaking premises were recorded when a clerk made out a list of the number of carriages for which standing could be provided, an important consideration in a busy manufactory which also took in carriages for servicing.[9]

Front Shop	11 carriages
Gang way	14 ditto
Yard, including right & left of	
Gateway in Cross Lane	14 ditto
New building in Cross Lane	14 ditto
Side of saw pit	3 ditto
Carriage painting loft	20 ditto
Total	**76 carriages**

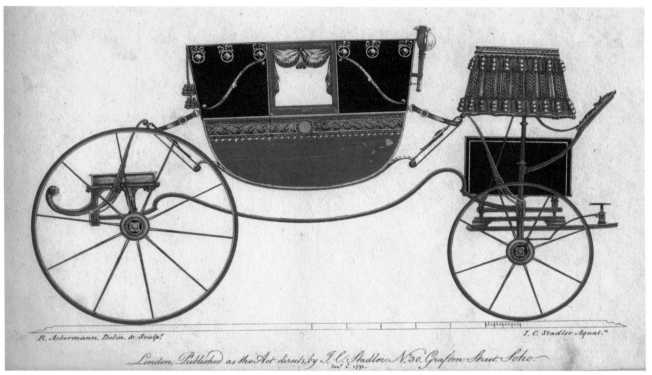

A crane-neck Landau, designed by Ackermann

A perch Landau with the black japanned hoods open, designed by Ackermann

Macklew, he had had the sole overall responsibility for decisions on borrowing and credit, on buildings, on product design, sales, marketing, and customer relations. He had employed Mr May as his chief clerk and Mr Hull as works supervisor but coachmaking was a business which depended for its success on the personality, taste and intelligence and drive of its chief executive.

Philip Godsal insured the value of cost of his stock in hand at any one time for the sum of £18,000,[20] (the insurance risks were high with the forges in close juxtaposition with the timbers and flammable paints and varnishes). The sum insured was about half the annual sales turnover, based upon the average annual payments made into his bank accounts.

Successful coachmaking businesses did not appear over-night. Philip Godsal was fortunate to take over a going concern but he still needed to borrow regularly (see chapter 'Capital and Creditors'). It is evident that to support this ratio of stocks to sales the profit margin on the sale of a new carriage or on a repair or service had to be high. Most businesses – and their bankers – look for a gross annual yield of at least sixty per cent – i.e. the profit margin attained multiplied by the number of times the value of stock can be turned round in a year. With the annual turn-round of little over twice – i.e. £18,000 stock value producing £36,000/40,000 sales revenue then the minimum profit margin would have to be almost thirty per cent. This would need to increase to take account of the charges for borrowing money and of the extended credit which was a feature of the coachmaking industry (discussed in chapters 'Customers and Debtors' and 'The Genealogy of Irish Debtors'). This theoretical profit margin can be tested later in this chapter.

It might be helpful first to examine the annual income of the Coachmaker himself, Philip Godsal, by now well established and successful. At the time the accounts for the first five years of his partnership with Baxter and Macklew were drawn up to December 1802 the profits of income over expenses were declared to be £40,000. However it was agreed that £6,000 should be reserved against the contingencies of 'not being able to get in certain monies' (although it was agreed that this was what we would now call a worst case scenario) and Godsal himself, a partner now in his old business and owning fifty per cent of that business, withdrew £17,000 and the other partners took out £8,500 each.[21]

The partnership had made a net profit of £34,000 over five years – an average of £6,800 per year on an average stock value of £18,000 (see above). This represents a net profit of just under thirty-eight per cent after all expenses are paid, all borrowings are paid for, all rental charges paid to the Mercers' Company, all the costs of new raw materials and all wages paid, lawyer's fees paid and the provision made for the extended credit and bad debts, the monies 'not being able to get in'.

To achieve this very healthy position the profit margin had to have been much higher than our theoretical thirty per cent (see above) and, although we cannot calculate the total of the business expenses it seems likely that the profit margin on each sales invoice was more like one hundred per cent in order to obtain the thirty-eight per cent net profit which the partners were able to share.

We have seen that Philip Godsal's annual average earnings from the partnership in the coachmaking business was £3,400 per year (i.e. £17,000 over five years). His highest paid employee was receiving no more than £200 and his average worker some £75. It can be said that if the highest paid employee in a modern private engineering business earned £50,000, then, on the same differential, its founding chairman might expect £850,000. This is not as far fetched an analogy as it may seem, for Godsal was being paid an agreed share of profits. And of course he had made a major investment of capital over the years. Our conclusion may need be no more than to acknowledge that, with all its attendant risks coachmaking could be a very profitable industry.

For Philip Godsal this was clearly the case as not only was he receiving half the net profits but he was also the landlord of the business premises, charging the partnership £1,000 per year and paying the Mercers' Company only £300. When he finally sold his half share to his partners in 1810 for £11,109 he remained the primary lessee of the Long Acre premises which he continued to let to his successors until his death in 1826.[22]

This was not quite the end of his income deriving from coachmaking. Two later chapters, 'Customers and Debtors' and 'The Genealogy of Irish Debtors' explain in detail the private banking arrangements he offered to his customers.

This annual nett profit of approximately £6,800/7,000 per year would have been entirely Godsal's until in 1797, at the age of fifty, he had let Baxter and Macklew buy into partnership to undertake much of the accounts and administration (Macklew) and the sales and production (Baxter). How did Godsal's income compare with his contemporaries in other employment?

In 1759 one Joseph Massie had compiled statistics of income divided by occupation. He did not include coachmakers but he recorded that £100 would cover the

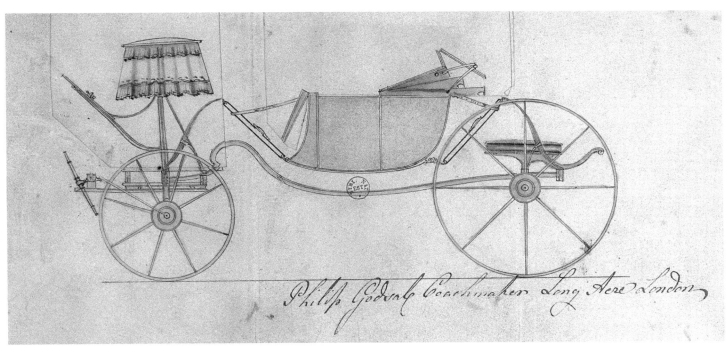

ABOVE: *A Landaulet with hood open, designed by Philip Godsal*
BEOW: *A Landaulet with hood closed, designed by Philip Godsal*

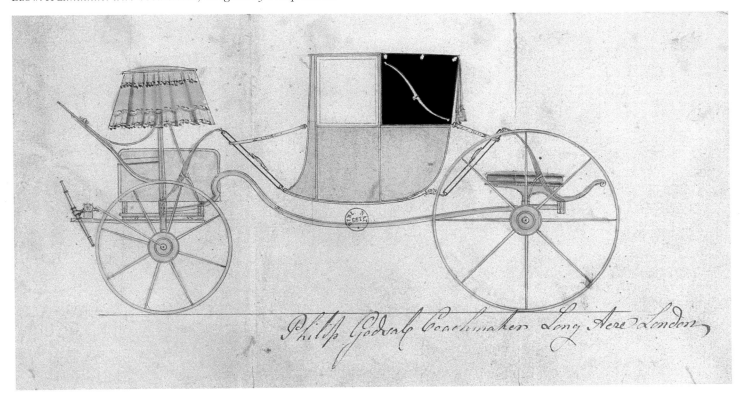

earnings of most clerics and army officers; a London based lawyer might reach £200 a year, earnings matched by some successful manufacturers and tradesmen. Only some few merchants were recorded as making as much as £600 per year and at the top of the pyramid of wealth were just ten families with annual incomes of almost £27,000. Even bearing in mind that it was over forty years since this particular systematic record was prepared, inflation had been modest and Godsal's annual income by 1802 is striking. In 1800 the Net National Income was only £230 million against the present day figure of £865 billion. As a proportion of the national wealth Godsal's annual income would put him in to-day's multi-millionaire bracket.[23]

Philip Godsal was in every way a merchant prince, enjoying every facet of luxury and fashion. He was, quite literally, 'living like a lord'. Nor was he the only coachmaker to achieve this standard of living. John Hatchett amassed great wealth and John Wright retired to a country house with a fine collection of art.[24] Of course these were the three men at the top of the profession. Many others no doubt earned less and it was a trade in which there were many bankruptcies.

Godsal, as a master coachbuilder, was a liveryman of the Worshipful Company of Coachmakers and Loriners (harness makers) from 1770 until 1806. In that period he registered ten apprentices, the last completing his seven year apprenticeship three years after Godsal's own retirement.[25] Philip Godsal, as heir to the coachmaking business, did not serve an apprenticeship, unlike his father, Thomas. Philip's mother, Susannah Godsal, née Lake, had herself been a master coachmaker, so designated when she took over the business after Thomas's early death.[26] Apprentices qualified as journeymen in one of coachmaking's various trades and the responsibility of the master coachmaker was the direction of the entire business.

Unlike his peers, John Hatchett and John Wright, Philip never served as Master of the Worshipful Company and it is clear that he took little active interest in its activities, which, already by the end of the eighteenth century, like that of most livery companies, were concerned more with education, charity, and social matters than with technical advances, the gaining of orders and the promotion of individual businesses. Godsal registered his apprentices with the Coachmakers' Company and attended their annual dinner to the incoming Lord Mayor but his own multifarious social engagements were rather at his two Masonic Lodges, his two Volunteer Regiment messes, the Soho Academy Old Boys Society, the Foundling Hospital, of which he was a Governor, the Westminster Dispensary, at which he served

as a Steward, and his three Hampstead clubs. Here he could both enjoy the rich social life he loved and gain new customers, which it was self evident he would not find in the company of his fellow coachmakers.

The Coachmakers' Hall incidentally could be hired for the holding of large public meetings, not connected in any way with the objects or interests of the Worshipful Company. Indeed two particular meetings had objects which clashed directly with the essentially conservative temper of all the livery companies. In 1780 Lord George Gordon hired the hall for the rabble rousing assembly which launched the fierce anti-Catholic Gordon Riots on to the streets of London. Ten years later the radical revolutionary and poet John Thelwell held a meeting there which resulted in the formation of the Corresponding societies, persecuted to extinction by Pitt's nervous government.

Philip Godsal was for a time a member of the Society for the Encouragement of Arts, Manufactures and Commerce.[27] The second half of the eighteenth century witnessed many inventions which improved the manufacture of carriages. Godsal invented folding steps which dropped to the ground when the carriage door opened and he himself is recorded in 1772 as paying Charles Varlo for 'twenty tickets of value £1.0s.6d. each for the liberty of making his friction boxes' (which appear to have been a means of automatically releasing oil on the axles of carriages to minimise friction).[28]

Like many other inventors, Varlo was a curious fellow. In 1784 he got it into his head that he was the lawful governor of New Jersey and lessee of two-thirds of its land. Unsurprisingly, when he arrived in America to claim his inheritance, he failed to convince the newly independent American courts, and returned home disappointed.[29]

John Hatchett registered a number of patents.[30] Advertisements by inventors appeared in the newspapers for concealed hinges for coach doors.[31] In the Midlands Erasmus Darwin and his young friend, the Irishman Richard Edgeworth, turned their fertile minds to carriage improvements, for one of which, allowing a smaller turning circle, they received a Gold Medal from the Society for the Encouragement of Arts, Manufactures and Commerce in 1769.[32]

In 1795 Godsal had a large claim made against him by his next door neighbour Lionel Lukin of 101 Long Acre, the former partner and now successor to John Wright. Whether the claim was for breach of a patent, (Lukin was a notable inventor [33]), or a boundary dispute, is not known. The case did not make the newspapers but it ended with Godsal having to pay Lukin damages of £900 and his costs of £75.[34] The trial must have been over several days for Godsal also

Nº 1.

Godsal was also a loriner or harness-maker

records paying £10.12s.0d for 'dinner bills for trial – Lukin and Godsal'. (Godsal usually paid about 10s 6d for a good dinner)

The London coachmakers had a considerable export trade. John Hatchett, famously sold a coach to Catherine the Great, Empress of Russia. Less well known Philip Godsal sold a coach to Napoleon's mother, 'Madame Mère', presumably during the brief resumption of trade with France during the Treaty of Amiens. In March 1803 he was writing to the Parisian bankers, Comte Peregaux, to obtain payment.[35] Joseph Farington had noted in his diary the problems English coachmakers had in obtaining payments after the French Revolution in 1789[36] but it seems that Godsal at least received his payment for this most curious transaction. This coach is possibly the one in which Madame Bonaparte drove to the coronation of her son in 1804.

Godsal advertised on his trade cards 'Both for Home & Foreign sale'.[37] His foreign market was to be found principally in India and the West Indies (not only was Continental trade difficult but the end of the American

Revolution had caused trade to look east rather than west). His arrangements with James Urmston, captain of an East Indiaman are described in a later chapter (page 58) as are his pursuit of debtors in Jamaica, Barbados, India, the United States and Italy. Rudolph Ackermann, who provided a number of designs for carriages built by Godsal noted that 'carriages for exportation, and in particular those for the East and West Indies, are in general gay, lively and pleasant colours, suitable for hot climates'.[38]

The Irish market had been lucrative for London coachmakers until the beginning of the last quarter of the eighteenth century when the Dublin coachmaking industry had developed apace. *The Times* reported in 1787 'The coachmakers report that home business is much less than for many years past and that the exportation of carriages to Ireland has very nearly ceased.' [39]

Philip Godsal was to buck that trend when he received the commission for the State Coach of the Irish Lord Chancellor in 1789 which is described in a later chapter. He had made carriages before this date for Irish customers but it was after completing the Lord Chancellor's commission that he obtained the majority of his fifty Irish clients who have been traced (see 'The Genealogy of Irish Debtors').

There was a flourishing trade in second hand carriages in London and in the provinces. Many were offered through classified ads in the newspapers and there were several large second hand dealers. 'The London Repository' in Golden Square, Soho advertised regularly

> The Proprietors beg permission to inform the Nobility, Gentry & the Public in general, that they have a great assortment of Modern carriages of all descriptions for sale both for Town & Travelling; amongst which are a variety of exceeding good Coaches, Chariots, Phaetons, and Post Chaises, all of which are available for immediate use. The proprietors will for six months warrant any carriage purchased at the Repository.
> N.B. Gentlemens' carriages sold at 2¼ % commission, or best price given.[40]

At Mackenzie's 'Rhedarium' in Park Street, Grosvenor Square, 'upwards of 150 carriages' were advertised and on one occasion offered 'a Crest chased – an arm and hand erect, holding a spur. Any gentleman whom the Crest suits may have them reasonable'.[41]

Gentlemen, including Philip Godsal, liked to decorate their personal carriages with coats of arms, to which they may not have been entitled.[42]

With regard to these second hand vehicles, no doubt the leading coachmakers would advise *caveat emptor* but it is doubtful if this thriving second hand market damaged their businesses. Rather was it an indication of the success of their trade and the growing market of individuals able to afford the running of the carriage, once bought. It is perhaps worth mentioning here that buying your carriage was one thing. You had to pay the licence fee and more especially buy the horse or horses and hire a coachman to drive it. As we shall see, the running costs of a gentleman's carriage could be every bit as expensive as the carriage itself. Carriages were still the preserve of the wealthy and the wealthy bought new carriages to impress their peers and keep up with the fashions.

Here were Philip Godsal's products and market, dazzling fashionable carriages for the aristocracy and gentry. They made him one of the richest men in England and it is time to look at some examples.

CHAPTER THREE
Fashionable Carriages

Travel by carriage, waggon or horseback, was the only means of personal transportation throughout the whole of Philip Godsal's lifetime. Mail and stage coaches offered a form of public transport, for those with the money to pay their fares, which were not inexpensive. Even more costly were post chaises, the hire cars of the time, which provided private transport with hired horses. If they had to travel, the poor went by waggon. Private carriages and horses were for the wealthy and for them the carriages were not only utilitarian but also the most public statement of wealth and fashion. A man might have the finest pictures, furniture and silver in his homes but few would ever see them. A rich man's carriage was seen by everyone and for those in the fashionable world it was therefore the ultimate fashion accessory.

Godsal was probably fortunate in having no royal customers for they were notoriously slow payers, even non payers. No doubt he was content to let John Hatchett, John Wright and Lionel Lukin petition the Prince, or his commissioners, for payment. One of Godsal's own tenants, Nathaniel Jefferys, jeweller to the Prince of Wales and to his brother, the Duke of York, was twice forced into bankruptcy through royal indifference to the payment of his bills.[1]

Without this doubtful privilege of serving the Royal family Godsal nevertheless drew his customers from the world of wealth and fashion. Almost all came from Byron's 'top ten thousand by whom the World is made'. Seventy-two of them were members of the Houses of Parliament, as many again were also members of the aristocracy and titled gentry.[2] Philip Godsal undoubtedly shared Josiah Wedgwood's belief that royal or aristocratic introduction was as necessary as real elegance or beauty to the sale of an object. 'The manufacturer must therefore bestow as much pain and expense gaining such patronage as on the design itself.'[3] Godsal's clientèle show that he was eminently successful in this regard.

Because members of the aristocracy were in the news, their *equipages* were often a matter of comment and there are vivid newspaper descriptions of many of Godsal's

fashionable carriages. Some few of Godsal's own specifications have survived in the Iscoyd Park Papers, and most notably in the archives of Lord Delaval of Seaton Delaval in Northumberland. They provide a thorough description of the basic make-up, and the customised improvement of a Godsal carriage.

On 21 June 1777 Philip Godsal sold a chariot (a 'half' coach with one forward facing bench seat) to George William Prescott, Esq

A new neat Crane neck Chariot, the body run with beads and scrolls, painted dark green with your arms neatly painted in mantles in relief on the end and on the door panels. The body oil varnished, the leather japanned and the brass round. The inside lined with fine green cloth and trimmed with fine lace, half landau back & sides stuffed & quilted. Best plate glass, mahogany shutters, oval behind, neat wainscot trunk under the inside seat & a carpet to the bottom. The Body, hung on a neat crane neck [under] carriage, run with beads & scrolls, Town made steel springs, iron axletrees with screwed nuts to the ends. Wrought iron pipe boxes, a platform before with side irons covered with leather, the [under] carriage & wheels coloured to match the Body & oil varnished. A handsome blank seat cloth with gimp [trimming of silk with wire running through it] & a fringe & green silk buttons & hangers.
Complete £ 115.16s.0d.[4]

On 9 April 1787 he sold to Lord Delaval a rather more expensive vehicle, a coach (with two facing bench seats) with some similarities in the specification but with a number of expensive extras.[5]

A new genteel coach, made of the best seasoned timber, the Body being neatly carved with raised mouldings and monumental scrolls, the roof and upper part covered with japanned leather. Lined with a superfine light coloured cloth, trimmed with raised lace. Polished glass and mahogany shutters, trunks under the seats and a

carpet. The Body hung with best leather braces with a handsome crane necked [under] carriage neatly carved, the cranes made with double bosses and worked with mouldings, ironed with the best Swedish iron, hand made German steel springs, iron axletrees with the boxes above...wheels. The ground colour of the carriage a fine olive green, the body painted fine patent yellow and the whole rightly varnished. A handsome hammer cloth. Every article of the best materials and finished with the utmost approved taste. Extras Double folding inside steps with treads covered by carpet. Handsome plated mouldings all round the roof and upper part. Plated door handles and brace buckles. Ornamental head plates, neatly chased. Plated rings for the check braces. Handsome plated square mouldings all round the lower framing with ornamental scrolls Trimming the body with rich broad lace worked in colours. Trimming all round the roof and pockets with ditto. Handsome full puckered falls to the seats trimmed with ditto. Ornamenting the panels all over with spots painted in relief & picking out body & carriage in colours. Painting an elegant border around the panels and footboard Providing a large platform with side irons covered with leather & large leather cover over. Round brackets with circular cuttings and fixing to foreaxle bed. Upright hind [rear] Standard [figure] carved with wings & footman's cushion made to remove at pleasure. A large Salisbury boot covered with leather finely japanned. Handworked plated mouldings all round the boot and round the step. A handsome full gathered hammer cloth of fine light coloured cloth lined with two rows of broad lace and ornamented with two rows of fringes worked in colours. Double set of broad laced footman's holders, with tassels and made up with plated buckles. Set spring curtains. Pair of handsome globular reflecting lanthorns, ornamented to match the panels and a painted border. A handsome set of mock joints strongly plated with silver. Reflecting lamp so constructed as to burn with oil, fixed with a frame to the guard light behind.
Complete £256.11s.0d.

Those extras certainly mounted up, and on this occasion Lord Delaval also chose to order four new sets of harness with octagon plates chased with his own crest at a cost of £48.

It was this ability to deliver the highest quality items that made Godsal's carriages amongst the most publicised and discussed in the newspapers. The great events which

attracted the carriages of the fashionable world were the birthday parades of George III and of his consort Queen Charlotte. That of the King was held early in June each year and the Queen's was on 8 January. New carriages out on the streets of London were noted at other times and reported upon but it was the birthday parades which attracted the most press coverage.

In 1782 the vehicles from Godsal's yard were reported as 'the smartest carriages we saw',[6] one of them, at the King's birthday, being for William Beckford, already, at the age of twenty-four, known as 'the richest man in England' but as yet without the scandalous reputation that was soon to attach to him.

But the coach 'surpassing all in elegance' in that year was that of the Duke of Northumberland which had silver heraldic decoration worked in *alto relivo*.[7] All Godsal's carriages were particularly admired for the method of varnishing used which produced 'a very high lustre, almost equal to a looking glass'.[8]

For the King's birthday parade of 1787 there was much publicity for Godsal when he produced a chariot for Sir H. Cosby decorated with spots.[9] The following January for the Queen's parade 'the greater part of the exceedingly tasty and elegant carriages came from Godsal & Co'.[10] The newspapers sent scouts to the coachmakers' yards in Long Acre before the parades to gain background information. The coachmakers, including Philip Godsal, were only too delighted to feed them their own descriptions, which naturally lost nothing in the telling. Rival newspapers criticised each other for falling in with this self publicity.

At the Queen's birthday parade in January 1790 *The Times* noted that 'we do not agree in the advertising account of the coachmaker [Philip Godsal] published in *The World* yesterday that the Earl of Massareene's coach could claim to be the most elegant'.[11] Having had a dig at its rival for re-cycling advertising under the guise of reporting, *The Times* went on to say 'While in point of richness the coach of the Earl of Massereene seemed to claim the preference, the panels are rich and gaudy and the mother of pearl ornaments out of style of coach grandeur'. It did concede however that 'the waved net work over the green mosaic ground has a pretty effect on the panels'.

Lumley Skeffington, Earl of Massereene was an Irish Peer with a reputation as a chronic debtor whose account with Godsal is discussed in chapter eight, 'The Genealogy of Irish Debtors'.

In this same procession *The Times* picked out the carriage of the Spanish Ambassador, which had a striped scarlet and gold body painted with decorative emblems.

LEFT:
An elegant crane-neck Town Landaulet with Canterbury boot and sword-case on rear of body, watercolour by Rudolph Ackermann

BELOW:
A highly decorated Town Coach, watercolour by Rudolph Ackermann

When the Spanish Ambassador had visited 103 Long Acre in the previous November to check on progress of his coach he had admired a watch stand in Godsal's office. He ordered a similar one which Godsal sold him for twelve guineas having bought it for £10.[12]

The annual Lord Mayor's procession was another occasion when the new coaches would invariably attract the notice of the press. The Lord Mayor, of course, rode in the City of London Corporation's own coach and it was the two incoming Sheriffs who commissioned new chariots for their year in office. There are records of Godsal making four of these between 1790 and 1803 and it is likely he made others. In 1790 he was actually in Ireland delivering the Lord Chancellor's State Coach when he notes in his memorandum book that Alderman Macauley's chariot was sent out from his yard.[13] It was extremely colourful and *The Times* was especially impressed, although no doubt itself drawing on the description provided by the coachmaker.[14]

> The body, a light olive and a painting in the middle – Commerce and Justice; the panels red with beading and carved work, burnished with gold and silver; the coach box supported by dolphins, the hind part supported by the cap of liberty and plenty…the hammer-cloth is a very rich blue and orange, and round it festoons of rich orange silk, with a beautiful border of lace, consisting of blue, orange, white, purple and silver; the inside lined with white silk, with fringe matching the colours of the hammer cloth. The horses, two French black stallions with black harness decorated with orange and purple ribbons.

This same year the other Sheriff's coach was also made in Godsal's yard. Alderman Glynn had clearly chosen to spend rather less than his colleague – there were no carvings at front and rear and its colours were rather less flamboyant, but *The Times* recorded his chariot as being

> very neat and elegant, the body is pale blue, on the panels a painting of Justice and Commerce, the borders of the panels silver burnished; the inside lined with white silk with silver fringe; the hammer cloth blue with white silk festooned at each end.[15]

The chariot Godsal made for Sir John Eamer, a Sheriff in 1794, survives in pictorial form in a drawing by the designer Rudolph Ackermann and is described in chapter six, 'Customers and Debtors'. Of the chariot made for Sheriff Powell in 1803 we learn only that it was amongst the finest carriages to be made and that it cost £1,000.[16]

Many other Godsal carriages are mentioned in the newspapers including that made for Lord Melbourne in 1788, 'a new carriage, very highly spoken of both as to taste and execution – its colour is dark green'[17] and on the same day, more an entry in a gossip column than a carriage review 'Colonel Tarleton has lately launched a *vis-a-vis* but we do not hear whether or not his old companion, *Perdita*, will condescend to take a seat in it'. The gossip about Colonel Tarleton, and his connections, and those of Lord Melbourne, with Philip Godsal are told below and in chapter six, 'Customers and Debtors'.

The year 1790 was perhaps Godsal's *annus mirabilis*. Not only did he complete the celebrated State Coach for the Irish Lord Chancellor and the chariots for the two Sheriffs but he also completed a carriage for the Hon Arthur Annesley with a border composed of heraldic bearings and the arms of twelve families, connected with the House of Valentia.[18] Annesley succeeded to the title of Earl of Mountnorris in 1793 and his son also became a customer of Philip Godsal. His story is told below.

In this same richly productive year he made at least two carriages for William Courtenay, Annesley's brother-in-law, who had just succeeded as Viscount Courtenay of Powderham Castle, Devon. The newspapers were unanimous. *The Public Advertiser* said of one that it was 'superlative and will astonish the gazing Town'. *The Oracle* said 'the *Vis-à-vis* is the most beautiful carriage ever seen' and *The Times* concurred, noting [19] 'Lord Courtenay has just launched a new coach which in point of magnificence is superior to any private carriage that has been seen for many years'.

Only a week later the same newspaper, which frequently made coded but clear attacks on homosexual public figures, carried another report. It should be said that Courtenay's boyhood infatuation with William Beckford which had led to the disgrace and temporary exile of the older Beckford, was public knowledge. And it may need to be explained that Morocco was infamous then, as now, as a haunt for homosexuals.

> Lord Courtenay's new carriage will cut a fine figure at MOROCCO, where it is said his Lordship is soon to go. The appearance of a magnificent nobleman cannot fail to be of service to the garrison…and his Lordship may have more private amusement…than any traveller of his age and rank.[20]

By the time of the King's birthday parade in June *The*

A Military Fly, designed and built by Philip Godsal in 1798

Times contented itself with complimenting 'the elegant v*is-à-vis* of Lord Courtenay and a new coach likewise belonging to his Lordship'.[21] This vehicle was painted in Godsal's 'patent yellow'.

There was no public record of the identity of the manufacturer of Courtenay's carriages but Philip Godsal's Diary reveals that in October 1790 he travelled to Powderham Castle and spent five days with Viscount Courtenay.[22] Courtenay's carriages in the 1791 parades were noted as 'the most splendid and expensive of any nobleman'.

One of his carriages had hub caps decorated with ornaments in ormolu which were said to have cost 100 guineas each. One hammercloth was said to have cost 300 guineas[23] and the splendours of Courtenay's carriages were said to have been much admired by the 'gay' world, an adjective whose particular relevance in this case now strikes us with even greater resonance.

Conclusive evidence that it was Philip Godsal who manufactured two other special coaches for 4,000 guineas each for Courtenay and his beautiful sisters (he had no fewer than twelve), and that Courtenay had been slow to pay, is the bond for the re-payment of £8,200 to Philip Godsal to be found in the Iscoyd papers.[24] Courtenay's debts to Godsal, and the scandals which pursued him, are discussed later.

Drawings or prints of several of Godsal's carriages exist. They include a fully signed drawing of a landaulet, showing the head, open and closed,[25] (page 29) and a print of a 'Military Fly'[26] (above). This vehicle is something of a curiosity. Drawn by four horses it was designed to carry twenty of the infantry men in a cavalry regiment. The evident lack of springing suggests they must have suffered considerable discomfort. The print was published in 1798 by the carriage designer Rudolph Ackermann although the design could be either his or Godsal's. The artist, Thomas Rowlandson, noted that it was 'inventit et excudit at Godsal & Co'. Shortly afterwards Philip Godsal became a mess member of the City of London Light Horse Volunteer Regiment to whom the print was dedicated and later received a captain's commission in another Volunteer regiment, the Hampstead Volunteers.[27]

A Berline, designed by Philip Godsal in 1783

CHAPTER FOUR

The Irish Lord Chancellor's Coach

The most celebrated of the many carriages made by Philip Godsal was the State Coach made for the Lord Chancellor of Ireland in 1789/1790. It generated enormous publicity in both London and Dublin and although not all the press coverage was complimentary it demonstrates the adage that no publicity is bad publicity for it was undoubtedly the means of making his name well known in both capitals and generating more business.

The genesis of the Irish Lord Chancellor's Coach is to be found in a model of a ceremonial coach made in London by a recently arrived German emigré, Rudolph Ackermann,

who after early training in Saxony, worked as a coach designer in Switzerland, Paris and Brussels before arriving in England in 1788 at the age of twenty-four. Although he had worked for Antoine Carassi in Paris and for Simons of Brussels, the leading continental coachmakers, it would not be easy for the young foreigner to break into the established London coachmaking business. As an advertisement of his skills the young Ackermann made a model of one of his designs and took it to Long Acre where Philip Godsal was so attracted that he bought the model and the accompanying technical drawing for the princely

The Irish Lord Chancellor's Coach

43

sum of £200 thus establishing Ackermann's fortunes and reputation at a stroke.[1]

For Godsal too it was money well spent, for the model was seen in Long Acre by Lord (John) Fitzgibbon who had recently been appointed Lord Chancellor of Ireland. He ordered a State Coach to be based upon the design. Godsal went to Dublin in the summer of 1789 for further talks with Fitzgibbon, dining with him on 21 July when 'I took his orders for the State Coach'.[2]

The decoration was discussed, the painting of the bodywork with the emblematic herald painting, the carving and gilding of the supporting figures, the roof entablature finial and the interior finish with its ceiling the site of a further allegorical painting. A price of £7,000 was agreed,[3] this figure apparently including the decorative elaborately chased harness for three pairs of horses. This was by no means the highest price asked for in the London coachmaking industry. The Nawab of Arcot was said to have paid John Hatchett fifteen thousand guineas for a coach only a few years before.[4]

Godsal himself is believed to have given the following description of the Irish Lord Chancellor's coach to *Faulkner's Dublin Journal*[5]

It is 11ft 6in high and 19ft 10in long. The body is hung by leather straps from upright or whip springs; at the base are curved supports, ornamental at each end with cornucopia, to which the ends of the leather braces are fastened, and in the centre, under each door is a head of Apollo surrounded by the rays of the sun. Running round the waist of the carriage is a broad band of arabesque ornament carved in relief and gilt showing a rich crimson ground under the gold design. On this, on the doors and the front and rear of the carriage are the Chancellor's arms, a saltire with three annulets in chief, the shield supported by a lion and griffin holding a scroll with the motto 'Nil admirari'. The pillars, which support the roof slope outwards, making the roof longer than the waistline of the body, and are carved with caryatides standing upon a caduceus. These figures hold a festoon which runs under the edge of the roof, and support at each of the four corners the crowned harp ornamented with palm leaves. On the centre of the roof are three figures of boys supporting a cushion with Lord Fitzgibbon's coronet.

On the fore and hind axles are carved seated figures representing at the fore end 'Prudence' on the near side and 'Justice', on the off side; and at the rear 'Liberality' and 'Concord'. From beneath these figures issue the upright springs.

The cranes are carved with oak leaves and acorns. On the front axle-bed or platform are carved heads of Solon and Numa. The footboard in front is framed with a wreath of leaves, and has on it the crowned harp surrounded with rays of glory. Two wolfdogs terminate the curved supports of the footboard.

The hind axle bed is carved with bull rushes and a large shell shaped ornament with the head of King Alfred beneath it. The head and those of Solon and Numa represent the three great law-givers.

The wheels have their spokes, inner rim and nave delicately carved; the caps are of ormolu. The buckles of the braces, the door handles and other metal ornaments are also of ormolu.

The lining of the interior is of crimson velvet trimmed with gold-fringe and shamrock patterned lace. The coachman's seat is covered with the same material with fringe and tassels.

On the panel of each door is an allegorical painting framed in an octagonal, carved moulding. The subject on the rear door panel is the Temple of Fame with figures of Britannia and Hibernia embracing and crowned with Peace and Plenty. These represent National Prosperity, which is proclaimed by Fame with her trumpet. The arms of Ireland are supported by the Genii of Immortality.

The off-door panel shows the Courts of Law and Equity, represented by Justice sitting on a throne, holding the scales in her right hand and the sword in her left, supported by Minerva. On one side appears Truth, a nude female figure with her right hand on an open book; on the other, Mercy stretching out her hands to Justice. At the foot of the throne of Justice are the Chancellor's purse and mace.

On the panel in front of the body of the carriage is seen a seaport, with ships loading bales of Irish manufacture at a wharf; in the foreground three figures typifying Europe, Africa and America with a statue of Mercury; the whole representing the Commerce of Ireland and her intercourse with all parts of the world.

On the hind panel Agriculture is represented by the triumph of Ceres, with boys, emblematic of the four Seasons, directing the car of the Goddess. Figures in the foreground bearing cornucopia typifying Plenty.

In the centre of the roof inside the carriage is a medallion portrait of King George III, supported by the allegorical figures of Virtue and Loyalty crowning the King with immortality.

These paintings executed by William Hamilton, R.A. at a cost of 500 guineas.

Roof Medallion in Lord Chancellor's Coach, painted by William Hamilton, R.A.

century French furniture mounts, and the bodywork background of stripes and ovals resembling contemporary wallpapers and materials, he did not know the identity of the designer.[6] These French influences derived in this case direct from France where Ackermann had been trained and had but recently arrived.

The detailed specification tells exactly how elaborate and unique the State coach was. It also indicates something of the man who commissioned it. The modern biographer of Fitzgibbon believes that he was as preoccupied with the trappings of power as with its exercise and remarks that 'he had an overmastering desire to create an elegant and aristocratic impression on the world at large'.[7] His State Coach provides a perfect illustration of this character assessment.

John Fitzgibbon was a clever Irish lawyer from County Limerick who rose to his eminent position by his brains and by his loyalty to the British crown. He received his due rewards. He was created Baron Fitzgibbon in 1789, appointed Lord Chancellor of Ireland in 1790, created Viscount Fitzgibbon in 1793, Earl of Clare in 1795 and in 1799 he was created an English peer as Baron Fitzgibbon of Sidbury.[8] Having decided early where his bread was buttered he delivered his country into Union with the country of his political masters in 1801.

That he should choose an English coachmaker, rather than an Irish one is in line with his character and was widely perceived as a political statement but the detailed specification of his State Coach suggests that there could have been few coachmakers who could have delivered on that specification even if they could have prepared it. In London there were probably no more than three or four[9] and it was Fitzgibbon's judgement that there were none in Dublin.

Before the vehicle was actually seen on the streets of Dublin in all its glory however there were many who took a different view. 'Suspicion and resentment of England's commercial superiority and a belief that every Irishman

The harness is of morocco leather with mountings of chased ormolu. The buckles are ornamented with the harp, the Cap of Liberty, the caduceus and the Chancellor's purse; the blinkers are edged with a pierced ormolu pattern, with the Harp in the centre. Other ornaments of sprays of foliage appear on various portions of the harness. The traces are attached to a breast-strap not to a collar.

When a later furniture historian noted the influence of French fashion on the design of the coach, with the acanthus frieze, the gilded caryatids echoing late eighteenth

ABOVE:
Lord Fitzgibbon, later 1st Earl of Clare, Lord Chancellor of Ireland. Print after Sir Joshua Reynolds, P.R.A.

RIGHT:
Prudence, one of four figures desiged by Richard Westmacott, for the Lord Chancellor's Coach

ought to patronise home manufactures had long been essential articles of the patriot/opposition creed'.[10] Thus the political battle lines were drawn almost before work had begun on the coach in Godsal's workshops in Long Acre in London. The rivalry was pointed up when on the very day of Philip Godsal's arrival in Dublin in July 1789 to reach a final agreement with Lord Fitzgibbon, the Corporation of Dublin voted £600 to provide a new coach for their Lord Mayor. A committee appointed to progress the matter immediately reported back that the sum allowed was entirely inadequate to support the dignity of the Chief Magistrate. The Corporation now agreed to provide £1,200

and the contract was given to one of Dublin's principal coachmakers, William Whitton of Dominick Street who began work in the autumn of 1789.[11]

The two rivals, Dublin and London, were now head to head but it is doubtful if this political aspect pre-occupied Philip Godsal. His yard was now preparing to meet the demanding specifications and particularly the unusually demanding amount of emblematic painting and of carved figures and symbols on the coach and the chasing and ormolu on the harness.

The painting of the bodywork was probably by Charles Ackroyd, whom Godsal believed to be the best in the business.[12] The heraldic and emblematic painting was in the hands of William Hamilton R.A. and his studio. It was the carving which caused Godsal the most concern in view of a delivery date to Dublin to allow the new State Coach to

had previously believed. That delightful model, on a scale of 1:6, is a copy of the coach, as finally built, and may well have been commissioned when the actual coach was completed. What more natural than that Fitzgibbon himself should commission such a model.

It seems possible therefore that there were two models; one by Rudolph Ackermann made after his design which was used as the basis for the finished Coach and one model made after completion of the actual Coach. That this could be the case is reinforced by the fact that 'a model in bronze of the State carriage, built by Godsal, of the Lord Chancellor, with painted panels and bronze figure by Lilla Chassern' was sold at auction in 1888 by the grand-daughter of Lord Fitzgibbon, the model having descended to her from the collection of Lord Fitzgibbon at Mountshannon, co. Limerick. It was sold again at auction in Christies on 20 January 1903 and was bought by the Lady Lever Gallery, Port Sunlight where it remains.[40]

If indeed the Lady Lever model is not the original model by Rudolph Ackermann on which the design was based then what happened to that model? Godsal's Diaries throw some light on this.

On 18 April 1804 Godsal writes 'Breakfast at Hampstead – Mr Tayler with me – delivered him the model of Lord Clare State Coach'

On 13 October 1804 he writes 'Paid Mr Tayler £20.3s.6d in full of all demands for completing the model of Lord Clare's State Coach'

Presumably Godsal by now kept Ackermann's model in his home and had sent it for repair fifteen years after it was made. There is more. On 15 July 1815 he pays Oliver £1.8s.0d for 'writing on model of Lord Clare's' (perhaps a description of the coach for displaying with the model in his home in Cheltenham) and in July 1816 he pays, Whitby, the furniture maker £5.12s.0d for '2 cases made of best 1¼ inch deal for Model of State Coach and glass cover of ditto containing 40 feet planed smoothed inside and out and put together with strong 2½ inch screws – 4 strong japanned lifting handles to each case'. Whitby's also billed Godsal for 2s for 'porteridge' of model Stand'.[41]

This is the last we hear of this model, (? the Ackermann model), some twenty-six years after it was bought and displayed in Godsal's Long Acre manufactory. Later, it had become a decorative feature in Godsal's homes, first in Hampstead, then at 243 Oxford Street and then at Montpelier Place, Cheltenham.

It is not mentioned specifically in his will. Perhaps, in 1826, his widow took it to her new smaller home in Addiscomb Street, Cheltenham or perhaps it stayed at Montpelier Place as his son Philip Lake moved in. Perhaps it was to him an unwelcome reminder of the trade that had made him the fine gentleman he had become. Certainly it was no longer of such sentimental significance as it had so clearly been to Philip himself and some years after his death it may have been quietly disposed of by Philip Lake.

John Wombwell, a nabob returned from Bengal, made a large investment in Godsal's coach-making business in 1789

CHAPTER FIVE
Capital and Creditors

In the later years Philip Godsal's coachmaking business generated cash which he was able to invest in the business itself, in property and a variety of investments including prototype banking in the form of cash loaned to customers against security. In the early and middle years of the business however it was Godsal himself who had to borrow capital from time to time to put into his business and to buy and extend his residences.

When this proved necessary he rarely borrowed from his bank, where his account was maintained in credit against which he would draw cheques for day to day business expenses. He borrowed instead from a variety of individuals or from other businesses who had cash available at the time. The Usury Act restricted the interest on such borrowings to five per cent so that negotiation for such borrowings was limited to the length of the loan, the security and, of course, an assessment by the lender of the character and commercial standing of the borrower.

Godsal inherited the coachmaking business from his mother in 1768 and there was therefore no requirement for start-up capital to create a business but he expanded the business in the later 1780s and it was at this time he took out a series of significant loans.

In July 1784 he asked his solicitor, Frederick Booth, to send the following letter to certain of his debtors.

Mr Godsal of Long Acre, coachmaker, being at present very much distressed for having been assisted some time since with a very large sum of money by his Banker which he was long since to have repaid & is now obliged & which he is entirely incapable of doing but by the assistance of those Gentlemens' accounts who are indebted to him'.[1]

Whether Godsal did indeed have a large bank loan at this date or whether this solicitor's letter was a wake-up call to get debtors to pay we cannot be entirely sure. But employing such wording suggests that such large borrowings were known to be a normal fact of business.

In April 1787 he borrowed £2,000 on a short term loan of eighteen months from Montague and Edward George Lind. He did not give security in the form of a mortgage on property but gave his bond, jointly with his brother-in-law, Charles Cole, for £4,000, twice the sum borrowed.

Bonds were formal legal agreements drawn up by solicitors and the sum indemnified by the borrower was twice the principal sum lest he should fail to pay the principal sum, any interest due and any legal expenses against their recovery. Interest however was paid on the principal sum borrowed and not on the sum indemnified.

Godsal repaid the Linds £1,000 of the principal within a year but agreed with them to extend the loan for a further five years, continuing to pay the annual interest of five per cent. The principal and interest were finally paid off in June 1793[2].

When Godsal bought the lease of 84 Piccadilly from Mrs Abington in 1788 he borrowed £1,000 from John Michie, a wine merchant of Craven Street, Strand who was also a Director of the East India Company. In this case he did not give his bond but mortgaged to Michie his property in Gower Street, redeeming the mortgage twelve months later.[3]

It was in 1789 that Godsal made his principal investment in the coachmaking business. Business was booming and the order for the State Coach by the Lord Chancellor of Ireland required a major investment in terms of workshops, skilled workers, and materials, including gold leaf. He needed £8,000 and he turned for this enormous sum to a Nabob, John Wombwell, recently returned from Bengal.

The fortunes to be made in the service of the East India Company were enormous and Wombwell had clearly 'shaken the Pagoda tree' to good effect. His cousin, George Wombwell, had been a Director of the Company in London, and John had already run through a fortune at home when he was sent out by his father in 1775 to be one of the inner circle of Philip Francis to keep an eye on the Governor-General, Warren Hastings.[4]

John Wombwell had more opportunity than most to make his fortune in this land of easy pickings, for in 1778 he was appointed 'Paymaster to the troops serving with the Vizier under British officers in the Province of Oudh'. At the same time he was appointed 'Auditor General of the accounts of the commissaries to the Vizier's troops and of all disbursements made in the Vizier's army except the pay of the troops'.[5]

The combined roles of Paymaster and Auditor General would now be seen as entirely improper but from Wombwell's point of view it was entirely satisfactory. The instructions of the Directors in London were that

the Paymaster and Auditor General do reside at Lucknow, visiting as he may see occasion, the different stations of troops paid by him, and that all monies issued from the Vizier to be advanced for the subsistence of any of his troops, be issued in the first instance to the Paymaster General aforesaid, to be issued by him to the said troops at their respective stations.[6]

The opportunities for making a fortune could not have been more clearly spelled out. Wombwell's opportunities were increased because his predecessor had carried off all the accounts and left him with no established system of financial control.

The requirement of residence in Lucknow was another benefit, for the town was, from a European's point of view, the most agreeable and civilised in the Province. The artist Johann Zoffany visited Lucknow at this time; his friend Paul Sandby said it was 'to roll in the gold dust'.[7] Zoffany pictures John Wombwell in several of his paintings including the celebrated 'Colonel Mordaunt's Cock Match', 1784-6 and Colonel Polier and his friends, 1786.[8]

For Wombwell things were to go from good to better. In 1783 the Accountant to the Residency at Lucknow was removed and ordered to hand over all his accounts to Wombwell who thus earned another salary.[9] He became responsible for receiving the payments required from the Vizier by the East India Company.

By 1785 however questions were beginning to be asked. First, the salary of his assistant was withdrawn and then Wombwell was asked to account precisely for the commissions he was paying himself both through the Vizier's accounts and the Company's accounts. It was decided by the Court of Directors that he could not hold his two salaries and in 1786 the Court removed him from his post as Paymaster and Auditor General which was then abolished.[10]

Wombwell was appointed Superintendent of the saltpetre manufacture at Purnea,[11] critical to the Company for its use in gunpowder. He decided to resign however in

1788 and brought back his fortune to England. Even at the end there was a whiff of scandal for when his final accounts were scrutinised in Calcutta it was noted that he had drawn his last quarter's salary from the Resident's office but had also paid himself at the manufactory. The Governor-General asked the Court of Directors in London to make enquiries of Wombwell in London over this discrepancy.[12]

It was immediately on his return to London that he agreed to make Philip Godsal the loan of £8,000. Though both men attended the same church of St George's, Hanover Square, the contact between the two was most probably made through Colonel Mordaunt of Lucknow, for whose brother, the Earl of Peterborough, it was likely that Godsal had made the famous coach described by William Hickey and discussed on page 40.

On 12 February 1789 in consideration for £8,000 cash at five per cent interest, Philip Godsal of Long Acre assigned to John Wombwell of Hanover Square his 'leasehold messuages and lands in Charles Street, Long Acre, Cross Lane, Castle Street, Nottingham Court and Gower Street in the parishes of St Martins and St Giles in the Fields and St Georges, Hanover Square in the County of Middlesex. The insurance lodged in Mr Wombwell's hands'.[13]

Thus it was that East India money financed the expansion and development of one of the three principal coachmaking manufactories in London.

The annual interest was £400 until it was reduced in 1795 when Godsal paid off £2,000 of the principal sum.[14] He paid off further amounts of the principal over the following years and in March 1801 he made a final payment of £715.19s.6d 'in full of all demands, principal & interest of the sum of £8,000 borrowed in the year 1789', thus redeeming the assignments on his properties.[15] On a re-calculation it was discovered that he had overpaid by £62.0s.0d which John Wombwell, Esq re-paid in full in May 1801.[16]

In the period of rapid expansion Godsal also borrowed £1,000 from Lewis Gilles in August 1790 against his bond for £2,000 and continued to pay the annual interest of £50 until 1800 when he paid off half the principal. He did not make the final payment until 1805.[17]

Meanwhile in 1793 Godsal had the opportunity to buy a property in Hampstead, next door to his residence Grove House. His friend and solicitor, Frederick Booth agreed to lend him the money on a short term loan without security but at the usual five per cent interest and Godsal borrowed £1,500 to buy Mr Ambrose's house.[18]

Godsal paid back the money quickly but then two years

later, when he bought Dingwall out of his lease at Hampstead (see page 83) he borrowed another £1,000 from Booth which he paid back within four years.[19]

In this same period, in 1794, he borrowed £2,000 from his bank, Messrs Pybus, Byde, Dorsett, Cockett & Pybus, which he had paid back by 1801.[20]

Even at the height of his business turnover Godsal continued to borrow money in the medium and short term, some of it for the coachmaking business and some for his proliferating property interests. One of the loans was to cause him some embarrasment.

In 1797, at the time he took Baxter and Macklew into partnership, he gave his bond for £500 to Charles Ackroyd, a man whom he described as 'the best coachpainter in the business and one of the best of men'. Three years later Ackroyd died and Godsal gave a gift to the widow.[21] However no interest was paid subsequently on the bond until 1814 when Macklew, who was an executor to Ackroyd, came across the bond in the papers at Long Acre and drew it to the attention of Godsal who wrote in his Diary, 'the bond of £500 due to the estate of Charles Ackroyd, deceased had escaped my recollection, having supposed it paid and charged to my account within the Trade, Long Acre but find it not paid and correct in Macklew's executors' accounts'.[22] He paid over the sum of £871.15s.8d.

In 1798 he borrowed £1,000 from Howell & Co, carpenters, against his bond, redeeming it in 1804 after he had purchased chambers in Albany.[23] In 1799 he borrowed £500 of Prescott & Co for three months[24] and from 1799 to 1801 he borrowed from, and re-paid, the woollen draper, John Wallace, a series of sums, one of which secured him the lease of Number 1 Clarges Street.[25]

In 1802 he borrowed £500 for three months from Mr Siveright.[26] To complete the purchase of his Oxford Street house in 1805 he borrowed from his solicitor Evan Foulkes the sum of £800 which he finally repaid in 1811 by which time he had borrowed £1,000 from the widow of his friend the late Jonathan Buttall in order to buy Montpelier Place in Cheltenham. This he repaid in full with interest in 1813.[27]

This apparently bewildering series of loans from a variety of individuals and tradesmen is explicable perhaps in the context that the banks did not fulfill the range of functions of the present day banks and there were as yet no building societies. And Godsal was himself lending money to his friends in the short and medium term at the same five per cent interest rate.

This was the period of the so called Industrial Revolution when the dynamic growth of manufacturing business was apparently achieved without the formal infrastructure which might be expected to have been in position to facilitate it. This was of course a period when the country was at war, and it appears that the banks found greater profits in financing the government's war efforts through investment in Government stock than in generating increased income through the encouragement and expansion of productive industry. Perhaps the truth has always been that the true British genius has been in the entrepreneurial spirit of its people and not in the structure of financial institutions that has grown up to feed off it.

That banks were very different institutions from those of the present day is shown by only the second banker's loan which Godsal ever took out. In 1803 he had changed his long standing account with Pybus & Co to Marsh, Sibbald, Graham, Stracey & Fauntleroy of Berners Street. He gave a Power of Attorney to the younger Henry Fauntleroy when he sold off £5,000 of Government Stock to pay for his son's commission in the Honourable Company of Gentlemen Pensioners[28] and over the years he became on friendly terms with Fauntleroy, inviting him to dine at his house and sponsoring him when Fauntleroy was elected a Freemason at the prestigious Somerset House Lodge.[29] On another occasion Fauntleroy gave Godsal six tickets for the Opera House.[30]

In 1814 Godsal borrowed £4,000 from the bank to pay for two pieces of land which were to form the major part of his estate at Montpelier, Cheltenham.[31] He paid the annual interest of some £200 per year until July 1824 when he paid off the last £3,000 of the principal sum.[32] Only two months later the bank suspended all payments and Henry Fauntleroy was arrested on the charge of forgery. He had been using existing Powers of Attorney and forging others to cash in Government stock lodged by customers with the bank. This fraud had been going on for some years, covered up by Fauntleroy paying out the annual interest due on the, by now, non existent stock.

At Fauntleroy's sensational trial at the Old Bailey on 30 October 1824 the losses were stated to be in excess of £400,000 and Fauntleroy was revealed as the greatest swindler in English history. Witnesses confirmed that he had bought a splendid house in Brighton where he maintained the attractive daughter of a Brighton bathing woman and where he drove about in high style in a splendid carriage – almost certainly made by Philip Godsal. He was also said to be paying annuities to a number of other young ladies. In his defence seven respectable gentleman spoke for his previously good character, although Philip Godsal was not one of their number. It was a hopeless case however, and Fauntleroy was found guilty and was hanged outside Newgate prison in the first week of November 1824 in the presense of a crowd estimated as being over ten thousand.[33]

Godsal was not present to see the execution of his old friend, fellow freemason and banker but a month later he wrote across his Bank Book 'Mr Henry Fauntleroy tried for forging several Power of Attorneys & found guilty at the Old Bailey Sessions Oct'r 30th 1824. Suffered the sentence of the Law'[34] and he recorded in his Diary loss of £751.6s.0d held in credit in his account when the bank's payments were suspended.[35] The treachery of an old friend and fellow freemason must have been a bitter pill for the seventy-seven years old Philip Godsal and it must have

been particularly galling as he had so recently paid back to the bank the balance of the £4,000 he had borrowed ten years earlier.

When the bankruptcy receiver completed his examination of the bank's accounts he declared a dividend of 6s 8d in the pound and Godsal at least recovered £250.8s.8d.[36] There was more bad news however for the collapse of one bank often led to the collapse of others and Godsal's Cheltenham bank and Tewkesbury bank also suspended payments occasioning him another loss, albeit small.[37]

For the last year of his life Philip Godsal opened an account, like so many gentlemen, with the respectable Thomas Coutts in the Strand.[38]

CHAPTER SIX
Customers and Debtors

In the coachmaking business there is less distinction to be drawn between customers and debtors than in many other businesses. The gentlemen and the members of the aristocracy who bought carriages expected credit, and almost invariably received it. Thus the customer became a debtor and some indeed became bad debtors. The coachmaker necessarily had to be a man with considerable capital reserves and also have a productive manufactory so that over a period of time cash was coming in at the same time credit was being given. Few new coachmaking businesses were established in London from the late eighteenth century. The established ones continued, or were sold on as going concerns, or went bankrupt. The worry about bad debtors was ever present. Most letters requesting payment were politely couched but the constant worries to the coachmaker are well caught in an informal postscript Godsal wrote to his solicitor in 1784 'By accident I see Tinker's chariot this day at a Painter's shop. I suspect he has sold it – he must be watched for he is doubtful. I know he cannot move without your knowing – I hope he will last good so as to pay me – pray watch him'.[1]

Given the extended credit customary in the trade, it was usual for the coachmakers both to charge interest on the credit account and to look for some sort of security, the commonest form of which was a bond, a legally executed document guaranteeing twice the amount of credit lest legal expenses should be incurred on collecting the principal and interest owing. Given this form of credit guarantee it was not unusual for the coachmaker to round off the carriage debt by lending a cash sum in addition. From this practice it became regular for a coachmaker's customers to borrow cash from time to time. Thus the coachmaker, and indeed other tradesmen with liquid capital available, served as private merchant bankers to the aristocracy and gentry. An acute German observer visiting one of the leading coachmakers, Hatchetts of Long Acre in 1786 noted this 'I was amused to see how the people played into each other's hands, and that a coachmaker has a counting house and a paymaster just like a banker'.[2]

Several banks developed from this vestigial or prototype banking, Curtis, the ships' biscuit manufacturer and Wood, the druggist were two of Godsal's London contemporaries whose businesses were transformed into banks.[3] Had Philip handed over his business to his son it is likely that the banking element of the business would have extended and perhaps, separated from the carriage manufacture. That is of course hypothetical, but the fact is that many of Philip Godsal's customers who bought carriages on credit also borrowed cash.

Customers included no fewer than forty-seven English Members of the Houses of Parliament in addition to the twenty-five Irish Members who sat in the Irish Parliament or the British Parliament after 1801 and who are discussed in a later chapter. These seventy-two members of the two Houses represent over forty per cent of all Godsal's customers whom it has been possible to trace, in the absence of a formal Debtors' Ledger in the Iscoyd Papers.

Members of the Houses of Parliament could not be declared bankrupt, nor imprisoned for debt and that privilege might be thought likely to lessen their opportunities to borrow, for the sanction of imprisonment for debt for ordinary debtors was a very strong deterrent indeed to non-payment. Most of them, however, were prepared to sign legal bonds for Godsal and, although he often had to work very hard to collect the debts, there were on the whole relatively few bad debtors. The Marquess of Blandford, later the 5th Duke of Marlborough, is the worst case and his relations with Philip Godsal are described in a separate chapter.

Some debtors were members of the Diplomatic Corps. Thomas Bruce, 7th Earl of Elgin, later to achieve immortal eponymous fame for the Marbles, bought a carriage from Godsal for £199 after he had returned from Berlin and before his departure to the Porte. The Hon Hugh Elliot, brother of the Earl of Minto, was a friend of Mirabeau, of Coleridge and of Marie Antoinette's sister, the Queen of Naples. While on leave from his post in the Leeward Islands and before taking up the post of Governor of Madras he paid £200 for a carriage he had bought over five years before.[4]

The Sheriffs and Aldermen of the City of London were important clients and better payers. There are records of the chariots bought from Godsal by four Sheriffs between 1790 and 1803 and there were probably more. From the twentieth century the Sheriffs have ridden in the Lord Mayor's procession in carriages owned by the Corporation but in the eighteenth and nineteenth centuries they rode in their own, and a new chariot ordered for the occasion was *de rigeur*.

The drawing of Sir John Eamer's chariot, designed by Rudolph Ackermann and made by Godsal in 1794, and now in the collection of the Huntington Library and Art Gallery in San Marino, California was mentioned earlier (page 36). Eamer's chariot is particularly elegant and the harness and plumes, designed by Ackermann, of the pair of greys, were made in Godsal's harness shop.

Such embellishments were no doubt appealing to Sir John Eamer who was to become one of London's most colourful Lord Mayors. At his inaugural dinner in 1802, which coincided with the temporary peace with France he invited the Prince of Wales and the Royal Dukes and, apparently to save money did not give his Sheriffs any tickets for their friends. The Sheriffs boycotted the dinner for the only time in the City's long history and Sir John became the subject of some splendid cartoons and the victim of a hoax when a considerable number of people called at his house carrying invitations to dine.[5]

Two years later he was court-martialled for conduct prejudicial to military discipline for his use of gross and ungentlemanly language to the officers under his command in a Volunteer Regiment. He was acquitted, but the next year he was found guilty of striking a waggoner with his whip, on which occasion his colourful language was again remarked upon by several witnesses. He was fined £10. Given his evidently choleric disposition it is no surprise that he met his end through becoming overheated, although this time it was on Brighton beach where he died as a result of sun stroke.

Godsal had overseas debtors too. In 1799 his solicitor billed him for work in connection with 'a debt due from Mr Chace of the Island of Barbados & giving Power of Attorney to Mr Hordle of that Island'. Towards the end of his life he gave a Power of Attorney to one William Powell to collect debts from two plantation owners on Jamaica.[6] There is no record that he was successful. However he did recover debts of £176 from William Cockell in Madras in 1799, £434 from Sir Robert Liston in Philadelphia in 1801 (he was British Ambassador to Washington), £230 from William Windham in Florence in 1803 (he had formerly been

Secretary for War) and £300 from General Rawstorne in Calcutta in 1804.

Godsal also traded with India through the medium of Captain James Urmston who carried Godsal's carriages and spare parts to the East on at least two occasions.[7] Urmston commanded ten voyages of East Indiamen between 1772 and 1803. Captains were permitted by the East India Company to carry a certain tonnage of their own trade goods and at their own risk. In 1772 the permitted tonnage was twenty-five tons, rising to ninety-two tons in 1791 and by 1797 up to ninety-nine tons. For this privilege the Captain was required to pay the Company £500. By this means a number of European luxury items, such as claret and madeira, millinery, glassware and carriages were shipped to India and sold principally to expatriates.[8] Carriages were manufactured in such centres as Calcutta and Bombay but the London made carriages were more fashionable and East India captains like Urmston helped supply the demand. It appears that he bought the carriage or carriages on credit and settled with Godsal on his return, some two years later.

One of the largest bonds Godsal received was for £5,400, to re-pay £2,700, from Sir John Boyd, M.P., a Director of the East India Company and his brother-in-law, John Trevanion, M.P. who was a West India merchant. The original bond had been taken out for £2,000[9] but was re-negotiated in 1800 when Sir John succeeded his father as the 2nd baronet. They proved to be amongst the most obdurate of debtors, paying the interest only sporadically. Trevanion died in 1810, and already by 1806 it was said that 'he has dissipated whatever property he had and bears in other respects a very broken reputation'.[10] Sir John Boyd died five years later and in 1818 Philip Godsal listed the joint debt as being £3,144.6s.0d. There is no record of any payment whatsoever in the Diary or in the Bank Accounts and it would appear this was one of the largest of Godsal's bad debts.

Others with fortunes based on overseas trade paid more promptly. William Beckford, M.P., owner of extensive sugar plantations on Jamaica, was widely believed to be the richest man in England when in 1785 he ordered a carriage from Godsal and paid his account without delay.[11]

In his public character, Beckford appeared to court notoriety, and there were other customers who figured larger than life in their contemporaries' perception. Richard Tickell and Richard Brinsley Sheridan had married the Linley sisters, two of the celebrated beauties of the day. Through his association with Sheridan, Tickell became a member of Charles James Fox's circle. A witty Whig

The Chariot of John Eamer Esq. Sheriff of the City of London & County of Middlesex.
September 28. 1794.

R. Ackermann Del.

Built by Mess. Godsal &c.

Sir John Eamer's Chariot designed by Ackermann and built by Godsal

pamphleteer, he was much disliked by his Tory opponents who found much to criticise in Tickell's personal extravagances.[12] In 1793 he bought a carriage and took out a bond with Philip Godsal for £992 to repay £446.[13] At the same time he was also borrowing money elsewhere and his mounting debts were believed to be the reason for his suicide, which he commited with ostentatious bravado by throwing himself from the balcony of his Hampton Court Palace apartments in 1795. His beautiful widow scandalised the Town, and most especially his creditors, by continuing to drive about in one of Godsal's unpaid for carriages.

Another of Fox's circle was Colonel Banastre Tarleton, M.P. who had distinguished himself in the American War of Independence and, on returning home, had taken as his mistress the actress 'Perdita' Robinson, in succession, as it were, to the Prince of Wales (see page 39). Tarleton became M.P. for Liverpool in 1790 and shortly afterwards bought a carriage and took out a bond with Godsal for £500 to re-pay £250. He made no re-payments whatsoever for many years at a time when he was reported to be spending £2,500 a year with Mrs Robinson. She ditched him in 1797 when he was said to have designs on her twenty-one year old daughter, but the following year he married an heiress, the illegitimate daughter of the Duke of Ancaster. However any hopes Godsal had of getting his money back as a result of the marriage were to be disappointed. He had to wait until May 1806 to receive what he noted in his Diary as 'the first money I ever received of the General'. Tarleton, who had been promoted to the rank of Lieutenant General in 1801, eventually paid up the principal and interest in full in 1807.[14]

Another close associate of Charles James Fox was Andrew St John, M.P. later Lord St John of Bletsoe. His first dealings with Godsal date back to 1782 and he bought a carriage in 1785 for £227.7s.0d. A strong supporter of Fox, in 1787 he was one of the Parliamentary managers in the House of the impeachment of Warren Hastings. Godsal remained his coachmaker and in 1793 St John gave his bond for £2,108 against a debt of £1,009. He paid no interest whatsoever on this debt for thirteen years until in 1806, with the Whigs back in the Government again he was given the sinecure of captain of the Honourable Company of Gentlemen Pensioners, the King's ceremonial but salaried bodyguard.[15]

It is unclear which of the two made the suggestion but in June 1806 Godsal records that he calculated with Lord St John that the unpaid interest on the loan amounted to £692. He agreed to abate this by £192 and St John paid the reduced figure of £500. St John thereupon recommended

Colonel Banastre Tarleton, a hero in the American Revolutionary War, became a long-term debtor to Philip Godsal. Print after Sir Joshua Reynolds, P.R.A.

Godsal's son for a vacant lieutenancy in the Band of Gentlemen Pensioners and Philip Lake Godsal was gazetted in September and sworn in at Lord St John's private house in January 1807. The following day Godsal lent St John a further £100 and St John paid no further interest until 1811 when he agreed both to start paying interest and to pay the insurance premium for a policy worth £1000 on his death. He died in 1817 and the Equitable Insurance office paid up the sum assured.

Godsal numbered other prominent Whigs amongst his

clients. George Stubbs's painting of the Melbournes and the Milbankes in 1770 hangs to-day in the National Gallery in London and pictures Sir Ralph Milbanke, M.P., the 5th baronet, his son John, his daughter, Elizabeth Lamb, seated in her 'tim-whisky' carriage, and her husband Penistone Lamb, who was to become the first Lord Melbourne in 1784. All three men were customers of Godsals as was the 6th baronet Ralph Milbanke, whose daughter Arabella was to marry Lord Byron in 1815.

The first to patronise Godsal was Sir Ralph Milbanke, the 5th baronet, whose Whig credentials were confirmed by his brother's marriage to a daughter of the 2nd Marquess of Rockingham, twice Prime Minister albeit for the shortest spells.[16] The first lawyer's letter which survives in the Godsal archives is written by Frederick Booth to Sir Ralph at Philip Godsal's request in 1780 asking for the immediate payment of his account. Milbanke replied that he was making every effort to do so and that his son John had been trying to raise money 'in the North' for this very purpose.[17]

The debt was converted into a bond of £1,835 for the repayment of £917.10s.0d as Milbanke continued to have carriages made or serviced by Godsal and when he died in 1798 the sum of approximately £700 remained unpaid and Godsal agreed to extend it in the name of his heir, the 6th baronet who paid off the bond in full in 1805 by which time he too maintained an account with Godsal. At the date of his daughter Arabella's marriage to Lord Byron in January 1815, when he devised £20,000 on the bride, Milbanke owed £835 to his coachmaker.

Sir Ralph Milbanke, the 6th baronet had married Judith Noel, daughter of the Viscount Wentworth, and Milbanke's financial situation was eased significantly when his wife inherited the Wentworth fortune, although not the title of her late unmarried brother in 1815. Milbanke now received the Royal Licence to change his name to Noel, and under that new family flag he finally paid off his account with Godsal in 1819 with a payment of £867.12s.0d.[18]

Milbanke/Noel's brother-in-law, Penistone Lamb, who had become the 1st Viscount Melbourne in 1784, became more celebrated as the cuckolded husband of Elizabeth, née Milbanke, than as a political figure in his own right. Lady Melbourne had a series of celebrated affairs but remained in Society as the leading Whig hostess of her generation. Melbourne bought his carriages from Godsal and around 1797 took out a bond for £2,500 to repay £1,250. He paid it off in full in March 1801.

Other Whig politicians who were Godsal's customers included Charles Bennett, Lord Ossulston, M.P., later the 5th Earl of Tankerville. A member of the Holland House set, and associate of the diarist, Thomas Creevy, Ossulston was known as 'little O' because of his size which Lady Holland described as 'insignificant and diminutive', although, she added, 'he aims at thinking and judging for himself'.[19] He had married in 1806 a Frenchwoman, Corisane de Gramont, a close friend of Georgiana, Duchess of Devonshire. Ossulton's father had not approved of the marriage and Georgiana's husband provided her with a dowry of £10,000. Ossulston paid his account with Godsal in 1817 in the sum of £411.

Ossulton's mother, the Countess of Tankerville, wife of the 4th Earl, had bought a carriage from Godsal in 1788 for £286.13s.0d and had never paid for it before the date of her death in 1816 when Godsal's lawyers pressed her husband, the 4th Earl for payment. He did not respond but when he died in 1822 Godsal submitted his account to the executors. At last in February 1825, thirty seven years late, the account was paid although the executors refused to allow any interest.[20]

A rather more occasional Whig, indeed he was accused of being a turn-coat, was John Lord Delaval, whose family seat was the magnificent Vanbrugh house of Seaton Delaval in Northumberland. With a particular love of carriages Delaval added an east wing with a lofty stable measuring sixty-two feet by forty-six feet with arches, stall divisions and hayracks all of stone. This screened a stable yard with the coach houses and harness rooms.[21] Lord Delaval was one of Philip Godsal's most important customers.[22]

Although he was an M.P. for twenty-two years his interests were rather in the social whirl, his carriages, and the theatre than in politics. Even when he was seventy Nathaniel Wraxall could still describe him as 'elegant, gay and pleasing in his manners, graceful of person and devoted to the pursuit of pleasure'. He was a friend of James Boswell and of the dramatist and theatre manager Samuel Foote, who said he was 'a man with all the decent externals of ignorance'.[23]

Delaval loved acting and on one memorable occasion in 1752, he rented the Theatre Royal, Drury Lane to mount a London production of *Othello*, with himself as Iago, and members of his family taking the other principal roles. It was a sell out and the House of Commons adjourned at 3 p.m. as so many of his fellow members had bought tickets. The Prince of Wales, later George III, was present, with four other members of the Royal Family. Of course they wanted to see Delaval perform, but there was great interest too in the two beautiful young West Indian creoles who played Ophelia and Emilia. They were Delaval's step-daughters,

John Hussey, Lord Delaval, was one of Godsal's oldest and best customers. Print after Sir Joshua Reynolds, P.R.A.

having been adopted by his wife as her wards, although Delaval's contemporaries insisted on thinking he might enjoy an even closer relationship.

Despite his raffish life style and reputation, Delaval proved an excellent customer of Godsal for over twenty years, ordering a number of carriages and he was more approachable on a personal level than most of the coachmaker's aristocratic customers. In October 1785 Godsal wrote to him

My Lord
Presuming on your Lordship's friendly disposition towards me I am emboldened to ask your recommendation to the appointment of being Coachmaker to his Royal Highness the Duke of Cumberland, as the late person, Mr John Foster who serv'd his Royal Highness is dead.

His Royal Highness has arrived from abroad on

Saturday in Town & the earlier the application is made the more likely of success. I understand General Garth to be the principal person in his Royal Highness's Household, but as I know the intimacy your Lordship has with both their Royal Highnesses, made me take the liberty to beg your kind interference in my behalf.

For whatever reason Godsal was disappointed in this application but it did not affect his relations with Lord Delaval who eighteen years later wrote to him heartily congratulating him on the marriage of his elder daughter. In acknowledging his letter Godsal wrote 'My wife requests me to add her very great obligation to Your lordship for your kind congratulations & to assure your Lordship she participates with one in all due respect and attentions'.

In the first fifteen years of their business relationship Lord Delaval paid promptly for his carriages and their subsequent servicing, but by 1797 he was suffering some financial problems, although he was unusually frank about them in his letters, and subsequently for the next ten years paid on the rendition of an annual account.

Delaval also introduced two of his sons-in-law, the Earl of Tyrconnel and George Touchet, Lord Audley, who both bought carriages and borrowed money from Godsal.[24] Tyrconnel married Sarah Delaval, who shortly afterwards excited Society by becoming the mistress of the Duke of York. Neither her husband, nor her father appeared too concerned. They lived in a fast set. Only the year before, in 1787, Delaval and Tyrconnel had taken out a joint bond for £2,000 with Godsal which went some way towards the purchase of Claremont, the house near Esher rebuilt on the site of a former Vanbrugh house with a garden by 'Capability' Brown. In the gardens they commissioned from Robert Adam a small house for Delaval to keep his mistress, Miss Hicks.[25] The bond, incidentally, was repaid in 1803.

Delaval's daughter, the Countess of Tyrconnel and formerly mistress of the Duke of York, was now living openly with the Earl of Strathmore, who had himself been married to a famous society beauty with connections to the Milbankes. This inter-connected web of Whig grandees drew in Philip Godsal, for the Earl of Strathmore was also a customer of his, paying off his account of £411.9s.6d in 1801.

Lord Audley, Delaval's other son-in-law, took out a loan of £2,000 from Godsal in 1795, mortgaged against one third of his holding of £29,277 in three per cent Consols. This was repaid in full in 1799. It seems likely that it was Delaval who made the introduction when his friend the Duke of Cumberland, son of King George III, borrowed £100 from Philip Godsal in 1799, repaying it the next year.

CHAPTER SEVEN

The Earl of Egremont

Of all Philip Godsal's customers few cut a more glamorous figure in the social world than George O'Brien Wyndham, the 3rd Earl of Egremont, who succeeded to the earldom and the splendid Petworth House at the age of only twelve in 1763. The boy earl was to grow up to be one of the most attractive men in London and one of the greatest patrons of art his country has ever known.

His father, the 2nd Earl was a Secretary of State from 1761 to 1763 in the short-lived ministries of the Duke of Newcastle and of the Earl of Bute. Indeed, it was Egremont's own premature death from an apoplectic attack which brought about the demise of Bute's ministry.

The young 3rd Earl became one of the early customers of the young coachmaker, Philip Godsal in 1776, when Egremont was twenty-five and Godsal was twenty-nine. The treasure trove of domestic documentation preserved at Petworth, chronicles the details of Egremont's coachmaking accounts with Godsal over a period of eight years in what is the most important coachmaking archive of the period.

Godsal's first bill, for the twelve month period from July 1776, amounted to £900.12s.5d from which Godsal subtracted £38, representing the value of a phaeton and an old post chaise 'traded in', to use to-day's parlance. Godsal also allowed a discount of £150 (curiously, he describes it as a 'disoblegen') in view of the large amount of business. This sum of £900.12s.5d was made up of the purchase of four new carriages, together with the servicing, repair and re-furbishment of existing vehicles. The new vehicles purchased by Lord Egremont were a Post Chaise for £136, a Phaeton for £70 and two Coaches, each costing £188.16s.0d.

The specifications for each vehicle are given in detail in Godsal's invoices preserved in the Petworth accounts. All had the bodywork hung on crane neck carriages, with 'best Town-made steel springs and iron axle trees'. The panels of the post chaise and the phaeton were dark green and those of the two coaches were 'painted a fine Noysette' [nut brown] colour. All were 'oyl varnished', and the second of the two coaches incurred the extra charge of £12.12s.0d for 'preparing the panels and high varnishing'. All had wainscot

trunks under the interior seats to store hats etc, carpeted floors and best plate glass windows, and all had 'Your Lordship's crest and coronet' painted on the panels and, in the case of the two coaches, engraved also on 'the tongues and braces of the Main Braces [the leather straps, securing the body to the springs]'.

The phaeton, being a high vehicle had 'double sliding steps under the bottom' and the interior was finished with 'light coloured cloth trimmed with cafoy lace'. The post chaise was a half landeau with the fold back roof made of japanned leather. It had mahogany shutters, the sides were stuffed and quilted for long distance comfort and warmth and the interior was 'lined with superfine striped Orleans and trimmed with cafoy lace'.

The two matching coaches were the luxury vehicles. Instead of wooden mouldings decorating the bodywork they had brass, and the metal cornice or frieze around the roof was gilt. At the back, the footboard was 'carved in imitation of a shell', on each side of which were twin iron decorative vertical standards. The interiors were lined with 'fine Dove coloured velvet and trimmed with yellow silk lace'. Godsal supplied new double harness for the two coaches. That for the first coach cost £16.16s.0d, and the second, bought five months later, cost £24.6s.0d, the brass work, including crest and coronets, being more extensive.

It would appear that Lord Egremont kept one of the twin coaches at Petworth and the other in London. The post chaise was used for travelling betweeen the two homes. The dangers of highwaymen at this time are confirmed by Godsal charging £2.16s.0d for 'a new pair of pistol holsters, lined and covered with fine [matching] Orleans & fixing them up inside the post chaise'. Egremont also had a house at Newmarket reflecting his passion for horseracing and the post chaise was employed for journeys there. The phaeton would be driven between residences during long stays.

This first bill of Godsal was not paid immediately by the Earl's agent, Tripp, and the sum was carrried forward to the second bill for the next six months ending December 1777. No new vehicles were bought in that period but there was much refurbishment and repairs and Godsal allowed £46.0s.0d for an 'old chariot' taken in part payment. Payment in full of the balance was made six months later in June 1778, two years after the first debts incurred. The aristocracy required extended credit and the coachmaker required deep pockets.

It was during this period that Lord Egremont became the lover of Lady Melbourne, two years his junior and the wife of Penistone Lamb, Viscount Melbourne (see page 61). Bizarrely, and almost certainly apocryphally, Lord Egremont was said to have bought her from Lord Coleraine for £13,000 of which both Lord and Lady Melbourne were rumoured to have got a share. Elizabeth, Lady Melbourne was the daughter of Sir Ralph Milbanke, the 5th baronet who was also a coachmaking customer of Philip Godsal at this time (see page 61). It may be presumed that Godsal was introduced to one by the other, although it is not clear who was Godsal's first customer. There is a note on one of his invoices noting an alteration for Lord Egremont on a carriage originally made for Sir Ralph. All successful coachmakers, and others in the luxury trades relied on word of mouth recommendations amongst acquaintances.

Lord Egremont's *affaire* with Lady Melbourne was no secret and he was, and is, universally believed to be the father of William Lamb (the future Prime Minister, Lord Melbourne) who was born in 1779 and conceived, the fact has some interest but no relevance, in the month when his father paid his first coachmaking bill to Philip Godsal!

Unlike his father, and indeed most Whig grandees, Egremont had little interest in politics but he was a noted figure in society, not only the lover of Lady Melbourne but the friend of Georgiana, Duchess of Devonshire. A highly eligible bachelor, although his inclinations did not turn to marriage, he was a frequent guest at many of the great houses, and the quality of his carriages was of the first importance. It is evident from Philip Godsal's invoices the trouble and expense incurred in keeping them up to the mark.

In the twelve months to December 1778 the invoices comprise eleven pages of closely written narration with expenses totalling £187.2s.0d. The new vehicle this year cost only £31.12s.0d, and was described simply as a 'new neat perch carriage (probably some kind of gig or whiskey) and was no doubt utilised around the vast estate at Petworth. The other items record expenses incurred to keep the existing vehicles up to the mark. Like motor cars, carriages require servicing which varied from the basic 'well cleaning the post chaise, cleaning and oiling the braces, greasing the wheels and new spare lynch pins 4s 8d' to the

more extensive 'taking off the undercarriage and lining the perch bolt-hole with leather and nails and putting a new leather washer between the transomes, fixing the carriage under, a new key to the perch bolt and putting a new double key to the other coach £6.6s.0d'.

In 1778 Lord Egremont bought from Godsal a 'Strong new sett [sic] of wheels' for £6.6s.0d to replace older ones, and a 'new sett of main braces made up with new brass buckles' to renew older ones at a cost of £6.6s.0d. He had the panels of the post chaise rubbed down and re-painted dark green, oyl [sic] varnished, 'the carriage and wheel colour to match the body 'for £5.5s.0d. He had 'a new Travelling Trunk to the fore part of the carriage of the post chaise, lined with linen & garnished with new brass nails' for £3.3s.0d.

Inside one of the two coaches he had 'a new false lining and fixing with hooks and eyes, to take out and put in occasionally'. This cost £3.3s.0d. In the other coach he was billed for 'putting all new silk to the spring curtains, 2 new sticks to ditto, & new brass eyes & fixing up the curtains, 4 new brass fastings & all new silk lines to ditto £1.18s.0d'.

On one of the coaches at the cost of £8.18s.6d the coachman's seat was given 'a new square cloth made up with velvet with a row of broad yellow silk lace and a row of binding lined with Russian drab and loops'. The footman, to the rear, was not forgotten; after all the *tout ensemble* had to be right. 'To a new sett of worsted Footman's Holders with tassles & silk button hangers – sewing them on to the staples & stuffing the footman's cushions fuller with flock £1.10s.6d'.

In 1779 Lord Egremont bought a new coach for £186.0s.0d and was credited with £31.10s.0d for one of the older ones bought back by Godsal. The year's expenses were £403.14s.0d, the usual expenses of replacement wheels, replacement braces, oiling, greasing, new perch bolt hole leather etc etc being incurred. The Agent paid the bill in full in June 1780.

Lord Egremont, approaching thirty, was now what Lord David Cecil has described as 'the pattern *grand seigneur* of his time, at once distinguished and unceremonious, rustic and scholarly, he spent most of his time at his palace of Petworth in a life of magnificent hedonism, breeding horses, collecting works of art and keeping open house for a crowd of friends and dependants'.

Like other grandees, his ambitions were unconfined. Because he liked pictures, he filled Petworth with Coreggios and Claudes. He was the patron of the sculptor Nollekens, of Flaxman, and later of Turner and Constable. He liked horses and owned an outstanding Arab Stud. He

Philip Godsal made a 'half-landau' or landaulet which could be coverted into a post chaise for the Earl of Egremont

liked women and had a number of children by various mistresses. When Georgiana arranged an outing to Vauxhall Gardens, he was the first to be invited. Charles James Fox said that when he was drafting his India Bill in 1783 it was Egremont's opinions he valued most. Indeed he seems to have been touched by the Gods and as a racehorse owner it was no surprise that he should prove to be one of the most successful of his, or indeed of any era. His first Derby winner, there were to be no fewer than five, was in 1782 and he also won the Oaks five times.

Such a connoisseur, unconstrained by financial limitations, must have the finest carriages and maintain them in the best condition. Godsal's meticulously itemised bills reveal Lord Egremont's ambitions in this regard. Every year he demanded the same care and quality evident in the extracts quoted above of the years 1776-1778. In 1783, the last year for which Godsal's bills are available, the last items include an item which indicates something of the style of Lord Egremont's travel accompanied evidently by outriders. 'To two best brown postillion saddles with deep skirts, polished stirrups, woollen frames with straps £3.12s.0d.' Another shows his sense as well as his sensibility 'To a new deep Coachman's Seat made of strong leather, stuff'd & covered complete £2.2s.0d'.

After eight years there are no further records in the archives of Lord Egremont's coachmaker's bills but the Petworth story is picked up in accounts of Lord Egremont's youngest brother, the Hon. William Frederick Wyndham. He bought carriages (unspecified) and servicing from Philip Godsal to the value of £1,277.2s.0d between the years 1788 and 1794 but made payments of only £33.12s.0d. To this significant debt Philip Godsal added interest at five per cent and despatched a series of letters and statements to Wyndham, having failed to get satisfaction. In February

1800 he wrote to Wyndham in Florence, the letter being 'sent by favour of Mr Broughton from the Secretary of State's Office'.

There was no reply but at last, after his return to England in August 1800, Wyndham came in person to Godsal's yard to dispute the bills, and a subsequent letter from Godsal sent to 'The Hon. William Wyndham at the Earl of Egremont's, Grosvenor Place' makes clear the the terms of trade which for the most part were observed between the patron and the coachmaker and which had been so seriously breached in this case of a debt, a part of which extended back twelve years.

Sir

The amount viz £1,230.18s.10d which my clerk gave you when you did me the honour of calling in Long Acre does not include any interest for length of credit. In my letters to you I have made a claim for credit beyond 18 months and the enclosed statement for £1,636.1s.4d will fully elucidate the business.

Wherever such unlimited credit has been taken it has always been allowed – not having met with any exception from any Gentleman – because it carries this conviction with it, that otherways the Tradesman would be a considerable loser instead of a Gainer by his business. I feel I had only to make this known to you and trusting to your honour make no doubt but you will readily allow the charge. I can only add how very much you will oblige me by a settlement
P. Godsal   August 21 1800

Finally, on 8 June 1803 Godsal received '£1,230.18s.10d of the Hon. William Wyndham by hands of the Earl of Egremont'. No interest was ever paid.

CHAPTER EIGHT
The Genealogy of Irish Debtors

Some forty members of the Irish peerage and gentry, the Anglo-Irish Ascendancy, provided an important and distinctive group of the customers of Philip Godsal's coachmaking and money lending businesses. Many of them can be traced in a genealogy of the families of two individuals, John Fitzgibbon, the Earl of Clare and John Foster, later Baron Oriel.

This chapter will focus principally upon the individual debtors of these two families but will first examine the earliest known Irish connection of the London coachmaker.

In April 1787, John Stratford, later the 3rd Earl of Aldborough of Baltinglass in County Wicklow, took delivery of a carriage made by Godsal in Long Acre, London. Stratford did not pay cash but took out a bond for £268.13s.8d bearing five per cent annual interest.[1]

There was already apparently some connection with John Dwyer, the private secretary of John Fitzgibbon, at that date the Irish Attorney General. In December 1788 Stratford paid the first year's interest on the debt to Dwyer for onward transmission to Godsal in London. The connection between Dwyer and Godsal is possibly related to negotiations between Fitzgibbon and Godsal for a State Coach to mark his installation as the Lord Chancellor of Ireland in 1790. In these negotiations Dwyer seems to have played a part. The story of the Irish Lord Chancellor's Coach is described on pages 43-51. It is about this time, 1789-90, that Godsal's business in Ireland appears to have developed rapidly.

In 1790, the John Dwyer connection was evident again when Francis Whyte of Red Hills, County Cavan, bought two carriages and gave his bond for £597.5s.0d agreeing to pay the interest through Dwyer.[2] In the same year Dwyer himself both ordered a carriage and borrowed money from Godsal although he made no payments until 1799 when he re-paid £635.[3] He was to prove one of the most intransigent of a difficult group of debtors and twenty seven years later Godsal wrote to him, 'a large portion of your unpaid debt is for the coachmaking work done for you, with the interest amounting to £512.12s.0d'. Dwyer failed to pay.[4]

Dwyer's position as private secretary to the new Lord Chancellor Fitzgibbon, had some part to play in encouraging the growth of Godsal's business in Ireland, but we must turn now to Fitzgibbon himself and to another important politician, John Foster, Speaker of the Irish Commons. Both were dominant figures in the last decade of the eighteenth century when Ireland still retained its own Parliament.

Amongst political groupings it is rare to find complete agreement and this was most certainly the case with the Protestant Anglo-Irish who dominated both the Lords and the Commons in the Irish Parliament. Two of the principal issues of the day were the proposed Union of Ireland and England and the possible emancipation of the Catholics who formed the great majority of the Irish population.

Fitzgibbon and Foster agreed on the subject of emancipation. They were against it. They did not agree however on the question of Union with England which would bring with it the dissolution of the Irish Parliament. Fitzgibbon believed that the British connection was vital and was strongly for the Union. Foster believed that the Anglo-Irish in Ireland should remain the independent government of Ireland, and was strongly against the Union. Fitzgibbon's side triumphed and the Act of Union came into effect on 1 January 1801.

Such political matters were only a backdrop to Philip Godsal's business in Ireland but they were a factor in a matter of more immediate concern, the growth of the Irish carriage making industry in Dublin during the last two decades of the century. This is discussed on pages 45-46.

Customers and debtors are seen by tradesmen rather as individuals than as members of political affiliations and it is time to turn to the individuals introduced to Godsal through the families of Fitzgibbon and Foster.

The Fitzgibbon Connection

No fewer than nine members of the family and relations by marriage of John Fitzgibbon, Earl of Clare, became debtors of Philip Godsal by buying carriages or borrowing sums of money.[5] They were Fitzgibbon himself; his wife Anne, née

Whaley; his brother-in-law, Thomas Whaley; the Earl of Cremorne, husband of Anne Fitzgibbon's niece; Fitzgibbon's sister Arabella Jeffereyes; her son, George; the first and second husbands of her elder daughter, Viscount Westmeath and the Hon. Augustus Cavendish Bradshaw; and the husband of her second daughter, Viscount Caher or Cahir, later Earl of Glengall. They were a very rum lot indeed.

Anne Whaley, an elegant beauty from County Wicklow, was the daughter of Richard Chapel Whaley, known as 'Burn Chapel' because of his peremptory way with the places of worship of the Catholic tenants of his estate at Whaley Abbey, Wicklow. Anne married John Fitzgibbon in 1786 and he remained devoted to her despite what many thought was her less than strict adherence to their marriage vows.[6]

On the death of her husband in 1802 the dowager Countess of Clare lived both in Ireland and in England, where, when she was not a guest of the Prince of Wales in Brighton, she lived in Savile Row. She was a friend rather than a rival of the Prince's wife, Maria Fitzherbert despite Maria's Roman Catholic beliefs and the previously strongly expressed Protestant beliefs of the daughter of 'Burn Chapel' Whaley.

Lady Clare had been left £1,100 a year in her late husband's will but found it insufficient for the glittering social life she enjoyed in England. She petitioned the government for a pension and was refused.[7] She had bought a carriage from Philip Godsal and now, in 1804, she turned to him to raise a mortgage on her house in Savile Row.[8] Godsal granted the mortgage for £650 repayable at £32.10s.0d per year and in 1808 agreed to increase the mortgage to £1,200 with an annual repayments of £60.[9] Lady Clare was punctual in her payments and redeemed her mortgage in 1814.[10]

Anne's brother Thomas, known as 'Buck' or 'Jerusalem' Whaley has been described as 'a man who perpetrated every undesirable stereotype of the insanely, irresponsible, recklessly self indulgent Anglo-Irish gentleman'.[11] One suspects 'Buck' Whaley would have taken this as a compliment.

In 1789 he took delivery in Dublin of a carriage, costing £229.10s.0d made by Philip Godsal.[12] At that date it seems unlikely that any Dublin coachmaker would have been willing to give him credit such was his reputation. In Paris he had lost a fortune, said to be £14,000, and had been forced to flee the city and return to Dublin in 1788. There, he recouped some of his losses by a series of improbable dares, including leaping from his drawing room window

into the first barouche to pass by and kissing the occupant. Then he took a bet that he would not travel to Jerusalem and play ball against the Wall of the ancient City. He won that bet too and returned to Dublin in 1789.[13]

If Godsal had been ignorant of these exploits when he sold his carriage on credit to Whaley, he would have soon woken up to Whaley's unreliability when he said he could not pay but took out instead a bond for £459.[14] Ten years later, and with no interim payments, Whaley finally paid the bill, including the interest.[15] Godsal agreed to a further loan but Whaley died of pneumonia within the year leaving Godsal with a claim against the estate.

Surprisingly, the 'half mad' Lord Camelford, a man no less reckless than his friend 'Buck' Whaley, agreed to pay off some of this second debt.[16] The details are not clear but Godsal removed Whaley from his list of debtors so was presumably paid in full.

Anne and Thomas Whaley had a brother John whose daughter Anne married Richard Thomas Dawson, an enthusiastic Abolitionist and Whig M.P. who succeeded as the Earl of Cremorne.[17] He went against the family tradition in favouring Catholic emancipation but acted like the rest of his family with regard to buying carriages and borrowing money and he incurred a debt of £1,000 to Philip Godsal. The principal and interest were paid off by 1821.[18]

Rackety as Fitzgibbon's relations by marriage were, they appear almost reliable when compared to Fitzgibbon's sister's family whom the Lord Chancellor was to specifically exclude from his will.[19]

Arabella Jeffereyes, née Fitzgibbon, married St John Jeffereyes, a wealthy landowner from Cork but her own social ambitions and extravagant nature were to make her chronically insolvent, 'the long bankruptcy of her life' has been one mordant epitaph.[20] In London and Dublin, pursuing her social ambitions in the demi-monde, she became a patron of the actress Frances Abington, from whom, no doubt coincidentally, Philip Godsal bought the lease of 84 Piccadilly in 1788.

Philip Godsal probably knew of Arabella Jeffereyes' reputation for the non payment of debts, yet he lent her £100, no small sum, in 1800. He was one of the lucky creditors for Arabella paid him back in full.[21] Unfortunately for Godsal her son George did not. He had a carriage for which he did not pay. He sent a bill at three months which bounced.[22] Later, however, the bill was paid.

Arabella's two daughters acquired a position in society by marrying into the Irish peerage, but their reputations were as tarnished as that of their mother and brother.[23] The elder, Marianne, married first George Frederick Nugent, the

7th Earl of Westmeath, unusually a supporter of Catholic emancipation, to whom Godsal lent £715 against his bond before Westmeath divorced Marianne because of her adultery with the Honourable, perhaps in this context better the Dishonourable, Augustus Cavendish Bradshaw, 'a pretty, little and delicate man' who was required to pay £10,000 damages to Westmeath for 'crim.con'.[24]

Despite this unlooked for windfall Westmeath was slow to repay Godsal who obtained a Warrant of Attorney against him in 1804. Westmeath still failed to pay, and even when Godsal agreed to accept an annuity Westmeath failed to honour it. Godsal had prudently insured Westmeath's life for £1,000 and on his early death in 1814 the debt was liquidated by the payment of the insurance company.[25] It was however, a squalid business.

The Honourable Augustus Cavendish Bradshaw had married Marianne after her divorce, and to replenish his coffers after his payment of the damages for 'crim. con', he borrowed £1,400 from Philip Godsal.[26] Cavendish Bradshaw

at least proved to have more financial probity than his wife's first husband for he had paid off his debt in full by 1802. Part of the debt was paid by the Hon. John Vaughan, later Earl of Lisburne, and himself a debtor to Godsal.[27]

Arabella Jeffereyes' second daughter, Emily, was a chip off her mother's domineering block.[28] Arabella had found in Paris a claimant for the vacant Viscountancy and estates of Caher, and even more remarkably persuaded the Courts to recognise the penniless young man. Less remarkable perhaps was that she persuaded the venal young man to abandon the Roman Catholic faith, and, perhaps no surprise at all, that she persuaded him to marry her pretty daughter, Emily.[29] The almost fairy tale element of this romantic story was no doubt lost on Philip Godsal for the new Viscount Caher, later to be the Earl of Glengall, was to prove one of the coachmaker's greatest worries for almost a quarter of a century.

Caher borrowed £2,000 from Godsal in 1797, agreeing to pay interest at five per cent and to pay the annual

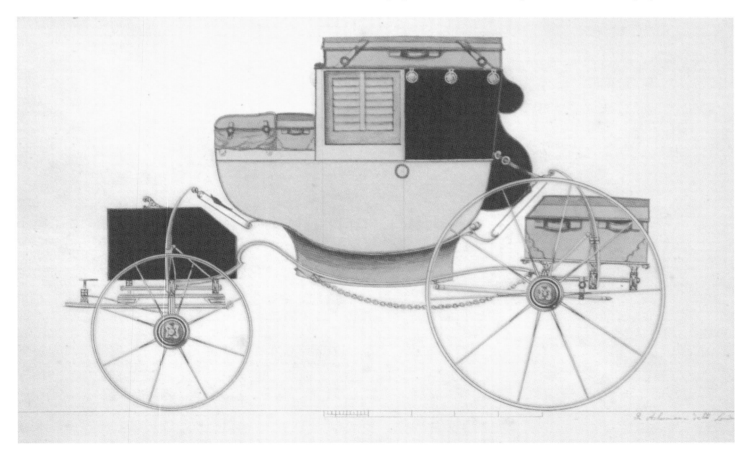

A custom-built post chaise was suitable for heavier loads. Designed by Rudolph Ackermann

insurance premium on his life. Caher got behind with his repayments and in 1803 his bill at three months bounced. It was a double embarrasment for Godsal who had discounted the bill with his wine merchant whom of course he now had to repay.[30]

Caher again failed to pay in 1804 but early in 1805 he repaid £1,000 of the principal sum.[31] Despite constant reminders he made no further payments until 1809 when he repaid the second £1,000 of the principal.[32] This still left the accumulated interest and the unpaid insurance premiums which had amounted to £899 by 1811 when Godsal agreed to pay him £101 and convert the loan into an annuity of £162 to be paid by Caher and a reduction in the insurance premium.[33]

When Caher failed to pay the first year, Godsal instructed his Dublin solicitor, John DeCourcy, to take out proceedings against his Lordship.[34] Thus encouraged, Caher paid the years 1813 and 1814 whereupon Godsal dropped the proceedings.[35] And whereupon Caher failed to pay in 1815 and 1816. And whereupon Godsal once again instructed DeCourcy to sue.[36] This predictable cycle came to an end when Caher, now the Earl of Glengall, died in January 1819.

The Rock Insurance office paid Godsal £1,400 on the life insurance,[37] and it seems that Godsal, now seventy-two years of age, did not trouble to pursue a claim against the estate.

The Foster Connection

The family and connections of John Foster were less raffish than the Fitzgibbons but, as Philip Godsal was to discover, they included a number of chronic debtors.

One was Foster himself. He was a very able man and it was generally agreed by his contemporaries that he was remarkably honest for a politician who was in a position to feather his own nest and those of his connections.[38] He had large land holdings, which however, failed to produce sufficient income to sustain his expenses. He had other financial problems. Lady Moira, who was well disposed towards him, wrote in 1796

His pecuniary distresses (not originating from himself but from his father), a hospitable and generous disposition, with a wife who in no degree attends to that regulation and economy which she has not the leisure to preside over, not only renders his situation uncomfortable, but obliges him to look for the loaves and fishes with avidity.[39]

She was not implying financial irregularities but had in mind the large loans he was taking out from Dublin bankers at that time.[40]

It was at this time that Godsal agreed to build a coach for Foster who paid Irish £400 instead of English pounds. Godsal's attorney wrote to Foster who paid in a further Irish £50 but observed that the original agreement had been for only English £200 but that Godsal had added £200 for some trivial extras.[41] It is perhaps appropriate, even ironic, that Foster's first concern on taking his seat in the British Parliament was to endeavour to combat the anomaly in the rate of exchange between Britain and Ireland.[42]

It should be noted that, as Speaker of the Irish Parliament, Foster was in receipt of the very large salary of £5,000 per year, which could clearly go some way to servicing his large borrowings. When the dissolution of the Irish Parliament ended his office as Speaker, the English Parliament voted him the continuation of his salary of £5,000 a year as compensation, in addition to a one off sum of £7,500 for his moiety of the disenfranchised borough of Dunleer. Within two years Pitt appointed him Chancellor of the Irish Exchequer.[43]

By 1806 however he sold this annual compensation for £30,000 cash in order to pay off his existing debts. Clearly it was not the prudent financial decision of a Chancellor of the Exchequer, but the desperate throw of a chronic debtor. In the same year he approached Godsal for a loan of £4,000 which was granted in return for an annuity of £200 a year until his death.[44] It was a generous offer by the coachmaker for Foster was already sixty-six years of age. In the event he was to live another twenty-two years and never failed to pay the annuity.

John Foster's nephew, the Rt Honourable John Maxwell Barry, later the 5th Baron Farnham, was another Godsal debtor. Foster's sister had married the Bishop of Meath, the Right Reverend the Honourable Henry Maxwell, and their son, John Maxwell succeeded to the estates of his godfather James Barry in 1798 and added the name Barry to his own.[45]

John Maxwell Barry, who was a Member of the Irish Parliament, bought a carriage from Philip Godsal at this time and paid for it in 1802. In 1806 he became a Member of the British Parliament and in 1810, with his brother-in-law, Viscount Valentia, also a Member of Parliament, he took out a joint bond of £2,000 with Godsal.[46]

In 1789 Maxwell, as he then was, had married the sister of George Annesley, who was to become Viscount Valentia in 1793. Three years earlier Annesley had married a sister of William 'Kitty' Courtenay, William Beckford's former catamite. Another of Courtenay's sisters had married the

Godsal's final property investment in London was **244 Oxford Street**, next door to his home at No 243. In February 1812 he paid the first rental of £150 per year to the same landlord, Mr Willan who insisted that a reluctant Godsal should buy the furniture valued at £272.15s.0d.[26] Godsal promptly re-sold it for £229.12s.0d and, after having the verandah coppered, the roof slated and the walls papered, he let the property to the Hon. Charles Bagot for £200 per year plus an initial payment of £1,050. Bagot was at the time Parliamentary under Secretary for Foreign Affairs and within two years he was posted to Paris as Minister Plenipotentiary.[27] The new tenant was General Taylor, who was posted to Ireland leaving Godsal to chase up the outstanding rent in Dublin.[28] Soon after his recovery from his operation for the stone Godsal negotiated with Mr Willans to hand back his lease.

Residential Property

84 Piccadilly is on the corner of Piccadilly and Clarges Street. Godsal bought the lease from Frances Abington, the actress, in an auction at Christie's on 29 January 1788 for £1,365.[29] Mrs Abington was close to her first retirement from the London stage but still active. *The Times* for March that year carried an advertisement for her performance as Beatrice in *Much Ado About Nothing* in which it promised that Mrs Abington would sing a favourite duet with Mr Johnson in Act II and oblige the audience with a song and mock minuet in a special Farce which would be performed after Shakespeare's play. Much was expected from favourite actresses.

The ground landlord and lessor of No 84 Piccadilly was Sir Nelson Rycroft to whom Godsal paid £52 per year. Sir Nelson lived just around the corner in Clarges Street. Westminster Council calculated the rateable value of No 84 Piccadilly as £60 and the property was subject to the following annual rates: £6 Poor Rate and Highways Tax; £1.10s.0d Watch; £4 Paving, Cleaning, Lighting. It was also subject to annual Government, or 'King's' Taxes of £14.9s.5d Window Tax for its forty-eight windows and £4.12s.0d for Land Tax. In 1789 Godsal mortgaged the property as part of the collateral for the loan of £8,000 by John Wombwell (see page 54).[30]

As its forty-eight windows indicate, 84 Piccadilly was a large four or five storey town house. It was in one of the most desirable situations, looking across Green Park to the Queen's House, now Buckingham Palace, with the Chelsea Water Company's reservoirs creating a fashionable promenade immediately opposite, inside the Park. This view was shared with his neighbours in Devonshire House, which was only fifty yards to the east along Piccadilly.

Philip Godsal bought 84 Piccadilly from the celebrated actress, Mrs Abington

Opposite Devonshire House was a busy coaching inn, which stood on the site of the present Ritz Hotel and provided bustle and excitement to the otherwise fashionable promenade that was Piccadilly. Philip Godsal commissioned views of the Park from his house from William Burgess, R.A. in 1789 but, sadly, these views have not survived.[31]

The fashionable nature of this area of Piccadilly is confirmed by an examination of the Westminster Rate Books.[32] When Philip Godsal moved in, the Duke and Duchess of Devonshire lived at Devonshire House, the Countess of Bath was a next door neighbour in Bath House and just beyond Godsal, to the west on Piccadilly, were the Earl of Egremont, the Earl Bathurst and the Duke of Queensberry, 'Old Q', the notorious old roué.

The streets in the immediate area running north of Piccadilly, Clarges Street, Bolton Street, and Stanhope Street were a veritable enclave of the aristocracy. There were some few wealthy commoners, leading tradesmen like John Boydell, the print publisher, and Joseph Bramah, the ironmonger and inventor, being joined by bankers Thomas Coutts and the Barings.

Philip Godsal lived at 84 Piccadilly from 1788 until 1794. Since 1792 however his principal residence had been Grove House, Hampstead and in 1794 he moved his town house from 84 to 83 Piccadilly.

From 1794 until 1796 he let 84 Piccadilly for £240 per year to Nathaniel Jefferys, M.P., at that time the jeweller to the Prince of Wales. 'I imagined my fortune made by his smile', Jefferys said later, but he found the Prince and his circle to be great buyers but poor payers. Mrs Fitzherbert, for example refused to pay a bill of £120 while Georgiana, Duchess of Devonshire, proved reluctant to pay a debt of £3,000, which she thought 'excessive'. While he was Philip Godsal's tenant in 1795 Jefferys received an order from the Prince of Wales for £50,000 of jewels for his intended bride, the ill-fated Caroline. The Prince failed to pay this huge sum, his financial affairs having been entrusted to commissioners, who clearly did not approve of expensive baubles. Jefferys had to vindicate his claim in King's Bench where he was awarded £51,000 out of his claim for £54,685. While awaiting receipt of this huge sum he secured a seat in Parliament on which he spent 'less than £4,000' by his own account and nearly £7,000 according to his opponents. It was at this point in 1796, and with the commissioners having failed to pay him a penny of the legally proven debt, that he ceased to be Godsal's tenant.[33]

From 1797 until 1816 Godsal let 84 Piccadilly to Baron Robeck, or Roebeck, or de Roebeck, as Godsal called him at various times. The rent remained £240 per year and for

nineteen years Robeck proved a satisfactory tenant. There were two occasions only when he failed to pay his rent on time. The first was in 1802 when he apparently visited Paris during the Treaty of Amiens which had brought the first period of peace in the long wars with the French. Godsal wrote to Robeck's bankers in Paris, Compte Peregaux at Rue Mont Blanc, and received his rent.[34] The second occasion was in 1814 when the Peace of Paris brought another opportunity to visit France. Again Godsal wrote to the same bankers in Paris and was promptly reimbursed.[35]

Robeck had a curious personal history. Born in Sweden he had fought with a French Regiment against the armies of King George in the American Revolution yet in 1789 'John Henry Fock called Baron de Robeck' was naturalized a British citizen by Act of Parliament and in the same year married Ann Fitzpatrick, the sole heir of the Hon Richard Fitzpatrick. She was to inherit large estates in county Kildare and now a member by marriage of the Anglo-Irish aristocracy Robeck commissioned George Stubbs to paint his portrait on horseback in 1791.[36] By 1810 the former enemy of the Crown was a guest of honour at a ball and supper in Weymouth when the statue of King George III was unveiled. He left 84 Piccadilly at Christmas 1816 after nineteen years as Godsal's tenant. Philip now arranged for the lease from Sir Nelson Rycroft to be transferred to his son, Philip Lake Godsal who paid the fine of £260 for the transfer and the sum of £26.5s.0d for the document.[37] Philip Lake had married in 1814 and had lived since then at 243 Oxford Street. He did not move into 84 Piccadilly until 1818 and in the intervening period Philip had commissioned, and paid for, a major renovation and refurbishment worthy of his son and the distinguished family into which he had married. Philip paid Appleford the builder almost £2,000, Crace, the decorative wall painter £153.13s.0d and Fricker & Henderson, the carvers and gilders £33.15s.0d, in all half as much as he had paid for the lease when he himself first occupied it nearly thirty years before.[38]

No 83 Piccadilly was leased by Philip in 1791 from Sir Nelson Rycroft at a rent of £105 per annum plus all taxes, approximately £157 gross. The following year he took out a new twenty-eight year lease on the same terms. In 1791 he had immediately let it to Lady Euphemia Stewart, the sister of the Earl of Galloway, at £200 per year.[39] She remained his tenant until he moved in himself in 1794 and it remained his town house until 1802.

It was smaller than Number 84 but still grand, with 28 windows, one of which was a bow. It was rated at £42 and Godsal was required to pay the Westminster Council yearly rates of £6.13s.0d for the Poor & Highways, £2.12s.6d for

Lighting, Paving & Cleaning and £1.1s.0d for the Watch. In addition he paid the 'King's' taxes of £16 for Windows, £7.10s.0d for the House Tax and £3.0s.4d for the Land Tax.

He had decorated the house for Lady Euphemia, with royal decorators Crace and Robson & Hale, and although he spent more time in this period at Grove House, Hampstead he did much entertaining at No 83, which, incidentally, he rather confusingly occasionally described as No 82 and even No 81.

When he decided to move to No 1 Clarges Street in 1803 he let it furnished to the Marquess of Blandford for £420, an excellent rent for the landlord, made only less so as the Marquess failed to pay for his three year tenure.[40]

On Blandford's departure in 1805 Godsal had another problem tenant, the unfortunate Nathaniel Jefferys who had been Godsal's tenant at No 84 some ten years earlier. In the interval Jefferys had been a fairly active M.P. in the Whig interest, had resumed his career as a jeweller, and had become an estate agent but whose rocky finances had gone from bad to worse. He had been forced to go bankrupt in 1797, and had started to voice publicly his reproaches to the Prince of Wales. He had lost his seat in Parliament in 1803 and although he received a part of the money due him for the Prince's jewels in October 1806 he was gazetted as a bankrupt for a second time. So Philip Godsal had a bankrupt as his tenant and one, moreover who now in 1806 published a pamphlet exposing the Prince and his relations with Mrs Fitzherbert. It sold 6,050 copies at 3s each in a fortnight.[41]

Meanwhile Jefferys continued living at 83 Piccadilly although he managed to pay only some part of the rent of £240 per year. Nevertheless he gave Godsal, as security, his lease on 11 Cadogan Place, which Godsal retained after Jefferys ceased to be his tenant in 1809. Poor Jefferys died in 1810 at the age of only fifty-one.

When Jefferys left No 83 in 1809 the new tenant was Mrs Delmar who paid rent £240 per annum for eighteen months before leaving in June 1810. The next tenant was the furniture company of Morgan & Saunders of the Strand who decided they could utilise the bow window as a shop window for a showroom in the West End. The venture was not successful but Godsal at least received compensation for taking back the lease after only four months by being paid £120 and the value of the furniture left in the showroom which he sold by auction for £239.8s.0d net.[42]

Finally, in 1811, one of Godsal's partners, Edward Macklew, paid him £3,000 for a lease premium for 20¾ years and an annual rental of £105.

No 1 Clarges Street had been leased by the wretched Nathaniel Jefferys for five years before Philip Godsal bought the lease from the landlord William Moreland for £262 plus £101.15s.6d for fixtures and fittings in November 1801. The ground landlord was again Sir Nelson Rycroft to whom Godsal was now paying £75 a year rent. Throughout the first half of 1802 Godsal let the house on short term lets at rents varying from seven to ten guineas a week until Lady Harvey took it for a year at £150. When she left Godsal paid a woman to look after the empty house and then had it re-decorated before taking over the occupancy himself when he moved from 83 Piccadilly in February 1803. He remained there for little more than a year before selling Grove House, Hampstead and moving to 243 Oxford Street which thenceforth became his only address until he moved to Cheltenham in 1814.

No 1 Clarges Street, although smaller than No 83 Piccadilly, nevertheless had twenty-seven windows and was rated at £40 by the Westminster Council. After he moved to Oxford Street Godsal let Clarges Street to Lady Harvey for £150 a year for five years. From 1809 to 1815 the tenant was William France, the upholsterer, and, from 1816 to 1822, William Miller, the well-known publisher and bookseller whose shop was in nearby Albermarle Street.[43]

243 Oxford Street was in the last terrace of five houses at the western end of Oxford Street on the north side. It looked almost directly down Park Lane and Hyde Park was just across the road. To-day's Marble Arch which would have enhanced, or obstructed the view, was not moved to the present site until 1851. The old Tyburn Tree, scene of public executions had been last employed in 1785 and in its place stood the Tyburn Turnpike which had just been leased by Lewis Levi for £12,000.[44] The area was in every way salubrious. Philip himself believed it to be healthier than Piccadilly, although there cannot have been much in it.

He bought a twenty-one year lease of 243 Oxford Street from William Willan for £200 per annum in June 1804 although he did not sleep there for the first time until November that year.[45] His Hampstead home was finally sold in 1805 and from that time 243 Oxford Street was his only residential address in London until he finally left for Cheltenham ten years later, in 1814.

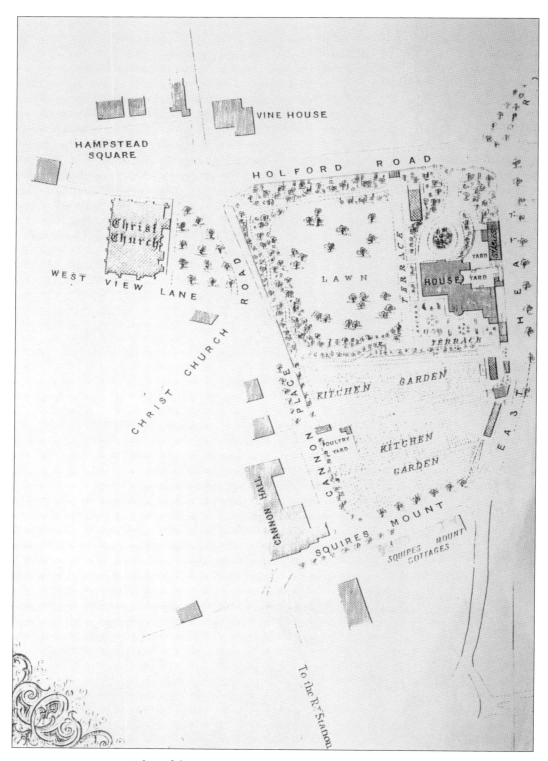

A plan of the Grove House estate created by Philip Godsal

framed mirrors above the fireplaces, chandeliers and 'a pair of 19 inch mirrors with eagles and chains, each with two candles in cut glass pans'. There was of course more furniture than in the ballroom: a pair of 8 feet 7 inches mahogany sideboards; a set of mahogany dining tables on pillars with claw feet and measuring 18 feet by 5 feet 6 inches; a pair of mahogany circular card tables; thirty-six japanned chairs; two sofas, each 6 feet 4 inches in linen and full flounced calico cases, in suite with the French window curtains which were lined throughout with full flounced valance, with draperies full fringed.

There were two pole screens to protect the faces of the ladies sitting near the black japanned register stoves and a magnificent room divider with all eight panels ornamented with scarlet serge and black velvet. Visions are called irresistibly to mind of Jane Austen's fiction, the facts of Holland House and the images of a host of Regency costume dramas.

These superb rooms were opened for the first time on 29 June 1807 for a 'Ball & Sandwiches' to which Mr and Mrs Godsal invited four guests, paying two guineas for the tickets.[39] Perhaps even more to Philip Godsal's taste was the first Proprietors' Dinner which was held ten days later.[40] It was a lavish affair costing £1.11s.6d per head and the Proprietors enjoyed it so well they arranged a venison dinner a month later costing £1.4s.0d each.

It was now nearly three years since Philip had left Hampstead but his appetite for his old friends had not diminished. He was still a regular visitor to the old Club and the Union Club and an occasional visitor to the Assembly Rooms. In 1808 he presented the Union Club members with six bottles of champagne and six bottles of East India Madeira.[41] In 1809 a local nurseryman reminded him of a debt of £23.1s.6d dating back to 1796-7.[42] In 1810 he presented the Assembly Rooms with a silver inkwell.[43]

He continued to dine privately with his old friends in Hampstead and entertained them regularly in Oxford Street. Indeed until his retirement to Cheltenham in 1814 the only extended periods when he did not enjoy their company were during his summer visits to South Wales, Bath, Cheltenham or Teignmouth.

Some old friends died. George Bogg, who left five guineas to each member of the Hampstead Society;[44] the rector Mr Grant for whose funeral Godsal joined the fellow members of the Society in paying the expenses,[45] Spencer Perceval, Prime Minister when he was assassinated in 1812 by a deranged merchant in the Russia trade.

Even when he moved to Cheltenham Godsal remained in close touch with Charles Holford and visited Hampstead once or twice a year on his London visits. As late as 1823 he paid Holford a cheque for fifteen guineas 'for my share of subscription towards the repair of the Hampstead Assembly Rooms'.[46]

His evident attachment to Hampstead is epitomised by the fact that for the remaining twelve years of his life after moving to Cheltenham he continued to pay the sum of 1s per week to the Poor of Hampstead. He considered this mandatory on those privileged to be, or to have been, members of the Hampstead Society.

Philip Godsal attended this review in which his future son-in-law took part

Chapter Eleven
Nelson's Attorney

Philip Godsal's first meeting with the young man who was to marry his younger daughter Maria was in the offices of the solicitor Frederick Booth in Craven Street off the Strand. Booth, who was also the Vestry Clerk of the City of Westminster, had acted as Godsal's solicitor since 1780 and had occasionally made loans to him for investment in the coachmaking business. Booth employed William Haslewood, a newly qualified solicitor from Shropshire, about the year 1790 and it was shortly after that that he and his future father-in-law first met.

Haslewood was clearly a bright young man and in 1795 Booth offered him a partnership in the firm which thus became 'Booth & Haslewood'. Three years later a social connection between Haslewood and Godsal began to be formed. The Volunteer Act of 1798 encouraged recruitment to Volunteer Regiments to prepare for the defence of England in the case of attack by the French. Both Godsal and Haslewood became members of the Light Horse Volunteers of the Cities of London and Westminster, a cavalry regiment and much the most fashionable and expensive of the fifty or so Volunteer Regiments raised in or near London. Henry Angelo called it 'the most respectable corps in Europe, nobility and gentry of the first rank of opulence'.[1]

It seems probable that Godsal had been introduced to the Commanding officer, Colonel Herries by John Wombwell, the wealthy nabob who was the major financier of Godsal's coachmaking business.[2] Wombwell had been a member of the L.H.V. since its formation in 1795 and it was possibly he who recommended Godsal to build a 'Military Fly' or troop carrier which was completed early in 1798.[3] Shortly afterwards the fifty-one year old coachmaker was offered Mess Membership of the L.H.V. and became an enthusiastic social member of the Regiment, regularly attending dinner at the Regiment's two messes, one at the Crown and Anchor in the Strand and the other at the British Coffee House in Birdcage Walk.[4]

Haslewood, a younger man, received the King's commission as a cornet in the L.H.V. on 10 May 1798 in time to command his troopers in a grand review by King George III on Wimbledon Common on 5 July.[5] Colonel Herries ensured that his regiment took their military duties seriously but that the L.H.V. was as much social as military is evident from the reminiscences of Henry Angelo, the swordsman and riding master, who was also a mess member.[6] Godsal and Haslewood now met frequently at the monthly dinners at which there was usually cheerful and patriotic vocal entertainment. In 1799 one of Godsal's favourite charities, the Westminster Dispensary, invited Haslewood's brother to deliver their annual Charity Sermon.[7]

For the young ambitious cornet, service with the L.H.V. was a useful way to advance his social position, and his professional career was boosted in 1800 when Admiral Lord Nelson asked the firm of Booth & Haslewood to act as his attornies. His immediate requirement was that they should pursue his various claims for prize money through the Court of the King's Bench.[8] Booth deputed his young partner to take the primary responsibility for the new client, already of course a national hero as the victor of the Battle of the Nile. Encouraged perhaps by his satisfactory social and professional advancement the young bachelor gave a rout at his residence in Devonshire Square in January 1801. He invited his friend Godsal and his wife who were no doubt impressed by a young man clearly destined for a fine future.

Haslewood was making himself useful and agreeable to Nelson, and quite literally getting his feet under the table. A week after the rout he noted 'I was breakfasting with Lord & Lady Nelson at their lodgings in Arlington Street and a cheerful conversation was passing on indifferent [sic] subjects'.[9] As it happened, this was to be the last time the Admiral and his wife were to meet. Deeply hurt by his obvious obsession with Lady Hamilton, herself a married woman, Lady Nelson left her husband never to return. Nelson's attorney now found himself having dealings with the mistress as well as the wife when Nelson resumed his sea command.

Lady Hamilton had determined that Nelson should buy an estate at Merton, near Wimbledon and Haslewood was instructed to complete the purchase at the price of £9,000. He communicated his unease to Nelson – the price was much too high, the property was in bad condition and Lord Nelson would be well advised not to proceed with the purchase. Nelson, who had never seen the place, was in the thrall of Lady Hamilton and ordered him to go ahead saying, rather weakly 'sailor-like, a few pounds more or less is no object. I never knew much got by hard bargains'.[10]

Haslewood replied that he had taken a surveyor to see the property and he enclosed a report which said 'it is a very slightly built, an old, paltry small dwelling...not the least privacy as a place for pleasure...the grounds are worn out, out of condition and through them runs a dirty, black looking canal which keeps the whole place damp. All in all the worst place I have seen pretending to suit a gentleman's family'.[11] Rather boldly, Haslewood added 'I am of course aware of the eminent tastes and talent of Sir William and Lady Hamilton but they could never take the trouble of a minute examination'.

Lady Hamilton was furious and Nelson was forced to defend Haslewood from her wrath by writing to her 'I suppose he is only doing what every lawyer should do in looking after the interests of his clients'.[12]

But Lady Hamilton insisted on her lover's prerogative and Haslewood was ordered to buy Merton forthwith. For all his 'client's best interests' he could never have hoped to beat Emma Hamilton. He himself had never been in love, certainly never consumed by a grand passion. Naively he was the the only person in London who believed that the relationship between Nelson and Emma was one of the purest friendship and that their love child Horatia, at this time only six months old, was Nelson's adopted daughter, the child of a mysterious 'Mrs Thompson'.

Within two months of completing the purchase of Merton it was Haslewood's turn to fall in love. He dined with the Godsals in Hampstead in December 1801 and for the first time he noticed Maria Godsal, still only sixteen and remarkably pretty. The kittenish charm so evident in her portrait by Hoppner, done when she was only five years old, had developed into a poised and modest beauty. She had been educated for a time in France, she played the piano and the guitar and she rode well, this last accomplishment especially pleasing perhaps to a young cavalry officer. Her family's love of the theatre had added to her social experience and it quickly became evident to Haslewood that this woman had all the qualities he might hope to find in a wife. Not least her father was extremely wealthy.

Philip Godsal quickly appreciated the situation and understood the value of what would be a good connection. Maria was given permission to write to Mr Haslewood on her seventeenth birthday on 1 January 1802. Haslewood was ecstatic. He returned home to Bridgnorth to tell his parents and he wrote to Philip Godsal on 6 January

My Maria's letter is like herself, correct, elegant, modest, unaffected, and although certainly delicate, free from all prudish censure. In permitting me to aspire to the happiness of calling such a lovely creature mine and by preparing her mind to receive me with more favour than I deserve from the kind sentiments in my behalf which friendship led you to express, an obligation has been conferred on me which I can never re-pay, but will never forget.[13]

A charming letter indeed, the last sentence of which was to be as ashes in the mouth of Philip Godsal in the last years of his life. But that was all in the future. For the present, all was sweetness and light. There was a flurry of dinner parties at the Godsal homes in Hampstead and in Clarges Street, Piccadilly. Haslewood was a guest five times in two weeks and introduced his father and his brother, the Reverend Mr John Haslewood.[14] It seems likely that it was now that the portrait of Maria by John Opie, R.A. was commissioned. The fact that the cost is not recorded in Philip Godsal's meticulous record of expenses suggests that it was William Haslewood who commissioned this wonderfully appealing portrait of his betrothed.

Regardless of all these happy distractions in his private life William Haslewood was extremely busy in the year 1802. It was an election year and Frederick Booth, as Vestry Clerk, was also Returning Officer for the large and volatile constituency of Westminster. Elections there were always hard fought and subject to abuses which the Returning Officer and his team were required to prevent. Haslewood was forced to write to Lord Nelson on 16 July

My Lord, I am sorry to be under the necessity of breaking my engagement to have your lordship's will ready for tomorrow but as I would not suffer anyone but myself to be acquainted with your intentions it was necessary for me to write the whole draft myself. And I have been so entirely engaged in the business of the Westminster Election as to have been prevented completing the draft – early in the ensuing week it shall certainly be ready.[15]

He was also active on Nelson's behalf in securing the

The presumed engagement portrait of Maria Godsal by John Opie, R.A.

prize money for the capture of French ships. In the same letter he was able to write 'Mr Tucker having consented to pay your Lordship a flag's share of the Mediterranean prizes I am preparing the indemnities involved'.

With the purchase of the Merton estate completed, Nelson was more than ever desperate for prize money and his letters to his Treasurer, Alexander Davison, confirm how much he appreciated Haslewood's efforts in these invariably long and protracted claims.[16]

Haslewood had other negotiations to undertake at this time for it was agreed that his marriage to Maria should take place shortly after her eighteenth birthday which was in January 1803. These negotiations of the marriage settlement and the details of the wedding are described in another chapter.[17]

The evident delight of the newly weds is made clear in a letter sent to Philip Godsal while they were on honeymoon in Bath .

Two persons were never more framed for each other than our Maria and her husband. The timid modesty which is her particular characteristic rendered the sweet maid diffident, silent, pensive and reserved. But the affectionate wife, with the confidence of wedded love, have given a continual smile to her face, with ease and vivacity for her language and carriage. Our tempers, tastes, habits and opinions entirely coincide. Whatever is proposed by one seems but the anticipation of the others project...[18]

There is more of the same. Haslewood, like Nelson, now knew what it was like to be in love.

The new Mr and Mrs Haslewood came to dine with Mr and Mrs Godsal immediately on their return from Bath and then moved into their new home in Fitzroy Square. In August they spent a holiday in Brighton with Maria's sister, Susannah Saxon and her husband, and with Philip Lake, Maria's brother. All was delightful save for an argument between Haslewood and his coachman on the morning of departure which led to the coachman being dismissed and the necessity of travelling by post chaise.[19]

Haslewood continued to impress Nelson with his zeal and commitment and was now often addressed as 'My dear Haslewood'. In 1803 he was explaining to a baffled Admiral the complexities of a new 'Proclamation for Granting the Distribution of Prizes' with which the Admiralty was obfuscating the whole issue of prizes, so important to sailors of all ranks.[20] In November Haslewood successfully steered through the case in the King's Bench which secured

Nelson £13,000 in prize money, previously awarded to Earl St Vincent.[21]

Haslewood's domestic life was as successful as his professional. Proof of the mutual passion of the honeymoon came with the birth of a baby boy to Maria almost exactly nine months from the day of the wedding. Her father presented her with a Bible with a dedication written by Thomas Tomkins, the leading copper plate writer.[22] On 6 February 1804 the Reverend Mr John Haslewood christened the baby Frederick Fitzherbert Haslewood, named after the two godfathers Frederick Booth, Haslewood's senior partner and Thomas Fitzherbert. The proud young father gave a dinner party for seventeen guests followed by what his father-in-law described in his Diary as 'a very large party in the evening – say 160 or more'.[23] Such extravagance had to be funded and shortly afterwards Haslewood successfully petitioned his father-in-law for a loan of £1,000.[24] It was to be the first of several.

Haslewood had high expectations of himself and of his employers, his family and his friends, and he was never backward in making them clear. At the same time of his petition to Godsal for the loan of £1,000 over and above the £5,000 he had just received by the terms of the marriage settlement he addressed a surprising petition to Admiral Lord Nelson

By your Lordship's most kind permission I take the liberty of putting the following memorandum in writing. Mr Collins, the Agent of Sir John E.Acton[25] is not a very temperate man. And if any accident should befall him, I should have every opportunity and, I need not add, disposition to do justice to the office he fills, having a little estate of my own in that neighbourhood [26] and being perfectly well acquainted with the county.[27]

It is almost breathtaking in its insensitivity and self regard. Poor Collins was still employed in his position and no accident should be wished upon him. Moreover Nelson's professional and domestic responsibilities might be thought enough to protect him from such solicitations of an employee. Perhaps Nelson took that same view, or perhaps the hapless Mr Collins survived his intemperance. In either case Haslewood did not obtain the position he sought and he was fortunate not to lose the regard of the patient Nelson.

The year 1805 began for Haslewood with the birth of a second child, a girl, and with increasing intimacy with Nelson. He was favoured with instructions about Nelson's love-child, Horatia,[28] with amendments to the will,[29]

Dear Sir

In a hasty line which I sent you this morning, I suggested the expediency of laying before Mr Seymour the circumstances attending my first introduction to your family, if you should feel reluctant to perform your engagement to me.

Allow me to add I should be equally satisfied with the matter being submitted to Lord Chief Justice Best [Philip Lake's father-in-law]. His sense of honour & knowledge of what is right would more than counterpoise any interested motive which might darken an understanding less acute.

Poor, poor Philip Godsal, now aged seventy-seven, to be so abused. He sent a brief response.[49]

Mr Godsal has read with the deepest regret Mr William Haslewood's two letters addrest [sic] to him on the 10th instant. Mr Godsal having made his pecuniary arrangements relative to his daughter Mrs Haslewood & her family under the most deliberate & anxious consideration it is not likely they will be altered unless Mr Godsal should experience a repetition to him of Mr William Haslewood's indelicate & unjustifiable application to him or to any other Person.

What else could he say? The facts of the matter, as we now know them, and as Haslewood suspected, were that the two daughters were to get no more at Philip's death than the original marriage settlement of £5,000 on which he had been paying them five per cent interest since the date of the marriage. At his death the capital sum was to revert to them. In 1818 Godsal had written a will in which each daughter was to have received an additional £3,000 on his death but in 1821, in a codicil, he had cancelled this provision. His recent discussions with Seymour had resulted in another codicil though this had nothing to do with his daughters' expectations.

However much Haslewood knew, or suspected, the fact is that Godsal was entitled to do whatsoever he wished with his fortune and he had clearly decided that it was not to be spent on Haslewood's debts or extravagant ambitions. But Haslewood, to his eternal shame, had more to say, and it was of a particularly offensive nature[50]

You decline to give me any satisfactory information on the subject of my letters. I sincerely lament this for your sake as well as my own. If you had done me no wrong, it would have been kind to relieve me from doubt. If you

have broken your faith with me you have condemned yourself to shame and sorrow; have banished peace from your pillow and your path, which must be haunted and beset by the image of your injured friend.

You threaten vengeance on your unoffending daughter, if I shall again invoke you to act justly and wisely. She deserves your kinder thoughts, for I am almost ashamed to say, she would rather her children and her husband should suffer wrong than one unwelcome truth be told her father.

You consider my application 'indelicate'. Alas, the task imposed upon me is the bitter fruit of a weak and faulty excess of delicacy. You would never have had the trouble, if I had not regarded your word, repeatedly and voluntarily pledged on the most sacred and solemn occasion as a security equal to your Bond.

When you promised a certain portion to your daughter on her marriage and the like amount on your decease if she could win my affections. I should have turned a deaf ear to your invitation had it not been accompanied by the strongest professions of warm attachment, deep respect and unlimited confidence. By these professions, more than by your promises, I was allured and entangled; let me never add, I was deceived and betrayed…

There is more but it is almost unbearable to read. How much more so for an old father to be told that his beloved daughter was married only for her financial expectations. Haslewood's bile, venom and downright wickedness is almost incomprehensible. Where is the undying gratitude he swore to Godsal for speaking to his young daughter on his behalf? Where is the gratitude for a succession of loans? His letters scatter pitch everywhere but chiefly on himself. He must have been in desperate financial circumstances and possibly suffering some sort of mental breakdown, presaged perhaps in Maria's letter early in the year about the state of his health.

Maria was distraught. Her husband had raged and informed her of the contents of his last letter. She wrote the most anguished of apologies to her father and had it delivered without her husband's knowledge

My dear Father

I hardly know how to express my grief and misery at learning that you were again subjected to a renewal of this, to me, especially wretched cause…The agony it gives me is not to be described, obliged to wear a composed demeanour while my heart is breaking within me. I had rather be reduced to the most abject poverty than to suffer the torture of mind I now endure.

I am most anxious that my brother should not be informed of what has taken place as I should ever wish to live with him in sisterly affection. I pray if you can conceal this from my dear mother as I would not for the world she should suffer on my behalf.[51]

Godsal returned a brief note by return and it can have brought her but limited comfort

My Dear Daughter
We are truly concerned for the cause that compels

you to address me circumstanced as you are. It is not a subject to be gone into with you – my arrangements as respecting your Family & your children have been made long ago & I trust you will have no cause for complaint – on no account would I have your brother know of what is passed for, if he did, he never more could enter your doors United love &c.[52]

There were no further communications between the two men before Godsal's death some eighteen months later. The Haslewoods received what they had been promised in the marriage settlement, and no more. It was perhaps more than William Haslewood deserved.

CHAPTER TWELVE
Marriage Settlements

Amongst the wealthiest families it had long been the practice to exchange legally binding marriage settlements to establish the guaranteed finances which each side would bring to the marriage. For the marriages of each of his three children Philip Godsal was a signatory to just such agreements and they provide an informative source for the family history. It might be mentioned, parenthetically, that he never learned the correct spelling of the word 'marriage' and throughout his Diaries and letters he invariably wrote 'marraige'.

The first of his three children to marry was Susannah, the elder daughter, and already thirty years old when she married Nathaniel Saxon in September 1802. Saxon was a solicitor or attorney, as they were often called at the time, who had been educated at Harrow and had qualified as a Bencher at the Middle Temple where he practised in chambers at Pump Court. Four years later he was to become for a short time, the Member of Parliament for the rotten borough of Ilchester in Somerset, the gift of his patron, Sir William Manners.[1]

Saxon and his future father-in-law had begun discussions of the marriage settlement with Godsal's attorney, Evan Foulkes, of Southampton Street, Covent Garden on 10 May 1802 and 'Heads of Settlement' were exchanged on 17 September the same year.[2] These appointed three trustees to administer the final 'Indenture of Settlement' recording in formal legal terms the informal agreement reached in the 'Heads'. The three trustees appointed were George Edward, Esq, an old friend of Philip; Philip Lake Godsal, the bride's brother; and George Blackman, Esq, a friend of Saxon who was later to succeed to a baronetcy as Sir George Hamage, Bart.

Nathaniel Saxon agreed to convey to the trustees a freehold wharf and two houses in Cannon Row, Westminster, the rent of which the trustees would pay to Saxon for his life, and thereafter to his wife for life should she outlive him. The children of the marriage would then inherit or, if there were no children, the properties would revert back to the Saxon family.

Philip Godsal agreed to provide the sum of £10,000 as his daughter's portion. Of this he agreed to pay the sum of £5,000 to Saxon within one month of the wedding and he gave the trustees his bond for the remaining £5,000 on which he would pay five per cent interest per year and pay this interest to his daughter every half year. In the event of his death the sum of £5,000 would be paid to Mrs Saxon from the estate. Should Mrs Saxon have children the sum would be shared amongst them on her death and should there be no children (and there were none) at her death the interest should continue to be paid to Saxon until his death, whereon the £5,000 would revert to the Godsal family.

Philip also gave his bond to the trustees that he would continue to pay direct to his daughter the interest on the three-and-a-half per cent consols which she had inherited from her grandmother.

Evan Foulkes and his clerk took the Indenture to Grove House, Hampstead for signature on 17 September 1802, where they were signed by Godsal and Saxon and witnessed by the clerk, William Wells, to whom Godsal gave £5 for his trouble.[3] He also gave his servants £8.18s.6d to celebrate the marriage.[4]

With regard to the £5,000 due to the bridegroom, Godsal gave Saxon £2,200 in cash and his promissory note for £1,000. The balance due of £1,800 was agreed by both parties to be the value of the house and stables at 39 Gower Street which Godsal transferred to Saxon and which became the Saxon family residence.[5]

The wedding took place at a quarter to nine on the morning following the signing of the Indentures at St George's, Hanover Square, fashionable then as now. Weddings were not the great social occasions which they have become, the focus being on the witnessing of the religious and civil contract of the vows. The only guests on the bride's side were her father and mother, her sister and brother, the trustees George Edward and his wife and Mr Fishwick, a friend of her father. The wedding breakfast was held at Mr Edward's house in Park Lane and the Saxons left immediately afterwards to travel to Winchester for the first part of their honeymoon.[6]

It was a time of mixed emotions for Philip Godsal, for on the following day he was at Villiers Street off the Strand where the body of his old friend, Thomas Devenish, was brought back for burial after his fatal accident in Loughborough where he had been thrown from his horse. On the day of the funeral, a few days later, Philip noted in his Diary that he had received the first letter from his daughter as a married woman.[7]

When the Saxons returned to London five weeks later, they moved in temporarily with the Godsals in Grove House, Hampstead while their own home in Gower Street was being re-decorated. Both families had much news to catch up on, the honeymoon of course, Philip Lake's first week up at Oxford and a visit to Hampstead by Susannah's old friend, Miss Jeynes, and her elderly beau Admiral Thornborough, who had announced their own forthcoming wedding. The Saxons stayed in Hampstead for a month before moving into Gower Street and they returned a month later when Ann Godsal gave a rout at which they were guests of honour.[8]

Before the year ended Godsal had received from Evan Foulkes a hefty bill for £220.17s.3d for the preparation of the Heads of Agreement and the Indentures.[9] He had also transferred to his daughter the £900 of consols which she had inherited and he generously rounded it up to £1,000.[10]

His generosity to the newly weds had not yet ended, for he presented them with a coach worth £315 and gave Saxon a pipe of port worth £101.[11] He also agreed to lend him the sum of £1,990 against Saxon's bond.[12] He also paid the half yearly interest of £125 on the £5,000 agreed in the Indenture.

No sooner was Susannah's settlement executed than negotiations began for the marriage of the younger daughter, Maria, to William Haslewood. Godsal's negotiations with Haslewood regarding the marriage settlement began in December 1802 and the marriage took place in March 1803. Godsal's commitments were essentially the same as those he made for his elder daughter, £5,000 to the bridegroom in cash and £5,000 invested paying interest at five per cent per annum for the bride and subsequently for any children of the marriage.

Haslewood brought to the marriage the income derived from two proprietory chapels held on leasehold, Bedford Chapel in the Parish of St George, Bloomsbury, and St Margaret's Street Chapel in Cavendish Square. Together they were said to produce an income of £400 per annum. In addition Haslewood's father gave Godsal and the trustees his bond declaring that a farm and lands in the parish of Higley, Shropshire were to be given to his son after the

death of himself and his wife. The trustees appointed were Philip Lake Godsal, brother of the bride, Frederick Booth, the senior partner in the law firm of which Haslewood was a member, and Thomas Fitzherbert, a friend of the bridegroom.[13]

The Indentures were signed by all parties on 7 March 1803 and Foulkes's bill this time was a more modest £116.7s.6d. Godsal intimated to the bridegroom his wish to present him with a pipe of port, but it was agreeable to all parties when Haslewood said he would prefer the money to be spent on jewellery for his wife.[14] Godsal gave him a coach, like Saxon's costing £315, and he gave Maria £20 for her clothes and a personal gift of £21,[15] an amount which he continued to give her each year for the rest of his life.

Maria's wedding, like that of her older sister, took place at St George's, Hanover Square, although Maria was married from her father's town house in Clarges Street. It was eight o'clock in the morning when father and daughter were driven to the church by the coachman and footman, both wearing new liveries and 'new round hats' bought for the occasion.[16] The service was conducted by the bridegroom's brother, the Reverend Mr J.D. Haslewood. The only guests on the bride's side were her mother and father and sister. Her brother Philip Lake was not present, having left for Oxford on the early morning coach. There was no wedding breakfast, as the couple left immediately after the ceremony to begin their honeymoon in Bath. There were some celebrations, however, for the Godsals entertained to dinner the Reverend Mr Haslewood, the Saxons, the Edwards, Mr Fishwick, Mr Foulkes and Mr Wilkinson, the banker.[17]

Again a marriage had taken place within a few days of a funeral, for the week before most of those attending the dinner had attended the funeral of the bride's uncle, Charles Cole, who had been buried in a vault of the self same church of St George's, Hanover Square.[18]

The newly weds returned to London after a month's honeymoon and were entertained to dinner by the Godsals in their town house at No 1 Clarges Street before they moved into their married home. Philip Godsal lent Haslewood £1,000 against his bond.

With his two daughters married within six months of each other it might seem that Philip had time to recoup his fortunes before his son married eleven years later in 1814. This was not strictly the case, for his expenditure on settling his son into society began shortly after the second wedding in 1803.

Philip Lake Godsal was already at Oxford when Susannah married in 1802 and he was registered at the Middle Temple in 1804. It was after his graduation,

Grace Ann Godsal, née Best, the wife of Philip Lake Godsal, by Samuel Woodforde, R.A.

however, that Philip invested £4,200 in his son's future by buying for him a commission in the Honorable Band of Gentlemen Pensioners. This was in June 1806 and eight years later, at the time of his marriage, Philip Lake was able to sell the commission for £4,675 which then formed a portion of the £15,000 which Godsal had committed to pay on the Indentures of his son's marriage in 1814.[19]

Before that date Philip Godsal had given his son £9,013 in 4 per cent stock in 1809 and £7,069 in 1812 as part of the sale of the coachmaking business.[20] These two payments were gifts and were not taken into account in the marriage settlement.

Under the terms of the marriage settlement of Philip Lake Godsal and Grace Ann Best, Philip Godsal agreed to pay to the trustees the sum of £15,000 which he paid by adding to the £4,675 resulting from the sale of the commission in the Gentlemen Pensioners a further sum of £10,000 in four and five per cent stock. Conveniently he had just received the last £2,000 in the series of phased payments for the sale of the coachmaking business. The bride's father, Serjeant Best, was committed only to £5,000 invested with the trustees for the maintenance of Grace Ann and any children of the marriage.

The disproportionate amounts paid by the two fathers reflected the social prestige conferred upon the Godsals by the Bests. Philip Godsal was certainly in no doubt of the advantageous nature of the relationship. His correspondence with Serjeant Best, which is noted on pages 118-119, makes that clear.

It is also evident that Best believed Godsal's fortune to be even greater that it was, for in November 1814, only four months after the wedding, Godsal received a letter from his own solicitor

I was not able to obtain an interview with the Serjeant before this morning when I obtruded myself upon him at breakfast & told him you had not the means of acccomplishing so large a purchase as £133,000. The Serjeant's idea was that as the Estates were to be taken at a valuation & as at the present moment, by the reduced price of corn, favourable to a Purchase, you might probably have had a Friend that was disposed to purchase a part of the Estate, & that with the assistance of your son's settlement, money which may be invested in the purchase of land or laid out upon a mortgage, the matter might have been accomplished & I rather understood he would not in that case have been disinclined to have made an advance of his daughter's fortune.[21]

It was not to be. Godsal did not have such funds, or such friends, at his immediate disposal. But the story illustrates the conception of deep wealth which Philip Godsal was assumed to have at his command. It is ironical that only four months later the Corn Laws were introduced, effectively guaranteeing the corn producers higher prices. Had Godsal and Friends bought the estate its value would have significantly appreciated almost immediately. The shrewd businessman for once missed a trick.

CHAPTER THIRTEEN

The Making of a Gentleman

Philip Godsal never intended his son Philip Lake to take over the family coachmaking business. Rather he was to be given a gentleman's education and a private income to enable him to take his place in society free of any taint of trade. Having determined this matter Philip Godsal set about organising his son's academic and social education with all the single minded efficiency that characterised him. This structured education lasted until Philip Lake was twenty-five years old at which time his father stopped making him an annual allowance and gave him instead a capital sum on whose interest he could live as a bachelor in a degree of civilised comfort.

Philip Lake was born on 29 January 1784, the fifth and only the second surviving child of Philip and Ann Godsal. His elder sibling was a girl. Susannah was already aged twelve at the date of Philip's birth and a year later the family was completed by the arrival of a second sister, Maria. Philip Lake thus had a childhood with a playmate close to his own age and a sister old enough to serve as a second maternal figure.

He had been christened Philip as were all the eldest boys in the Godsal family and his second name Lake after the maiden name of his paternal grandmother, who as a widow, had run the family coachmaking business until his father had been old enough to take it over.

The earliest impact which the three Godsals may be said to have made upon the world outside their own family was in 1789 when their father commissioned John Hoppner, R.A., already appointed as Portrait Painter to H.R.H. the Prince of Wales, to paint a joint portrait of the three children.[1] Susannah was then aged seventeen, Philip Lake aged five and little Maria aged four. It is a delightful picture which was exhibited at the Royal Academy in 1789 under the title 'Portrait of a young lady and two children'. Philip paid the painter £45. (Its undoubted quality was simply confirmed when two centuries later the Huntington Museum in San Marino, California acquired it to join their superb collection of eighteenth century portraits.) The publisher, J. Young, contracted to make a mezzotint of the portrait and in December 1790 the proud father bought twelve copies for £7.13s.0d. to distribute to family and friends.[2]

It can be said that the painting and the print represented the only presence in the parental home at 84 Piccadilly of the two youngest children, for in April 1789 both Philip Lake and Maria were sent to boarding school in Parson's Green.[3] This early withdrawal from the comfort and security of home must have had an emotional effect on the two children. Even such reassurance they could draw from each other's company was withdrawn when poor little Maria, still only six years old, was taken by her father to board at Miss Semple's Academy in Calais.[4]

Philip Lake was to live at boarding schools for the next thirteen years and this early and continuous separation from parents and siblings may well account for that emotional coldness which was sometimes evident in his adult life. From the ages of five to ten Philip Lake lived with Mr Sketchley who was paid £42 per annum for his board and education.[5] At the age of ten he changed schools, going to Mr Chauvet in Kensington where he stayed until the age of fifteen. It seems likely that Chauvet was a Frenchman and that Philip Lake learned to speak French at this time.

Mr or Monsieur Chauvet's fees for education and board were £68.12s.6d per half year[6] and when Philip Lake was fifteen these were supplemented by additional fees for extra-curricula activities. He was taught to ride by Mr Hall[7] and was taught to play the violin by Mr Mullian.[8] There is good evidence that he became a good horseman and, as he continued his violin lessons for two years, that he became a competent violinist.

It was when Philip Lake was fifteen years old that his father began to play a part in his social education, taking him on a fortnight's tour of great houses, historical sites and fashionable watering places. Father and son visited Blenheim, Oxford, Bath, William Beckford's Fonthill, Stonehenge and the old family home in Tewkesbury.[9]

Philip Lake now went to Harrow School, lodging with Professor Lloyd[10] and at the age of sixteen he was registered at the newly established Royal Institution in Albermarle Street.[11] Six months later his father arranged for

Richard Sullivan to propose him as a Proprietor of this most august institution.[12] He was accepted and Godsal paid the subscription of £52.10s.0d.[13] Sullivan had worked for the East India Company in Canton, where he had entertained William Hickey, and had then made a fortune in Madras.[14] Returning to London he now held a Government sinecure and his connection with Godsal was probably as a fellow Freemason.

Philip Lake must have been one of the youngest members of the Royal Institution which had been formed in 1799 and received its Royal Charter in the following year just before Philip Lake became a proprietor. The purpose of the Institution was declared to be 'diffusing the knowledge and facilitating the introduction of useful mechanical inventions and improvements and for teaching by courses of philosophical lectures and experiments the application of science to the common purposes of life'.

It had something in common with the established Society for the Encouragement of Arts, Manufactures and Commerce of which Philip Godsal had himself been a member but it quickly eclipsed the older society in prestige and Philip Lake found himself in the presence, if perhaps not yet the company, of some of the brightest intellects of the age, including the founder, the extraordinary American Count Rumford and the brilliant young chemist and polymath Humphrey Davy who began his celebrated lectures the following year. Davy's equally dazzling young friend Samuel Coleridge was shortly to lecture there.[15]

It sounds a daunting experience for a schoolboy but Philip Lake was later to delight his Oxford tutor with his intelligence and application and this early exposure to these luminaries may have assisted his own intellectual development.

Father and son's second summer tour was to Canterbury, Margate, Ramsgate, Hythe, Dover, Hastings, Tunbridge Wells, Penshurst and Sevenoaks where they visited Knole, seat of the Duke of Dorset.[16] At sixteen Philip Lake was getting an excellent introduction to the fashionable world. A young schoolfellow was invited to join them for a part of the tour which doubtless pleased the young men.

Two days after his seventeenth birthday Philip Lake went to board with his final schoolmaster.[17] The Reverend Mr Dixon lived at Storrington, a small town, little more than a village, to the north of Worthing in Sussex. Philip Lake by now had his own horse, whose livery was added to Mr Dixon's bills to make a total of £62.7s.6d per quarter. Father proudly noted that on one occasion his son had ridden from Storrington to Hampstead in one day, a

distance of some fifty miles.[18] It was at this time that he took fencing lessons to add to his gentlemanly accomplishments.[19]

On one visit home at this time Philip took his son to an old school re-union dinner of the Soho Academy.[20] These convivial dinners, so dear to his father's heart and stomach represented another part of the young man's education.

One of the reasons why the Reverend Mr Dixon had been selected was because of his excellent Oxford connections and he duly delivered to Philip Godsal his dearest wish when his son was accepted as a commoner at Oriel College. Father and teacher accompanied him to Oxford for the ceremony in the Sheldonian Theatre on 31 May 1802 when the Vice Chancellor admitted 'Philippus' Lake Godsal 'in statu pupilari' having 'subscripsit Articulis Fidei & Religionis'.[21]

They stayed at the Star Inn in Cornmarket, then the principal coaching inn in Oxford and they attended a service in the University Church of St Mary's in the High Street. The vicar of St Mary's was the Reverend Mr Edward Coplestone who was to be Philip Lake's tutor although the service that day was taken by the Reverend Dr Nott of All Souls. The coachmaker was delighted to be presented to the don after the service and later it was to be Nott's turn to be delighted when Godsal bought some of his drawings of Rome.

Before leaving Oxford Philip paid his son's Caution money of £22 to Oriel (a large sum but young gentlemen could be boisterous in drink). Father and son met the Reverend Mr Edward Coplestone for the first time. Philip Lake's tutor was thirty-two and already an important figure in the University. Not only the vicar of the University Church he was also the Professor of Poetry and a celebrated Latin scholar. Together with the Provost of Oriel he had developed the course in *Literae humaniores*, or 'Greats', the celebrated Oxford Classics degree. He sustained this brilliant career by succeeding Eveleigh as Provost of Oriel, reforming the University examinations system, making Oriel's Fellowships the most prized in the University, and was later appointed Bishop of St Asaph. This was in the future but it is important to recognise his qualities for he is the principal witness to Philip Lake's career at Oxford.[22]

Although now formally entered as a pupil at Oxford Philip Lake did not go up to Oxford until the start of Michaelmas Term in October 1802. In the intervening five months he continued to live with Mr Dixon and not at the family home in Hampstead. He did however accompany his father on the third of their summer tours. They left their

The Godsal Children in 1789 by John Hoppner, R.A. was also published as a mezzotint

Dr Eveleigh, Provost of Oriel when Philip Lake was an
undergraduate

horses at Portsmouth, taking the ferry to the Isle of Wight where they hired a post chaise at Ryde to travel round the island for five days.[23]

Philip Lake paid a brief visit home for his sister Susannah's marriage to Nathaniel Saxon at St George's Hanover Square.[24] Once again he returned to Storrington to study with Mr Dixon, rather than staying at Hampstead. He did not return home again until 9 October, as his father said 'for to go to Oxford'.

Godsal accompanied his son to Oxford, chose the furniture for his set of rooms in Oriel paying the handsome price of £46.[25] Philip Lake was clearly not going to suffer by comparison with any noble scholar or commoner. His termly allowance from his father was £75, precisely the same sum as the present writer received from the State when he was a commoner at Oxford 150 inflationary years later. Godsal also agreed to meet livery costs and of course support his son in the vacations. Having settled his son in Godsal returned to Hampstead well pleased and gave his servants £1.10s.0d 'for my son going to College'.[26]

When he came down for the Christmas vacation Philip Lake did not spend much time at home but instead went to stay with the Reverend Mr J.D. Haslewood to whose brother his sister Maria was shortly to be married.[27] When the wedding took place however Philip Lake did not attend the ceremony but chose to return to Oxford on the 9 a.m. coach, having paid only a quick overnight visit to see his sister.[28]

One may guess that his mother at least would have wanted to see more of her only son and the reason why Philip Lake spent so little time at home throughout his childhood and student days might seem to be a lack of close emotional ties within the family. There is no specific evidence of this but there is very strong evidence that Philip Lake was a very hard working and commited student. Such creatures did, and no doubt, still do exist and there is no better witness to Philip Lake being one of their number than his tutor the Reverend Mr Edward Coplestone, whose academic and personal *bona fides* we have noted earlier.

In a series of letters to Philip Godsal, Coplestone paints a graphic picture of an unusually dedicated student. Towards the end of the first year Coplestone wrote

Your son's conduct in College has been highly meritorious and has gained him the esteem of every person under whose authority he has been placed. I am not in the habit of communicating with parents upon these subjects and I hope therefore you will not consider what I say as mere words. I mean to assure you that I have never derived more satisfaction from any pupil than him, and from the steadiness of his conduct and the manly principles of which he is possessed I have not the least doubt of his continuing to deserve the same unqualified commendation.[29]

Bearing in mind Coplestone's position, experience and reputation it can only be described as an astonishing communication but only one month later he wrote again 'How heartily I congratulate you on the prospect you have from him. I have no doubt of his diligent attachment to his studies and of his liberal and virtuous disposition and I have ventured to hint to him occasionally that he would be better if he amused and relaxed his mind more'.[30]

Perhaps because of this, but more likely as part of a long term strategy, Philip paid for a subscription, not yet a commission, for his son in the fashionable Cities of London and Westminster Light Horse Volunteers, a cavalry regiment of which he himself was a mess member.[31] Dedicated student though he was Philip Lake obviously had some potentialities as a cavalry officer. He was a good horseman and he had been taught to fence. He also had the money behind him for the attendant expenses of a very fashionable regiment. Within a week of paying the £37.12s.6d subscription Philip Lake was in the ranks when Lord Harrington reviewed the Light Horse Volunteers on Wimbledon Common on 25 August 1803.[32]

No doubt his tutor approved this diversion from a life of study as he would have approved of Philip Lake accompanying his sister Maria and her husband William Haslewood on a seven week visit to Brighton, then at the height of its prestige as the coastal resort of London society. It became a real family holiday when Susannah Saxon arrived with her husband Nathaniel, bringing with them a gift of £20 for Philip Lake from his father and the loan of his pony.[33]

The party took a house in the new Steyne to the east of the town overlooking the sea. Philip Lake had much time for reading but he also found the time to ride out to Devil's Dyke to join 'an elegant throng' on the Downs to watch a review by General Lennox of the South Gloucester and Hampshire Regiment. Philip Lake also rode over to Storrington, north of Worthing, to see his old tutor and Oxford sponsor, the Reverend, Mr Dixon.

He returned to Oriel for his second year at the end of which his tutor wrote again to his father in terms no less complimentary than at the end of his freshman year

I cannot suffer your son to return to you without an assurance from me that the experience of another year

has only been to raise him in my estimation and in that of the College. At the close of term he received our thanks for his exemplary conduct and most regular attention to his studies. One important object of a liberal education he is in a fair way of acquiring – I mean the power of expressing his thoughts on any subject with ease and propriety in his native language – I speak now from the improvement I have seen in his compositions. His acquaintance also with the Greek and Latin classics is much enlarged – and his taste more directed to those authors.

I believe I may with safety repeat a suggestion I made before – that during the vacations he stands rather in need of exhortation to amusement and company than to study.[34]

What father would not have been delighted at such an encomium to his son's academic progress? The hint that he remained a little too serious and not entirely sociable with his fellow students would have given him little concern.

Philip Lake spent most of the long vacation away from home once again, this time travelling to Harrogate, another fashionable watering place, for two months. He travelled up on the York Mail while his groom hacked up with the horses.[35] Meanwhile father renewed his son's subscriptions to the Royal Institution and the Light Horse Volunteers and paid a hefty tailor's bill of £48.3s.6d, the first intimation of Philip Lake's undoubted taste for fashionable dress.[36]

It was clearer than ever to Philip that his son should not take over the family coachmaking business but should pursue his career as a gentleman and to this end he entered him as a student of the Middle Temple, with Nathaniel Saxon and himself acting as the securities.[37] A career in the law, especially in the upper reaches, was entirely suitable for a gentleman and also offered the possibility of a political career.

On his return from Harrogate Philip Lake spent little time at Hampstead and went almost directly to Oxford to begin his final year. During the Christmas Vacation yet again he spent little time at home returning to Oxford three weeks before the start of the Hilary term. It seems that he may have been working too hard and it may have contributed to his illness for much of that term. However he was well enough in the Trinity Term to take the examination for his Degree. The as yet unreformed Oxford Finals were certainly not as demanding as the thirty-six hour ordeal they later became and Philip Lake took his degree as a Bachelor of Arts in the University of Oxford at the Ceremony in the Sheldonian on 15 June 1805.[38]

His father showed his delight by giving him the huge sum of £100 and a bay gelding costing £57.15s.0d.[39] The horse was put to good use immediately for Philip Lake did not stay at home but set off immediately on another extended tour, this time to Devon in the company of the Reverend J.D. Haslewood, his sister's brother-in-law.[40]

While he was away his father received another letter from Edward Coplestone which must have given him the greatest gratification.

Your son has now finished his academical course and acquitted himself throughout with great credit to himself and satisfaction to me. I feel this satisfaction so strongly that I cannot omit endeavouring to add to yours by assuring you that he has gained the esteem of the whole society in which he was placed and has deserved it. His moral conduct has been exemplary and I do not recollect that he has ever incurred the slightest censure for any breach of discipline. Of his attention to his studies I have often assured you, and the best proof is the very honorable manner in which he passed his public examinations in the Schools. His conduct towards me has been such again as to gain my sincere regard and esteem which I shall ever retain, and I trust will be mutual throughout life.[41]

This series of letters from a College tutor to the father of a student is quite remarkable and given Coplestone's own outstanding gifts doubly so. The partiality towards Philip Lake of which Philip was later to be accused by his son-in-law, William Haslewood, was based on a conviction, for which he had been given every reason, that his son was an outstanding young man and destined for a high place in society. That he should choose to devote his financial resources to promote his son's future rather than that of his married daughters is not altogether surprising or unusual.

It would appear that Philip Lake might have taken Holy Orders and possibly become an Oxford Don like his mentor Coplestone, a career which offered the opportunity of continuing the intellectual life to which he was clearly well suited. Instead he decided to pursue a career in the law, studying at the Middle Temple.

His father now gave him the generous annual allowance of £500, a sum it may be said that exceeded the annual earnings of most solicitors, clergymen and army officers and was nearly ten times that of most clerks and all labourers. He now had the means, and was beginning to show the inclination to live the life of a gentleman. His father commissioned the artist Isaac Pocock, a pupil both of

Romney and Sir William Beechy, to paint a full length portrait of this young man about town.

Pocock was only two years older than the twenty-two year old sitter but he had already exhibited subject pictures and portraits at the Royal Academy for four years. He was able to charge £52.10s.0d for the portrait and Philip paid an additional £22.12s.0d for the carved and gilded frame.[42]

The portrait was a highly competent full length, three quarter face in the current fashionable pose with the subject resting his arm on a classical plinth. At a later date the bottom third was cut from the portrait. The evidence suggests that Philip Lake was wearing long hessian boots, favoured by Beau Brummell and the Dandies at that time. There is a record of Philip Lake paying for the repair of just such boots at this time. It was perhaps later, when the style of Brummell had become passé that the canvas was cut and the picture re-framed as the three quarter length it is to-day.

The portait was handed over in December 1805 and the following month Philip Lake attended the great State Funeral of Admiral Lord Nelson in St Paul's. Tickets for this event were much sought after and Philip Lake's appears to have been obtained by William Haslewood who played a part in the ceremony as a member of Nelson's household.

Philip Lake retained the ticket as a souvenir and it is clear that the ticket was originally written in the name of Philip

It appears that Philip Godsal passed this invitation to take part in the procession on the occasion of Nelson's funeral to his son Philip Lake

CHAPTER FOURTEEN
The Marquess of Blandford

For the last twenty-five years of his life Godsal's financial affairs were interwoven with those of George Spencer Churchill, the Marquess of Blandford, who succeeded as the fifth Duke of Marlborough in 1817. Blandford was entirely without scruples with regard to the payment of his debts and Godsal needed all his experience and persistence to avoid being ruined. As it was, it was a close run thing, and on his death there remained problems for his son to resolve. It has to be said that some actions of the fifth Duke brought shame to his title.

All those problems were in the future when Blandford first became a coachmaking customer, probably some little time before 1796 from when the first coachmaking account survives.[1] Blandford had already by this date resigned as a Member of Parliament for the County of Oxford, a role which he had filled for six years. He was a Pittite Tory but politics were by no means the driving force in his life.[2] He was self indulgent to a degree, living above his means represented by an allowance from his father, the fourth Duke of Marlborough. Blandford by now rarely visited Blenheim and lived both at Parkbury Lodge, St Albans and at Whiteknights, Reading. Although married, he took as his mistress a married woman, Lady Mary Anne Sturt, by whom he had a child. In 1801 her husband, Sir Charles Sturt sued Blandford for *crim con*. The case was widely reported, and to general surprise, including that of Blandford himself who had planned to flee to Switzerland, he was found not guilty.[3]

It was immediately after this acquittal that he approached Philip Godsal for a cash loan, although, as was his wont, he had not paid his coachmaking bill. Even by the standards of the coachmaking industry, where extended credit was not unusual, Blandford was exceptional. He now needed to borrow money to meet his many extravagances which included not only maintaining a mistress but indulging his twin collecting passions for rare books and rare plants.

Godsal agreed to this first request and lent him £502.10s.9d on 10 June 1801[4] and it appears to have been unsecured, although Godsal was in communication with Joseph Brooks, attorney to the fourth Duke of Marlborough, who explained that Whiteknights was not owned by the Marquess who 'actually pays his father for it upwards of £1,000 per annum together with £340 for Caversham Farm'. Brooks continued

> If this be deemed a sufficient security Mr Foulkes [Godsal's solicitor] or yourself will have the goodness to draw such a lease from the Duke to his son as may be most pleasing & His Grace will accept it, but as I have said before, this proposal, if it be not satisfactory, another Title must and will be found & will be divested to accomplish this business.[5]

This communication appears to have satisfied Godsal, perhaps because it was clear that the Duke was aware of his son's borrowings and was prepared to consider offering Whiteknights or other properties to secure them. Godsal did not go down this route but instead now accepted a 'Warrant of Attorney' whereby Blandford bound himself to re-pay his debts to Godsal against specific penalties for non-payment. The Warrant was signed on 6 April 1802 against a penalty of £10,000. Prudently, Godsal registered the Warrant immediately with the Court of Chancery.[6]

Godsal's attorney also examined the Act of Parliament which had granted the first Duke of Marlborough and his heirs forever an annual pension of £5,000 paid from Post Office revenues, to see if it could be assigned as security.[7] The answer was that it could not.

Godsal now decided that it would be prudent to insure Blandford's life against that of his father, for should the son die before his father, then the Blenheim estate, which was entailed on the heir, would pass to Blandford's brother who would certainly not use his private resources to pay his spendthrift brother's debts. With some reluctance Blandford agreed to pay the premiums for such insurance but then provided incorrect information with regard to the dates of birth of both his father and himself. Anyone but a member of the aristocracy might have expected to find himself under arrest for this particular falsification and Evan Foulkes, Godsal's solicitor, had to make no fewer than eight visits to Blandford's solicitors before verifying the true dates.[8] At that point Godsal took out £5,000 of insurance on Blandford's life with the Westminster Insurance Company and £500 with the Equitable.[9]

Godsal now agreed to lease his house at No 83 Piccadilly to the Marquess at a furnished annual rent of £480, which was charged to Blandford's account and accrued interest as he did not choose to pay. No 83 Piccadilly was a handsome town house, looking across Green Park, only a few doors from Devonshire House. It had been decorated for Godsal by the Royal decorators Crace and Robson & Hale, and this stylish furnished accommodation suited the Marquess well, particularly as he did not feel constrained to pay the rent. He needed a town house at this time because in 1802 he had again been elected as a Member of Parliament. Remarkably, certainly ironically, this notorious debtor was included in William Pitt's government as a Commissioner of the Treasury.[10]

Between 1802 and 1806 Philip Godsal acted as a private banker for his tenant, allowing him to draw cash against an increasingly overdrawn account. Godsal now agreed with his understandably nervous partners, Messrs Baxter and Macklew, that he himself would take the personal responsibility for securing Blandford's debts to the coachmaking business, which in 1805 alone amounted to £1,069 for new coaches and repairs.[11] Despite paying £2,986 in 1805 towards his various accounts with Godsal he stood overdrawn to the amount of £4,652.10s.9d by the time he lost ministerial rank following the death of Pitt early in 1806.

Blandford's need for cash however was becoming ever greater and in the same year Godsal agreed to grant him a mortgage on Marlborough House in Pall Mall for the amount of £11,360.[12] This was as much cash as Godsal could raise at the time, and as the Marquess wanted more, Godsal agreed to stand security for a further £3,850 lent to Blandford by Godsal's bankers, Marsh, Sibbald & Fauntleroy. Blandford indemnified Godsal by giving him his bond for this amount.[13]

This escalation of debt is almost dizzying. Blandford never paid the rent for his Piccadilly house, he never paid the interest due on the Marlborough House mortgage, he never paid for any of the life insurance premiums, he never paid any of his coachmaking bills (these amounted to £1,765 for the years 1808 to 1810 alone), and he repaid little of the cash he borrowed.

In summary, by 1810 the Marquess of Blandford owed Philip Godsal £20,286.16s.8d including the compound interest which continued to mount because of the lack of payments. The only copper bottomed collateral was the mortgage on Marlborough House and the life insurances. At this time Blandford gave a second Warrant of Attorney, this time for £7,700[14] and Godsal now had apparent collateral in excess of the money owed him. However the two Warrants of Attorney and the Bond, while being proper legal documents, were by no means guaranteed should the Marquess die before he inherited the Dukedom. It was widely known that he was borrowing large sums elsewhere and, in the event of his death, Godsal would join a long queue of creditors looking for large sums against a limited estate.

Godsal now ceased to lend further money and Blandford had by now left No 83 Piccadilly. Godsal also took out £900 more of insurance on Blandford's life although Blandford did not pay the premiums and they too were adding to the account which was still increasing by five per cent per year. Godsal must by now have been holding his breath. Blandford continued to borrow elsewhere on *post-obits* on his father's death. What did he spend these enormous sums on? If he may properly be said to be notorious as a debtor then he was celebrated as a connoisseur collector. He collected both rare books and rare plants.

At the beginning of the nineteenth century there were three notable collectors of rare books; George John, the second Earl Spencer, William Beckford, and the Marquess of Blandford.[15] Their competition in the sale rooms pushed prices ever higher and dealers were not slow to play off one against the other.

Earl Spencer, brother of Georgiana, Duchess of Devonshire, and ancestor of the late Princess Diana, retired early from a promising political career to build up one of the finest private libraries in Europe at Althorp. The scandalously bi-sexual William Beckford, whose fortune was based on sugar, was the archetypal connoisseur of architecture, paintings, books and *objets d'art*, and was both celebrated and derided as the owner of the gothic extravaganza of Fonthill.

The reputation of Blandford as a collector is perhaps less well known to-day but Beckford's waspish description of the 'bibliomaniac' Blandford gives an idea of contemporary opinion. Writing just after Blandford had succeeded to the Dukedom but had put his Whiteknights collection up for sale, Beckford wrote 'The Greenhorn Marlborough has had his reign. He has for many years enjoyed the omnipotence of having all he wanted whatever the price...now we'll see issuing from Whiteknights torrents of treasures, books, porcelain, bronzes, ivories, agates …with £10,000 one could get treasures from this mine'.[16]

His apotheosis as a book collector came in 1812 when he paid £2,260 for the only known copy of the 1471 edition of Boccaccio's *Decameron*. It was the highest price ever paid in England for a single volume, and it remained so until 1880. In its reckless way the purchase was also heroic, for the underbidder was an agent of the arch-enemy, the Emperor Napoleon.

Sadly, Blandford was spending not only his own money but that of his creditors. And it was not only on books and *objets d'art*. The garden at Whiteknights contained the rarest of plants acquired careless of the cost. It was a time when new specimens from the Americas were reaching England and Blandford found their acquisition irresistable. His collection of new plants was exceeded only by King George III whose gardeners and superintendent he badgered incessantly for cuttings and seeds. His *magnolia grandiflora* cost one hundred and ten guineas and every square foot of his magnificent Whiteknights garden was filled with specimens on this expensive scale.[17] It was said that he bought the only three specimens of a new geranium and stamped on two saying, 'Now, I have the only specimen in England'.[18] Although doubtless apocryphal, the story suggests the public perception of his character.

In 1811 Blandford found a new way to spend his inheritance. He paid a significant portion (exactly how much is not known) of a £50,000 re-building of the Pantheon, or 'Winter Ranelagh' as Horace Walpole called it. The Pantheon opened briefly as a theatre, but it was deemed unsafe and closed. When it opened again in 1813 it was unlicenced and Blandford and his friends were prosecuted and fined.[19] It never opened again.

This folly marked perhaps the turning point in Blandford's apparently charmed life. His father, the Duke, began discussions with Thomas Coutts, the banker, to mortgage Whiteknights, which Blandford had assumed would descend to him unencumbered. Philip Godsal took fright and applied to the Chancery Court for the enforcement of the Warrant of Attorney for £10,000 which had been registered with the Court in 1802. This was granted against the Whiteknights estate but before receiving any of this sum Godsal, unaccountably lent the Marquess another £1,000.[20] This however was to be the final loan.

In Trinity Term 1813 Godsal applied to the Court and received judgement in his favour for both the Warrants, totalling £17,700.[21] He did not however as yet make application for Execution of the judgement, presumably anticipating Blandford would now pay.

Godsal's own financial situation changed at the end of 1813 when his son, Philip Lake proposed marriage to the daughter of Serjeant Best, later Lord Wynford and presently Attorney to the Prince Regent. As a good father, and as one conferring social prestige in return for money, Best looked to Philip Godsal for a hefty marriage settlement. On 23 December 1813 Godsal wrote to the Marquess of Blandford at Parkbury Lodge

My Lord
My son being on the eve of forming a matrimonial alliance with the daughter of Serjeant Best, I was requested by the Serjeant to state the particulars of the fortune I intended to give my son, as well for his personal support as for a settlement upon the young lady.

In turning my thoughts to the subject it was impossible to pass over the large debt [at this time it had reached £27,000] owing to me by your Lordship – having no other means. When I communicated the nature of the security I held from your Lordship, the learned Serjeant – I am sorry to say – did not think it such as could with propriety be made the subject of a settlement and he expressed his desire that I should inform his Lordship that to render it so, he wishes to have a mortgage given for the debt and the interest regularly paid.

As the proposed alliance is highly creditable to me & of the utmost importance to the welfare of my son, I venture to hope that from the expressions of regard your Lordship has so frequently & kindly expressed for me that you will have the goodness to comply with my present request for by so doing your Lordship will be rendering me the most essential service…[22]

Godsal cannot have been surprised, though he was undoubtedly greatly disappointed, at the immediate reply. If Godsal could be said to have advanced behind the cloak of Serjeant Best, the Marquess simply hid behind his Trustees: '…as I am placed, I can only be considered a passive, or at the most a neutral party in any of the deliberations of my trustees. As such I can recommend a measure but have no power to enforce it'.[23]

It was quite breathtaking. Blandford could borrow money without the sanction of his Trustees but, even with a Court judgement against him he could not pay it back without their approval. Further letters were exchanged. But Godsal's patience was at an end. His final letter looked to sever a relationship which had existed for twenty years

Your Lordship has been pleased to observe that I have money to purchase estates, and to advance on mortgage, and yet I have not a farthing when a reversionary interest is proposed. Is there anything extraordinary, allow me to ask, in such a circumstance? I have not designated myself to be a pauper. It is very true I could continue to make further advances, but then I must make them upon such terms as will immediately yield either a rent, or interest for the support of myself & family.

Can your Lordship seriously think that I could advance so large a sum as £30,000 – in addition to what is already owed me – without receiving either rent or interest? If such an idea has entered your Lordship's head, it cannot be too swiftly removed.

I do not feel myself at liberty to trouble your Lordship with further importunitites and I shall therefore (with great reluctance, I own) adopt those measures which I shall be advised to pursue.[24]

When Blandford, through his attorney wrote another stalling letter, asking for a recapitulation of his accounts with Godsal, Godsal, having consulted Serjeant Best, responded 'You are already in possession of the particulars desired in your letter and it would not now be of use to send you a copy for wearied out by my unceasing endeavours for a long period…I have at last yielded to the importunities of my family and given directions to enforce the payment'.[25]

Philip Godsal had been under distressing pressure from his son and Serjeant Best. Both had clearly intimated that he had been foolish in his dealings with Blandford and that this foolishness and financial incompetence might prejudice his son's future. Poor Philip now felt himself constrained to write a *mea culpa* in a most emotional and uncharacteristic letter to the Serjeant

I have not the language to express my sincere thanks to you for your kind advice and more powerful orders in directing this unpleasant and most vexatious business. Among the good events that have occurred to my declining years I place the introduction my son has enabled me to form with your excellent Family & the completion of the Union of the Young Couple is of the happiest import as it contributes so largely to fill up the measure of our Earthly happiness.

My boundless ambition for the promotion of my son's future welfare was the means of bringing me into this sad dilemma, but I woefully experience that I built my Castle on a sandy foundation. If any privations were necessary I most willingly would take it upon myself – For as a Father I would not inflict my errors on my Son. The education he has received & expectations he has been led to form shall not be narrowed by my improvidence but I trust my means are such as to make neither suffer. In pursuing the steps necessary to obtain my demand I fully appreciate my Son's disinterested opinion in whatever I might hereinafter obtain for him when he is in the plenitude of his power.

In taking what will be termed hostile steps I much expect from the Marquess all possible opposition & were I not as well & ably supported I confess I should tremble not for the consciousness of my accounts being in error but from the influence of such Men of Rank hold in this world of Adulation…[26]

Insofar as his fears that he might have jeopardized the marriage, Best was content that the wedding should take place and was therefore evidently sanguine that the debt, or the greater part of it would be recovered over time.

The threat conveyed in the last sentence of Godsal's last letter to Blandford had some teeth. After his consultations with Serjeant Best he screwed up his courage to face Blandford's opposition and instructed his solicitors to send in an Execution in respect of the original Warrant of Attorney given in 1802 for £10,000. Best recommended that they held off sending in the 1810 Execution at the same time and Godsal and his solicitor were embarrassed by young Philip Lake insisting that they should do so, in contradiction of his new father-in-law.[27] In the event they did not.

On the instructions of the Chancery Court the Sheriff of Berkshire distrained goods and chattels at Whiteknights and in January 1815 the long awaited £10,000 was paid over to him by the Sheriff of Berkshire and in the same month Blandford paid him £1,077.19s.5d against the £1,000 borrowed with interest in 1813.[28]

In February 1815 Blandford's attorney paid a further £780.7s.10d representing four-and-a-half years interest on the bond which Blandford had taken out with Godsal when the coachmaker stood as guarantor for Blandford's loan from the bank. A further £173.4s.6d followed in July being further interest on this same bond.[29]

This represented progress for Godsal, but in December 1815 Serjeant Best conveyed the bad news that as Blandford had not paid the bank their interest on the loan, then Godsal himself, as surety, was due to pay.[30] The new year started with more bad news for it was common gossip in 1816 that Blandford had borrowed the enormous sum of £50,000 on a *post obit* from John Farquhar, formerly the supplier of gunpowder to the East India Company and now a partner in a London bank (and incidentally, the future purchaser of Beckford's Fonthill).[31] At the suggestion of the Serjeant, Godsal now commissioned an Opinion from a leading barrister on the case of Godsal versus Blandford. It ran to eleven pages, and as a result of his views, Godsal's solicitor applied for judgements in the Court of Common Pleas for two separate sums.[32]

At last, in January 1817, came the news that so many had awaited with such eager interest. The fourth Duke of Marlborough died and the Marquess of Blandford came into his inheritance as the fifth Duke. He wasted little time in mourning his father but he soon discovered that his, and no doubt his creditors', sanguine expectations of solvency were not to be. Initially the signs were favourable. Godsal's solicitor wrote to his client

> I have seen the Serjeant and Mr Pinnegar [the new Duke's solicitor] several times and expect such a arrangement will be made for securing the money due to you from the Duke of Marlborough as will meet with your approbation without his executing any further Warrants of Attorney for I have signed judgements in the two actions commenced in Michaelmas Term last so that you have judgements more than sufficient to cover the whole of your demand which was made up to January last as £20,069.12s.8d & you have three judgements – one for £7,700; another for £10,941 & a third for £6,097 making together £24,738. The proposal made to Mr Pinnegar is that your charge upon Marlborough House with these three judgements will be declared to be a security for the whole sum due to you upon your undertaking not to issue execution for six months. The Serjeant approves of it.'[33]

Six weeks later Godsal was granted an interview with the new Duke in Marlborough House. The Duke was affable and promised payment but nothing was forthcoming that year, or the next.[34] The new Duke's trustees forced him into a series of unwelcome measures. Two estates, Parkbury Lodge, St Albans and and Syon Hill House, Brentford were sold immediately.[34] The new Duke was even forced to sell his celebrated library at Whiteknights. Boccaccio's *Decameron* was sold for half the price he had paid only seven years earlier. Even worse, it was bought by his great rival, the Earl Spencer.[35]

Later his beloved Whiteknights, with its 280 acres of landscaped park, its grotto, arbors, its treillaged tunnel and its botanic garden, were surrendered to Thomas Coutts and his fellow mortgagors. Godsal enquired of his solicitor regarding the possibility of some repayment from the furniture in Whiteknights but was informed that it did not belong to the new Duke but to the executors of his father.[36]

As for Marlborough House, some of its complicated leases were surrendered to the Crown in 1817, the year the Princess Charlotte and her new husband Prince Leopold took up residence. The Princess died in childbirth shortly after but the Prince continued in residence. Philip Godsal had granted a mortgage on Marlborough House and his rights do not seem to have been affected, although matters became ever more complicated. In December 1819 he received a letter from his solicitor 'The Prince Leopold has had Marlborough House for two years only – not three as you say & the greater part of the rent due from him has been paid into the Court. – it now remains in the hands of the Accountant General and no person can receive any part of it.'[37]

In the same letter Thomas Walford added 'I suppose you have heard that the Gold Plate has certainly been disposed of & most probably melted – something will very shortly transpire on that subject in the Court of Chancery'. This referred to the extraordinary effrontery of the Duke who had taken to London, for melting down and sale, one of the greatest heirlooms of the Duchy, the great gold service presented to John Churchill, the first Duke of Marlborough by the Emperor of Austria. It was entailed, and by breaching the entail Marlborough had broken the law and was now sued by his own trustees.[38]

In 1820, still with only a derisory total of £277 having been paid since 1815, Godsal became excited by the rumour that the new Queen Caroline, albeit estranged from her husband George IV, was negotiating to buy Marlborough House.[39] It was yet another *ignis fatuus* of hope, appearing but soon disappearing. In October the same year the Duke had the brass neck to send Godsal a hare and a brace of pheasants.[40]

Finally in 1821, the Receiver appointed to administer Marlborough House, the Accountant General, announced that he had £8,396 to divide amongst creditors with claims to £66,609 and he therefore declared a dividend of 2s 6d in the pound on Marlborough House.[41] Godsal received the sum of £2,002.10s.7d on 13 August 1821.

From this point on Godsal began to receive significant sums. The Accountant General paid to him the amount of £699.19s.6d for each of the next three years and £578.6s.11d in 1826. These were dividends in respect of Marlborough House. From 1822 Godsal also began to receive approximately £250 a year from farm rents on the Blenheim estate. In 1823 he received £231.3s.9d from the sale of jewels by the Duke.[42]

Nevertheless, at the time of Godsal's death in April 1826 he was still owed considerable sums by the Duke of Marlborough for which judgements had been made in his favour but executions not taken out. Yet the Legacy Office, looking at the papers, estimated that the value of the security on Marlborough House was worth only £4,712.[43]

It appears probable that the decision was taken that the cost of legal fees in seeking execution would exceed the amounts of goods available to the Duke to be surrendered. The Blenheim papers in the British Library have evidence of other creditors trying to seize what was to be seized but being confronted, as were the local tax collectors in Woodstock, by the fact that the contents of Blenheim Palace were either entailed and in the charge of the Trustees or that the other furniture had been hired and could not be seized.[44] In neither case therefore was it owned by the Duke.

There is evidence that Godsal may have made the decision not to go for execution of remaining judgements and that, after his death, his executors endorsed that decision. In a bitter letter to his solicitor, written six years after his father's death, Philip Lake Godsal was responding to a charge from his brother-in-law, William Haslewood, who had apparently claimed to the solicitors that the executors had 'shrunk from maintaining a claim in order to guard their father's memory from obloquy'.[45] Properly resentful that Haslewood should 'appear to mean that I may know more than can be prudently disclosed with regard to my father's honorable character' Philip Lake added 'If he means to allude to my disinclination to have produced to the Court of Chancery (that School of patience) the security on Blenheim Park, I have to observe that I am I trust guided by a sound discretion and act under professional advice…and that you assure me by withdrawing my claim to the fund in Court I shall not impare my securities on Marlborough House, Blenheim Park and the Insurance Policies'.

There we must leave the Blandford affair which has now become Philip Lake's business, save to note that the life insurance policies on the life of the wretched fifth Duke of Marlborough were paid to Philip Lake on the Duke's death in 1840 at the age of seventy-one.

CHAPTER FIFTEEN
Traveller and Sightseer

Philip Godsal was an inveterate, even insatiable traveller and sightseer. Although we learn of his travels on business and for pleasure only after the age of forty-two, when his Diary begins, he subsequently records travelling to France and Belgium, to Ireland, to the twelve counties of Wales and to thirty-seven of the thirty nine counties of England. Some of these journeys were on business but it is clear that he could not pass by a cathedral, a castle, a stately home or a noted beauty spot, without stopping for a little sightseeing.

There were few of the many popular spas which he did not visit to take the waters, and he travelled around the whole coastline of Southern England, from Margate on the north coast of Kent right round to Teignmouth in Devon. He pursued the 'picturesque' from the Wye Valley and mid Wales to the Lake District, the Peak District and the Yorkshire Dales. Even to-day, with the aid of rapid travel by car, train or coach, such comprehensive sightseeing is uncommon and it was even more unusual at a time when few who had the means to travel were so energetic or so curious.

Godsal's extensive travels were made on horseback, by mail coach, by private carriage and by post chaise and he gives fascinating records of the mechanics, the logistics and the expenses of his journeys. He is more sparing of recording his emotional responses to the sights he saw and of providing detailed descriptions but on occasion his Diary entries give a flavour of his thoughts which no doubt informed his conversations around his dinner table and in the intimacy of the masonic lodges, the regimental messes and the clubs where he spent much of his social life.

Godsal rarely travelled longer distances on horseback but on occasions a groom would ride his saddle horse ahead of his coach or chaise so that it was available for local excursions from his inn or hotel. This was usually the case when he travelled on holiday, staying for a week or more at hotels in Bath, Cheltenham, Brighton, Margate or Teignmouth. The saddle horse did not accompany excursions to the Lake District, for example, where he was staying each night at a different inn. On these occasions he would travel in his private coach or chariot, or in a post chaise.

Employing his own carriage horses meant that they had to be rested every two hours or so, limiting a day's travel to no more than thirty miles. This was suitable for excursions when sightseeing but not when speed of travel was the essence. Travelling in his own coach also enabled him to take two servants, usually Mary Chapman, the laundry maid and Thomas Parkin, the footman (the cook, Sarah Davis was left at home to look after the house). Of course he had to pay for their accommodation, and for that of his coachman, and for the stabling and feed of his horses.

When Godsal used his town coach for travelling he converted it by removing the Salisbury boot from below the coachman's seat and replaced it by a box called a platform boot which carried luggage inside. The decorative and expensive hammer cloth which covered the coachman's seat for town driving was not employed for dirty and dusty travel. At the rear, the vertical decorative stands were removed together with the footboards for the postillion or liveried footman. In their place he substituted a rumble, or boot with seats for the two servants and another luggage box underneath. Flat trunks, called imperials, were carried on the roof. The inside seats had already had space beneath, called wainscots, for further luggage.[1]

When he travelled in his own coach from London to Cheltenham, a distance of ninety-three miles, he would spend the first night at High Wycombe, and the second at Oxford, reaching Cheltenham on the third day. The cost of accommodating himself, his wife, and the servants for two nights and the stabling and feeding of his horses cost approximately £10.[2]

When speed was of the essence then the post chaise came into its own. The post chaise was much the quickest form of private travel as fresh horses could be obtained at every post stage and the journey, theoretically at least, could be continuous. Where this theory could break down was if there were no fresh post horses available on arrival at the next stage. Other travellers may have arrived earlier and the horses and the post boys who rode them, were out or had returned but needed to recover. Parson Woodforde describes just such an occasion when he encountered the Prime Minister himself, William Pitt delayed at a stage post waiting for horses and boys to become available.[3]

Pitt's was perhaps a last minute journey for, with some forward planning, rich men like Pitt and Godsal would have a groom ride ahead to secure horses against their arrival. The groom could also pay any turnpike charges to avoid his master's post chaise having to stop to pay the toll. If the journey were well planned, travel by post chaise could be very rapid. William Hickey described a journey he made from London to Portsmouth

At a quarter to five I was seated next to Emily in her own post chaise. We had four excellent post horses. Tearing away at a great rate we reached Kingston, our first stage, in an hour and a quarter. Two grooms, a man of thirty and a boy of sixteen set off with us, the boy riding in advance to prepare fresh horses and the man following in another chaise to pay the turnpike. We got to Guildford by seven thirty, breakfasted and at eight we went on to Godalming, then Liphook where we changed horses for the last time and from thence to Portsmouth which we reached at two o'clock.[4] [a journey of some sixty-five miles in 9 hours]

Employing post horses, Philip Godsal regularly travelled from London to Cheltenham, a distance of ninety-three miles in the day light hours of one day. Uxbridge, after sixteen miles was the first stage, then High Wycombe, fourteen miles, then Tetsworth, thirteen miles, and then Oxford, twelve miles, where he would have dinner [i.e.lunch]; on to Witney, ten miles, Northleach, sixteen miles and finally Cheltenham, twelve miles.[5]

The cost of 'posting' for Philip and his wife on this journey was initially £7.14s.6d, made up of ninety-three miles at 1s 3d per mile and 2s 6d per boy per stage plus 14s for turnpike tolls. By 1820 the cost had risen to 1s 6d per mile.[6]

Philip's post chaise was a town chariot converted for out of town travel. No coachman was employed as the post boys rode the lead horse. The Salisbury boot and hammer cloth were removed, as in the travelling coach conversion, with luggage space created, but here the essence was lightness, and the rear was unchanged, and if more luggage was required it was sent down in the charge of the servants on a stage coach.

The mail coach offered Godsal a third option for the London to Cheltenham journey and he chose this mode of travel when on short visits for one or two nights and carrying just hand luggage. The Cheltenham Mail left London at 8.30 p.m. and travelling through the night, arrived in Cheltenham at 10.15 a.m., a journey of approximately fourteen hours. The return journey to London left at 6.15 a.m. arriving at 8 p.m. Godsal, of course, chose to travel more comfortably as an inside passenger for which the cost of the return ticket was £5.[7]

Travel was expensive. The cheapest means employed by Godsal for the Cheltenham run was the mail coach and the price he paid for a return ticket represented some six weeks' wages of one of his own labourers, or two weeks wages for one of his highest paid craftsmen. For them perhaps the alternatives were the slow waggon, or not travelling at all.

The London to Cheltenham examples have been chosen to compare Godsal's travelling options and their relative costs but of course he travelled widely elsewhere using all these methods and sometimes a mixture of them. For example he might take a mail coach part of the way and hire a post chaise and the necessary horses to complete a journey. In these various ways he travelled all over England and Wales on roads of varying quality.

Much of his travelling was done before the effects of the Macadam and Telford road improvements which did not take effect until after 1800. But Macadam and Telford did not revolutionise road making, they perfected it, and for the last quarter of the eighteenth century stone chippings had already provided a decent surface on the important roads out of London to the main towns. The Turnpike Trusts had much credit for that and by the time Godsal was sixty in 1807 they maintained 20,000 miles of roads in England and Wales. The roads on which Godsal travelled were widely admired as the best in Europe, and he makes few complaints in his Diary except in Wales where he commented adversely on the state of some of the country roads.

Certainly on his trips west to Cheltenham and Bath, south to Brighton, and north-west to Warwick, or north to St Albans and Luton, the roads presented few problems although it cannot have been entirely comfortable, whether in mail coach, private coach or post chaise. As always however, it must be remembered that it is fruitless to try to explain historical experience in modern terms and suggest that, had Godsal known better, he might have made more complaints.

In these various carriages and on these roads he travelled the length and breadth of the country. In the

LEFT:
A Chariot converted for travelling but driven by a coachman designed by Ackermann

BELOW:
A Coach converted for travelling to be drawn by post-horses designed by Ackermann

While travelling Philip Godsal enjoyed many such inn meals as portrayed by James Pollard

1790s his favoured destinations for longer stays (he never used the word 'holiday') were Margate, Brighton and Bath. Margate had been fashionable enough until the new century when it was customary to satirise it as the choice of the 'cits', those Londoners who had just enough money to spend to seek to enjoy the pleasures of their betters. One cartoon of 1803 notes the miscegenation of the two classes when Milord meets a 'cit' walking along the front at Margate and says 'Your face is familiar'. The man replies, 'I made your breeches, my lord' and his lordship responds, 'Major Bridges, I'm happy to see you'.[8]

The 'cits' usually travelled to Margate, the cheapest way, by sea in a vessel known as a 'hoy' which carried mackerel and herring into London and inevitably smelled of its inward cargo on its return voyage.[9] The 'quality', by contrast, travelled by private coach. Philip Godsal stayed at Rochester or Canterbury on his Margate visits, returning via Tunbridge Wells.

He travelled to Margate several times with his family and friends. They stayed either at Mitchiner's, the best hotel in town, or took a private house. Mitchiner's provided an 'excellent bedchamber and very good sitting room, commanding a full view of the pier and the roads with the ships passing up and down'.[10] Philip records paying 7s 6d per head for dinner and supper 'and wax light' (superior, of course, to tallow candles). On two of his visits he makes a particular note that he had venison for dinner.

Margate was the port of embarkation for Ostend and there was plenty to see out at sea, where both outward and homeward bound East Indiamen and men-of-war provided a splendid spectacle. Margate too had one of the most important of provincial theatres where the stars of the Theatre Royal Covent Garden and of Drury Lane played during the summer season when the London theatres were closed. Godsal saw the precocious Master Betty play Hamlet there in 1807.[11]

Margate was a good centre for excursions to nearby Ramsgate (which was becoming more fashionable as Margate's visitors increased) and to the coast towns of Deal, Dover and Hythe. In 1800 Godsal and his party looked over a man o' war in Deal harbour.[12] On that family holiday Philip himself had to return to London on business for a few days. His coachman dropped him at Rochester where he returned to London by the stage coach. On rejoining his family he travelled again by stage coach and then hired a pony and rode down to Margate. That particular family holiday of four weeks for himself, his wife and daughter Susannah cost him £130 'including keep of four horses and board wages for Coachman and groom & for my journey to Town and back'.

This was his second visit to Margate in the same year. Earlier he had taken his sixteen-year-old son, and the two had travelled on further round the coast to Winchelsea and Bexhill where they had ridden out to see the barracks, this at a time when there were fears of a French invasion and troops were being moved to south coast garrisons. On their return they stayed at Tunbridge Wells and visited the Duke of Dorset's seat at Knole. This trip for father and son, with three horses and two servants, had cost £56.14s.0d.[13]

Brighton's fashionable reputation waxed as Margate's waned, and the Godsals became regular visitors from the last years of the century. Brighton was only some forty-five miles from London and the mail coaches took little over four hours. When the Godsals travelled in their own coach they would stay overnight at Sutton or Reigate. In Brighton in 1801 they took a private house on the front from William Tuppen, an interesting man, who at that time was a seaside landlord and was later to take over Walker's Marine Library and to become, in time, one of the Town's Commissioners.[14] The cost of a three week rent was a modest £18.10s.9d but it cost almost as much again for stabling the horses elsewhere.

The presence of the Prince of Wales had by now made Brighton the most fashionable of seaside resorts. The 'cits' were not to seriously disturb the aristocracy and gentry until the advent of the railway in 1841. Godsal continued to visit Brighton regularly and in 1819 he was one of the earliest visitors to Nash's new Royal Pavilion which had replaced Holland's old Pavilion.[15]

If Brighton was the Prince of Wales's resort, then Weymouth was his father's favourite spot. Neither chose to disturb the other's peace of mind by paying an unwelcome visit to the other. Like many of King George III's other subjects, however, Godsal paid several visits to Weymouth, staying at Stacey's Hotel. When the king was in residence he could be observed each evening walking up and down the Esplanade until dark, content to acknowledge the bows of the male vistors and the bobbed curtsies of the ladies. Godsal made a point of noting in his Diary that the Esplanade was three-quarters of a mile long.[16] And like the King, Godsal attended the theatre in Weymouth from time to time.

In September 1801 Godsal noted in his Diary 'The country from Southampton to Weymouth by Poole &c has most excellent roads and beautiful views of both land & sea. Poole Harbour & Quay is very fine. The Old Antelope, kept by Mr Blaney is a very good inn and Mr Blaney is a most intelligent man'. Further west along the coast he paid an interesting visit to a monastery. 'Near Lulworth Castle is a Monastery of the Monks of La Trappe. The building is newly erected on land given to them by Mr Weld, the proprietor of Lulworth Castle. They do not eat any animal food, nor eggs. They never speak to each other and practise great austerities. They work in the garden and till the ground'.[17]

It must be said that few lifestyles could be more unlike an ascetic monk than that of Philip Godsal, a prodigious winer and diner, and the most conversational of men.

In 1809 he paid the first of what were to be three extended stays in Teignmouth in Devon, a seaside resort which had perhaps been put on the map of polite society by Fanny Burney, who wrote of the joys of renting a country cottage there in her *Teignmouth Journal* of 1773. On their first visit the Godsals accompanied their friends the Edwards and George Edward liked the area so well that he decided to retire forthwith to nearby Bishopsteignton. Both the men formed a friendship with Thomas Luny, the marine artist, who had gone to live there in 1810[18] and from whom Godsal was to buy four seascapes, two of which remain in the family to-day.

Godsal toured the Lake District, the Peak District and the Yorkshire Dales but if any one area could be said to have caught his imagination it was probably the Wye Valley and the mountainous country of mid Wales. He made extended tours to the this part of the world on three occasions and, when there, his Diary entries become noticeably fuller and more responsive than the often ecomomical record he made elsewhere.

This was pre-eminently 'picturesque' country, the topographical subject of the first of the Reverend Mr William Gilpin's several books of travel which gave the word 'picturesque' its contemporary meaning and resonance. The immense mountain, the precipitous rocks, the solitary lake, the crashing waterfall, the wind-shaped tree were the scenes of nature which Gilpin believed most

Godsal became a friend of Thomas Luny and bought several of his paintings

elevated the mind and produced the most sublime sensation. A distant ruin and moonlight added to the potency of the mix. The Wye Valley had all these picturesque elements.

Artists and writers followed Gilpin's steps. Joseph Farington recorded his visits in his Diaries and in his watercolours and Coleridge and Wordsworth recorded theirs in their notebooks and poetry. Philip Godsal recorded his in his Diary, and there is no doubt that he was familiar with Gilpin's books and his definitions of the picturesque. Gilpin's favoured words, 'sublime', 'awesome', 'terrific', 'immense' 'romantic', 'ruin', 'grand' etc occur quite regularly in many of Godsal's Diary entries. One example will suffice. 'Llandaff Cathederal fine – the ruin park [sic]

very fine & worth seeing – the ride to Caerphilly over immense mountains, truly grand & sublime – Caerphilly Castle immense in size – a noble ruin not yet so good as Ragland'.[19] Predictable stuff but of course he was no poet; indeed why should he be? One entry records simply 'Chepstow to dinner/ inn good but not civil/ slept there/ went to Tintern Abbey by water/ 28 miles'.[20]

For Wordsworth, the ruined Abbey inspired not merely 'picturesque' observations but reflections on the passage of time, the 'still sad music of humanity', the primacy of Nature and the love of a sister. But one might as well say Godsal was no poet as to say that Wordsworth could not summon into being an elaborate ceremonial carriage or an elegant fashionable landaulet.

CHAPTER SIXTEEN
The Regency Theatre

Philip Godsal was educated at Soho Academy where the boys performed in celebrated productions of Shakespeare, and it may have been this experience that stimulated his first interest in the theatre. In his early days as a coachmaker, his most important customer was the stage-struck Lord Delaval and this too may have had some influence.

There is other evidence of an interest in the theatre. He bought, and had specially bound, the thirty-four volumes of Bell's *British Theatre*, which comprised the major published collection of English plays. He bought for himself, and as gifts for others, complete sets of the Boydells' celebrated. – and highly expensive – Shakespeare prints.

But the clearest evidence of a real passion for the theatre is the investment as a shareholder in both the Theatre Royal Drury Lane and the Theatre Royal Covent Garden and his frequent attendance at both theatres. In July 1792 he noted in his Diary 'bought of Mr Harris [Thomas Harris, the patentee] an admission and seat rent charges on Theatre Covent Garden for seven years from this date at a cost of £140'. Eighteen months later, when Richard Brinsley Sheridan, re-opened the newly enlarged Theatre Royal Drury Lane, Philip Godsal paid £500 for a share for one hundred years.

A 'renter', as the theatre shareholders were known, had various entitlements. Godsal received 2s 6d per night return for every evening there was a performance in each of the theatres. For the seven years of his Covent Garden share he averaged £21 per season from an average of 167 performances. From Drury Lane he averaged £23 per season from two hundred performances between 1794 and 1812 despite the theatre being closed for a season and a half consequent on the fire which burned the theatre down in February 1809, with Godsal, as we have seen, an eye-witness (see page 128).

When he decided to sell his Drury Lane share in 1812 it still had eighty-two years left to run and he received £215 after paying commission on the sale. Including his annual receipts he thus received a total of £629 (£215 + £414) on an investment of £500 over eighteen years. On his seven year Covent Garden share he received £147 against his outlay of £140. Not the most profitable rate of return perhaps, but unlike many investors in the theatre he had not made a loss.

Moreover, as a 'renter', Philip had received other benefits or privileges which included 'a free admission to any part of the House before the Curtain (except Private Boxes), a Silver Ticket transferable, and a power to give Orders each night for the free admission of any two persons'.

Philip made occasional use of these benefits to give his servants or employees a night out at the theatre but he himself never chose to sit anywhere but in a Private Box for which he had to pay. Although the London theatres were democratic to the extent that all social classes could and did attend, nevertheless there was a separation of classes, effected by practise and by cost.

The gallery was the home of artisans, servants and soldiers and sailors of the lower ranks. The pit was occupied by the middle classes and professionals and the boxes were occupied by the upper classes and gentlemen. By always sitting in one of the boxes Godsal saw himself, and was clearly seen, as a gentleman.

The newspapers, in their theatre or gossip columns, frequently mentioned the occupants of the boxes. Philip Godsal himself was not of sufficient public interest to be mentioned but the company he kept in the box lobby on many evenings is often recorded. On the evening in November 1803 when he attended a performance of *Macbeth* at Covent Garden *The Times* reported 'The House overflowed in every part at an early hour. Among the Company that graced the Boxes were the Earl and Countess of Cholmondeley, the Earl and Countess of Essex, the Countess of Jersey, Ladies Alvanley, Millman Hammet, Ann Windham, Lord John Cavendish, the Hon Mr Paget & Mr & Mrs Whitbread'.

Although it is most unlikely they would have talked shop had they bumped into each other in the crowded lobby, yet the probability is that the Alvanley, the Windham and the Earl of Essex's carriage had been made by Philip Godsal.

Only the boxes could be reserved in advance of a performance. For all other seats, except on benefit nights, payment was made only on the night. Even for the boxes, particular seats could not be guaranteed but were at the discretion of the box-keeper. When the theatregoer arrived in the box lobby at the theatre, he or she examined the box-keepers' box-book to see the places allocated. It followed that the box-book keepers of both Covent Garden, James Brandon, and of Drury Lane, Thomas Fosbrook, were very important individuals and the regular theatregoer was wise to be well aware of that fact. Both men were institutions. Brandon served in the role at Covent Garden from 1782 to 1825 and Fosbrook was at Drury Lane from 1782 to 1808. They were also the house-keepers of their respective theatres,

Godsal took good care to give generous tips to the box-keepers at both Covent Garden and Drury Lane

supervising and paying the cleaners, and they were the custodians when the theatres were dark, or closed for the off-season in the summer.

Philip Godsal was assiduous in supporting the benefit nights of both Brandon and Fosbrook, recording them in his Diary quite specifically in addition to noting tips made to them at other times.

These annual benefit nights were highly rewarding, confirming the status of the two men. Fosbrook's benefits brought him in between £125 a year to £369 but Brandon's popularity was reflected in an average of no less than £400 during the years of Godsal's attendance.

Even in the private boxes the conditions for the audience would be quite unfamiliar to modern theatre audiences, although those at rock concerts might find them more acceptable. After the relative tranquillity of the assembly in the separate box lobby, the box-holder would

enter the theatre to a bedlam of noise from those below in the pit and above in the galleries. Even when the performance began there was frequently a disturbing level of noise, and the box-holders often chattered amongst themselves.

Godsal was present at a performance of *Macbeth* at Covent Garden in November 1803 when *The Times* reported the following incident

Shortly after the drawing up of the curtain, a very great tumult arose in consequence of a foreigner, who had seated himself in one of the front boxes on the lower tier, having been obliged to give up his place to the party to whom it was engaged. Several persons in the galleries insisted upon him resuming his place, and their inference appeared to be the result of a generous emotion in favour of a stranger...Mr Kemble at length appeared and assured the audience that this person who had been obliged to relinquish the seat, had climbed over the back boxes into that which was kept for the ladies who at that moment filled it. This assurance was confirmed by great numbers in the Pit, and the tragedy proceeded without any further interruption.

Occasionally such indiscipline turned to riot or worse. Philip Godsal had attended Drury Lane twice in May 1800 although he was not present on the fifteenth when a disaffected soldier, James Hadfield stood up in the pit and fired his pistol up at King George III who was in one of the boxes. The King escaped unharmed and on Godsal's next visit to the theatre he joined in heartily with the loyal songs now incorporated into the performance.

Both Covent Garden and Drury Lane closed in the summer, for the principal reason that many of the nobility and gentry moved to their country estates or travelled out

Godsal saw the great Sarah Siddons in many of her most celebrated roles in both London and Cheltenham

of town, reducing the potential audience which, unlike to-day's West End audiences was usually comprised of London residents and was therefore already finite in potential numbers. It was uneconomic for these huge theatres (both seated in excess of 3,000) to employ their large companies of actors, musicians and back-stage staff to small houses so they simply closed down.

The actors followed their audiences to the provinces and Philip Godsal at various times attended the theatre in Margate, Ramsgate, Brighton, Weymouth, Bath and Cheltenham and saw such luminaries as Sarah Siddons, the child prodigy Master Betty, and Madame Catalani, the great Italian *prima donna.*

In the provinces, the power of the Lord Chamberlain was writ small but in London itself only the Theatres Royal of Covent Garden, Drury Lane and, for the summer season, the Haymarket enjoyed his licence to perform spoken drama as distinct from musical performances. This explains their metropolitan dominance and to a degree dictated their repertory.

Between the years 1794 and 1807 when Godsal was a regular member of the audience the general format of performances at both Covent Garden and Drury Lane would feature double, or even triple-headers, a practice long abandoned in the theatre although not unfamiliar to those who went to the cinema before the 1970s and saw the main film, the 'B' film and the news and cartoons.

In Godsal's day there could be an initial piece, perhaps a short farce, or a musical piece; then the principal production, perhaps a Shakespeare play, a ballad opera, a restoration or early eighteenth century or contemporary tragedy; and finally a farce or pantomime. Even during the intervals the band would play or there might be a comic monologue or some mimicry. At the end of the main piece, and often at the end of the final piece, there would probably be a 'tag' or epilogue in which the cast lined up across the stage and either resolved a complicated plot or made a moralistic comment. Audiences to-day at performances of *Don Giovanni* will experience this once familiar convention.

It is evident that the evening's entertainment lasted much longer than an audience to-day would expect, or perhaps indeed tolerate. Less than four hours seems to have been unusual and it could stretch to over seven hours. When Philip Godsal saw *A Winter's Tale*, starring John Kemble and Sarah Siddons in 1802 it was part of a double bill with *My Grandmother*, a musical farce by Prince Hoare with music by Stephen Storace. He saw *Antony and Cleopatra* in 1813 in a double bill with a pantomime,

Aladdin & the wonderful lamp which starred the great clown, Joey Grimaldi, then at the height of his popularity. It was a triple bill when Godsal saw John Kemble in *Richard III*. It was preceded by Oulton's farce *All in Good Humour* and followed by *The Purse, or the Benevolent Tar*, a musical comedy by John Cartwright Cross.

There were few of Shakespeare's comedies in repertory. Philip Godsal records seeing only *As You Like It* and *The Merry Wives of Windsor*. The most performed of Shakespeare's plays were *Hamlet, Macbeth, Richard III* and *Henry V*. Godsal's Diary records him as seeing all of these with the exception of *Henry V*. In all he saw fourteen of Shakespeare's plays including *King Lear* in December 1800 shortly before poor King George III had another attack of insanity and the play was tactfully dropped from the repertory.

When Godsal attended a rare performance of *Measure for Measure* in November 1811 *The Times* wrote 'We cannot yet see that this play is fit for representation; and so long as it is performed, we must think that a gross, premeditated, and insolent affront is offered to the habitual propriety of an English audience. It ought never to have been performed and ought to be immediately withdrawn'.

What *The Times* particularly objected to was that 'the main incident is an offer of prostitution to a nun'. We might remind ourselves that it was only seven years later at the height of the Regency that Thomas Bowdler published his expurgated *Family Shakespeare*.

Many of the Shakespeare plays which Godsal saw featured Kemble and Siddons, the brother and sister who dominated the dramatic stage of the period. Mrs Siddons playing Lady Macbeth was one of the celebrated performances of that or any era and her brother's performance as Coriolanus received equal acclaim. When Godsal saw it, he was so impressed that he immediately saw it again and then penned in his Diary the only piece of dramatic criticism he ever essayed 'Coriolanus by Kemble – not in the Annals of the Stage no like – beyond the powers of description – Play got up in a Stile [sic] of unprecedented grandeur and Classical taste – Mrs Siddons ag'y [?acting] great'.

He was too kind to note that Mrs Siddons had by now become rather large and her voice had gone but perhaps it would be fair to note that few of us write like Hazlitt or Tynan in our memorandum diaries. But Philip Godsal was fortunate to attend many of the celebrated productions in the history of the English theatre. He saw Mrs Siddons in many of her finest roles, not only in Shakespeare, but as Euphrasia in Arthur Murphy's *The Grecian Daughter*, as Zara in Congreve's *The Mourning Bride* and in the title roles in Pye's *Adelaide* and *Jane Shore* by Nicholas Rowe.

Godsal saw John Kemble not only as Coriolanus, Macbeth, King Lear and King John but also as Zangara in Edward Young's tragedy *The Revenge* ('very fine') and as Rolla in von Kotzebue's *Pizarro*, brilliantly adapted by Sheridan, the patentee of Drury Lane. Godsal saw the première in January 1800 of what was one of Sheridan's most successful productions. It was a time when Britain seemed to stand alone against Napoleon and appeared to be in the gravest danger of invasion. The subject of the play was the brave stand by the Incas against the wicked Pizarro and the power of Spain but the audiences were readily persuaded of the analogy of brave England facing the power of the wicked Napoleon and the French. *The Times* summed up the mood 'Mr Sheridan has felt the nature and pulse of the time...with a tirade of brilliant, patriotic and loyal sentiments in all the pomp of phraseology which no man can better dispose than himself'.

As a man full of patriotic and loyal sentiments Philip Godsal returned to see the production a second time. These sentiments, shared by so many, accounted for another resounding success the following year when Thomas Arne's version of Metastasio's opera *Artaxerxes* was performed in October 1801 immediately after the peace preliminaries had been concluded at Amiens on 1 October. Britain had been at war with France for eight years and when the great soprano Elizabeth Billington as Mandane sang the aria, 'The soldier tired of War's alarms' she was cheered and encored by an audience which mirrored the feeling of universal relief which had seized the nation. The production was clearly one to be seen and Philip Godsal took a party of six to his box on 3 November.

Godsal witnessed other individual performances which have come down in theatrical history. He had seen John Kemble declaim the role of Richard III and one of his last recorded visits to the London theatre before his retirement to Cheltenham was to see the new phenomenon Edmund Kean who made the role his own with his naturalism of voice and movement. Kemble by now was coming to the end of his long and distinguished career but the rise of Kean brought a reappraisal by the public of his acting style.

Kemble had suffered a similar unfavourable comparison a decade earlier when the extraordinary boy actor, Master William Betty took London by storm in 1804. His popularity with the public, at the expense of Kemble, gave the caricaturists a field day. Philip Godsal was too great an admirer of Kemble to turn his coat so readily but he did see Betty in two of his most famous roles, as Hamlet and as Norval in John Home's *Douglas*.

Because Godsal's Diary does not begin until he was forty-two in 1789 we have no knowledge if he attended the theatre before that time. It seems likely that he would have done so, if not with the frequency he did later as a shareholder in the two Theatres Royal and when his success in the coachmaking business had made him a wealthy man and one who had more leisure and social ease.

Godsal was already thirty when David Garrick made his last appearance on the stage and it is likely that Godsal saw this great figure who dominated the British stage for so long. But it was Kemble whose personality and style dominated the period when Godsal was a regular theatre-goer from 1792 to 1814.

To understand the conventions of the theatre as Godsal experienced them between 1792 and 1809 it is necessary to note first the practical facts of the two principal theatres. Both were re-built or remodelled at the beginning of this period and both houses burned down at the end. In 1792, when Philip Godsal first became a 'renter' or stockholder in the Theatre Royal, Covent Garden it had just been re-modelled by Henry Holland to seat 3,000 members of the audience. (It might be noted here that to-day's Covent Garden seats only 2,200 and that no London theatre seats more than 2,600). The reason for the extension was purely commercial.

When Godsal bought his hundred year stock in the Theatre Royal, Drury Lane in January 1794 it had just been re-built also by Henry Holland to seat 3,600. In other words both theatres were huge, and the intimacy of a smaller theatre was simply not possible. The style of acting had to reflect the size of the auditorium. Given this size, and the larger number of a relatively undisciplined and noisy audience, the actors simply had to speak loudly in order to be heard.

The distance between the actors and many of their audience dictated also that gestures and facial expressions required to be more distinctive in order to be clearly seen. Already one can see the constraints under which the actors performed. The intimacy and naturalism of David Garrick inevitably had to give way to the more mannered style of John Kemble, which Philip Godsal witnessed as the norm.

There were other notable changes at this period. The new stages were larger and permitted more spectacular effects which audiences came to expect. These effects were achieved through improvements in lighting and in the invention of new techniques. De Loutherbourg's innovations in the use of transparencies and gauzes were already in use when Godsal began his regular theatre-going. Somewhat paradoxically the new larger stages gave the actors less room to move because of the encroachment of the scenery. This too had its effect on acting styles.

But Godsal was certainly accustomed to some spectacular stagings. When he attended *Alexander the Great* at Covent Garden in April 1799 the play-bill advertised the spectacular set pieces, 'In Act II The Grand Triumphal Entry of Alexander into Babylon; in Act IV A Grand Banquet'. In Kemble's *Lodoiska* which Godsal attended, the actress Mrs Crouch was rescued from a tower, which on the first night accidentally burst into flames. This accident proved so popular that it was dangerously incorporated into subsequent performances. Even the end pieces and pantomimes had what to-day's audiences would find extravagant sets.

For a famous production of *Caravan* by Frederick Reynolds which Godsal attended on 10 December 1803 the stage was flooded to allow a large Newfoundland dog named Carlo to dive in to rescue a child. Given the demands on the stage crew it is the more surprising that *Caravan* was the underbill to *The Merry Wives of Windsor*. Only three days later Godsal witnessed perhaps the most spectacular effect of all in the ballad opera by Thomas Dibdin, *The English Fleet in 1342*. It proved immensely successful and *The Times* described it, for once mentioning the ingenious designers by name

> Mr Harris [the patentee of the theatre] has, in the scenery, dresses and decorations, spared no expence, which could strengthen the piece, and contribute to its popularity. The taste and skill of [John Inigo] Richards [the scene painter, machinist and designer] and [Thomas] Phillips [scene painter], have been finely exemplified in several instances; and the last scene, representing the English fleet, executed by [Samuel] Whitmore [machinist and decorator], is one of the most striking exhibitions of this kind the stage has presented to public view. In this scene the range of vessels, both in their heads and sterns, is admirably conceived and executed, and the perspective of the whole from the fort to the extremity, is preserved in a finished manner.

Given the ambitious complexity of many of the stage sets at this time (Godsal saw a pantomime, *Merry Sherwood* with twenty-one scene changes) it is made the more remarkable because almost every production was a short run. Ten performances in a season was unusual. The principal reason for this was that the number of London theatre goers was finite. There were no overseas tourists or coach parties from the provinces to allow the long runs of to-day's West End. Ten performances in a full house at both Covent Garden and Drury Lane meant that 30,000 people would have seen the performance. There were usually some 150 individual productions in one season.

A typical week at Covent Garden in November 1801 offered *The Will* and *Lodoiska* on Friday; *Jane Shore* and *The Son in Law* on the Saturday; *Richard III* and a comedy on Monday; *Pizarro* and a musical farce on Tuesday; *Artaxerxes* and *Honest Thieves* on Thursday. All these productions had period costume and elaborate sets. Latter day Repertory Companies would think themselves fortunate not to be subject to such demands, and stage crews would probably have walked out before the end of one week.

Godsal attended one production at Covent Garden on 30 October 1800 which has claims to be the shortest ever run. This was an opera, *Virginia* which, despite a fine cast, 'rich and splendid dresses and decorations and scenery judiciously suited to the occasion' was unable to complete its finale because of adverse audience reaction. Jack Bannister stepped forward to announce that it would be performed again but was booed from the stage and then John Kemble appeared to announce that no further performances would take place. 'He retired amidst universal plaudits.'

How did such factors as large auditoriums and a constantly changing repertory affect the actors? There was certainly little time for rehearsals and the role of to-day's director did not exist. As members of a company, familiar with each other's techniques and mannerisms, the actors worked things out for themselves, if necessary under the overall guidance of the senior actor in the production. In matters of dispute, there could be appeal to Kemble at Covent Garden, or the patentee Sheridan at Drury Lane.

There were simple conventions for movement, for example the actor crossing from stage left to stage right went behind one crossing the other way. In performance there were stereotyped gestures expressing particular emotions. If you were sad in *Hamlet* your gesture was probably the same as your 'sad' in a farce. It was of course absolutely necessary to speak loudly and face the audience when speaking so that your words would not be lost. This stage convention, which holds good to-day, surprised a German visitor to the London theatre, who noted with surprise that the English actors never spoke when in profile to the audience.

One effect of such a huge repertory of productions was that the actors were all required to be 'quick studies'. In other words they had to learn a succession of parts without

ever having the comfort of a long run. The role of the prompter was self-evidently important and it was recognised by the management who awarded benefit nights to these essential members of the Company. Joseph Glassington, the Covent Garden prompter was paid £5 per week and his benefit for one season brought him as much as £506.

The intimacy with the audience, which was a notable part of Garrick's style was simply not possible for the actors in Godsal's time as a theatregoer. John Kemble and Sarah Siddons, the leading luminaries of Godsal's theatrical experience declaimed their lines with a classical nobility of stance and movement. Kemble lacked the smaller Garrick's active grace of movement but his height conferred an advantage in the heroic or noble roles as Rolla or Coriolanus. This nobility was well captured by Lawrence's two portraits. Kemble was something of a classical scholar and he conveyed what Charles Lamb called 'a weighty sense'.

Philip's Godsal's favourite actors in the heavy dramatic roles were undoubtedly Kemble and Sarah Siddons but he was also a fan of Alexander Pope, supporting several of his benefits, and incidentally commissioning a portrait from the actor who was also an accomplished miniaturist. Leigh Hunt has left a graphic, if uncomplimentary account of Pope in action

Here is an actor without face, expression or delivery…There is however an infallible method of obtaining a clap from the galleries, and there is an art known at the theatre by the name of *clap-trapping*, which Mr Pope has shewn great wisdom in studying. It consists in nothing more than in gradually raising the voice as the speech draws to a conclusion, making an alarming outcry on the last four or five lines, or suddenly dropping them into a tremulous but energetic undertone, and with a vigorous jerk of the right arm, rushing off the stage.

The Times on the other hand wrote of his performance as Othello which Godsal witnessed, 'Some of his bursts in the last act proved uncommonly impressive'.

Of course most actors specialised in particular types of roles (Jack Bannister, a favourite of Godsal was unusual in his versatility). Godsal saw Dorothy Jordan, mistress of the Duke of Clarence, in several of her 'breeches' parts and, he was evidently particularly fond of the character comedy actors John Fawcett and 'Gentleman' William Lewis (who had a characteristic squint), supporting their regular benefits.

Philip Godsal's Diary suggests that of the various forms of theatrical entertainment his particular favourites were the ballad and comic operas which were performed as the main or the supporting feature. He saw no fewer than seventeen of the works of the leading practitioners, nine by Thomas Dibdin, four by Prince Hoare and four by the blind John O'Keefe. Many of these featured Godsal's favourite, the tenor Charles Incledon with whom he became on terms of personal acquaintance, in the Light Horse Volunteer Mess Nights and in Hampstead (see page 140). Godsal is on record as having supported no fewer than five of Incledon's benefits.

Although not the greatest actor, Incledon had a splendid tenor voice, admired by Hadyn himself (although he felt he over-used his comic falsetto). He played leading roles at Covent Garden in the pre-dominantly musical productions such as *The Beggar's Opera, Fontainebleau, Sprigs of Laurel, The Poor Soldier, Robin Hood* and *The Woodman*, all of which Godsal saw.

Incledon was also featured as the musical interlude in numerous straight plays including those of Shakespeare. This practice of introducing extraneous songs into plays was particularly popular in the years of Godsal's theatregoing and was advertised on the playbills to attract more interest. In the years 1798 to 1805 in particular, these songs were often patriotic ballads and it was in these that Incledon was at his incomparable best. A production of Sheridan's *The Critic* which Godsal attended in April 1800 advertised 'To conclude with a Grand Sea-fight and 'Rule Britannia' by Messrs Incledon, Townsend, Hill & full Chorus'.

In the production of *Fontainebleau* which Godsal saw in April 1803, not only did Incledon play his role but the play bill advertised 'In the course of the evening Mr Incledon will sing The Thorn, The Battle Song, Tom Moody, Black-eyed Susan, The Storm, The Dinner of Love & Admiral Benbow'.

Even Philip Godsal could not have felt short changed. 'Black-eyed Susan' and 'The Storm' were perhaps his two greatest hits, and he sang them at all his own benefits. 'The Storm' was delivered in the character of a sailor, without accompaniment and with a graphic scenic background.

Incledon was a theatrical phenomenon. An obituary noted

He had a voice of uncommon power, both in the natural and in the falsetto. His natural voice was full and open, neither partaking of the reed, nor the string, and sent forth without the slightest artifice; such was its ductility that when he sang pianissimo it retained its original quality. His falsetto was rich, sweet and brilliant and he could use it with facility and execute ornaments with volubility and sweetness. His intonation was much more correct than is common to singers so imperfectly educated and he had a bold and manly manner of singing, mixed with considerable feeling which went to the heart of his countrymen. He sang like a true Englishman.

Godsal met him in his social hours at the Volunteer messes and doubtless sang along with him when the cloth was removed for the singing which marked the end of the convivial mess nights. No doubt he was well aware of Incledon's 'amorous propensities', so well described by Henry Angelo.

Godsal's love of a good voice took him to many theatrical performances of two other tenors, Charles Dignum and John Braham and to performances by the two leading sopranos of the era, Elizabeth Billington and Angelica Catalani.

By 1815 however Philip Godsal's days of regular theatregoing were over. He retired to Cheltenham and went only occasionally thereafter, although the opportunity was there, both in the provincial theatres and on his many return visits to London. Theatre historians believe that about time there was a relative decline in the social and cultural golden age of the English stage. Other than Sheridan himself, who wrote only two plays, there had been no great dramatists for several generations. There had been, and indeed continued to be, many great actors but whereas before 1815 it had been fashionable to attend the theatre, afterwards it was less so.

There can be no doubt that Philip Godsal's social and cultural aspirations played a significant part in his investment in, and attendance at, the theatre. He was a man of his times and for him theatregoing, while undoubtedly giving him much pleasure had served also to confirm his place in society.

Godsal served as a Steward at a Masonic Dinner in honour of the Earl of Moira

CHAPTER SEVENTEEN
A Most Clubbable Man

The eighteenth century had witnessed the foundation of a proliferation of clubs and associations of all kinds. Philip Godsal proved to be very much a man of his times in becoming an active member of a wide variety of lodges, societies, messes, institutions, clubs and associations. Some were directly related to the furthering of his business, others purely social, and others a combination of the two. Their number and variety indicates that he was quite evidently a most clubbable man.

Naturally enough Godsal was a member of the livery company of his trade, The Worshipful Company of Coachmakers and Loriners, although he did little more than register his apprentices there and enjoy the occasional annual dinner when the Company of Coachmakers entertained the new Lord Mayor. Surprisingly, perhaps, he never became the Master and there is very little mention of it in his Diary or in any of his papers. Perhaps there was some personal animosity with a fellow liveryman (we know that Lionel Lukin successfully took him to Court for some unrecorded claim); perhaps he preferred not to talk shop in his social hours or perhaps the Company had little social activity. There is no evidence.

In 1783 he was elected as a member of the Society for the Encouragement of Arts, Manufactures and Commerce (now the Royal Society of Arts).[1] When Godsal became a member meetings of the Society were actually held in Beaufort Buildings which stood on the present site of the Savoy Hotel, while the celebrated lecture hall in nearby Adam Street was being decorated with James Barry's striking murals. The aims of the Society were indicated in its name, and for both a practical manufacturer and an individual with a lively intellect, it was a place where he could meet men of like minds.

When the Royal Institution was granted its charter in 1800 its aims seemed to replicate to some degree those of the Society of Arts, Manufactures and Commerce, but it became quickly evident that its principal thrust would be pure science. Recognising that its intellectual distinction might prove beyond his own capacities, Godsal arranged for his Oxford undergraduate son, Philip Lake Godsal, to be

nominated as a founder proprietor[2] and he had the opportunity to attend Humphrey Davy's lectures on chemistry and witness the dazzling intellect of Samuel Coleridge.

More obviously purely social clubs were the Enfield Club of which Philip Godsal was a member at the time he owned his property in Enfield Chase,[3] and also the Soho Academy Society of which he was an Old Boy and at whose annual dinners he served as a Steward.[4]

Neither of these were of equal significance in Godsal's life to his membership of the freemasons. By its very nature as a closed society it is difficult to learn much detail of freemasonry but Philip Godsal's Diaries give in outline at least his own role as a mason. He was admitted to the Somerset House Lodge in 1798. By 1801 he was serving as Grand Steward at a dinner at Cumberland Lodge where the Earl of Moira was President.[5] Moira was at that date one of the closest friends of the Prince of Wales who was also a freemason.

Godsal records dining as the President of the Grand Stewards of the London Lodges the same year and recorded that the expenses of serving as President cost him the large sum of £30.13s.4d.[6] It should be noted that Grand Steward is by no means the highest degree in freemasonry, but nevertheless it encompassed social and committee duties which brought its holder significance in the Lodge.

Godsal's Diaries record his regular attendance at monthly Lodge meetings, at both the Somerset House Lodge and the Blue Apron Lodge, to which, as a Grand Steward, he had also been admitted. He was a great supporter too of their charitable music concerts. Freemasonry was evidently very important to him and it would perhaps be naive not to suggest that it did his business no harm.

He arranged for his son, Philip Lake Godsal, to be admitted to the brotherhood,[7] and also his nephew, Charles Cole,[8] and his friend Collinge of Hampstead.[9] Regrettably also he also sponsored his banker, Henry Fauntleroy, when he became a mason.[10] Fauntleroy offended all the tenets of freemasonry and of friendship, and indeed the law of the land, by forging powers of attorney of his bank customers, for which offence he was hanged in 1825.

Philip Godsal records his own appointment as Provincial Grand Master of Carmarthenshire, which did not appear to require any fraternal, or paternal visits to the lodges of that Welsh county.[11] In December 1808 he attended on the Prince of Wales as Grand Steward when the Prince laid the first stone of the new Covent Garden Theatre and on 13 May 1813 he noted 'Attended the Duke of Sussex installed Grand Master of Masons at Willis Rooms, King Street, St James's'[12] and on 27 December 1813 'the junction of the Ancient & Modern Masons'. This last was a most significant occasion in the history of freemasonry as the two strains of English and Welsh Freemasonry, the 'Antient' and the 'Reformed', were merged. And he was present, together with the five Royal Dukes, at the farewell dinner given to Lord Moira on the eve of his departure to India as Governor General in 1813[13].

Godsal remained an active member of his two lodges until his retirement to Cheltenham in 1814, at which point he resigned from both. There was a flourishing masonic lodge at Cheltenham but, although he gave generously towards the cost of the purchase of jewels for the lodge, Godsal was no longer an active mason. It had been an important part of his social life and his business life for twenty years and had brought him into contact with many men of rank and influence. It would perhaps be as easy to overemphasise the commercial potential of these contacts as it would be to ignore them.

During this same period he had been a member of another exclusive social group, the Light Horse Volunteer Regiment of the Cities of London and Westminster of which he was a mess member. It seems possible that he may have been recommended by John Wombwell, the major investor in his coachmaking business, and who had been a member of the Regiment since its establishment in 1795. Indeed it may have been Wombwell who had sponsored him also as a freemason. Both the masons and the officers of the Light Horse Volunteers were amongst the most likely customers of the carriages which Godsal manufactured, and Wombwell, with £8,000 invested in the business, would not have been insensible of the potential.[14]

In 1797/8 Godsal designed and built a 'Military Fly' for the transportation of the Regiment's foot soldiers (see page 37) and it may indeed have been during these negotiations that the Commanding Officer, Colonel Herries decided Godsal would make an agreeable mess mate. The L.H.V. mess was one of the most expensive 'clubs' in London with a subscription of ten guineas a year, also monthly and subscription dinners at least once a month. These cost anything between 7s 6d and £1.11s.6d.[15]

Whoever it was who introduced him, Godsal became a very enthusiastic participant in the social activities at the two L.H.V. messes, one at the Crown and Anchor in the Strand, and the other at the British Coffee House in Birdcage Walk. He dined there sixteen times in the nineteen months between October 1799 and April 1801, missing one only because he was giving a rout that day at his Hampstead home, and the others because he was away on business.

At mess dinners the food and drink were of the finest and Henry Angelo, who was a regular guest, recorded that

> the conviviality, which was usually protracted to a late hour, was such as no military society that I have yet known could match. At these meetings, after the cloth was removed, a table was placed at the upper end of the room with a bottle and glasses at which two trumpeters took their seats and blew tan-ta-ra-ra between toasts. The delight the singing of songs afforded when elevated to the pitch of the second bottle of claret was truly exhilerating to behold.

The entertainment was often provided through the employment of the Theatre Royal Covent Garden singers, Charles Incledon or Charles Dignum. A talented amateur, Captain Morris, was himself a member of the Regiment, and took little persuading to add his voice with a topical, patriotic ditty.[16]

Godsal loved these occasions. He struck up something of friendship with Morris, and became a regular supporter of Dignum and Incledon's theatrical benefits. It was only in July 1801, when he himself was commissioned as a Captain in the Hampstead Volunteers, that he became less regular in attending these L.H.V. occasions.

However, he bought his son a commission in the L.H.V., which also cost him the price of an excellent horse, a uniform and a joining subscription costing £37.12s.6d.[17] It was one of Godsal's proudest days when his son and his Regiment were reviewed on Wimbledon Common by Lord Harrington in August 1803. Godsal retained his very expensive mess membership of the L.H.V. long after he had resigned his commission in the Hampstead Volunteers and long after many of the other Volunteer Regiments had been disbanded after the fears of French invasion (which had brought them into being) had receded.

Godsal's membership of the Hampstead Volunteers is discussed elsewhere as is his membership of no fewer than three other Hampstead clubs, the Hampstead Society, the Union Club and the New Assembly Rooms of which he was a founding proprietor.[18] Here it is sufficient to note that he was assiduous in his attendance at all these bodies of which he became a member between the years 1798 and 1810 during the whole of which time he was running one of the largest and most successful coachmaking yards in London.

It was in 1805 that the Russell Rooms were opened by the Bedford family for musical entertainments and despite Godsal's innumerable social commitments he immediately signed up to yet another membership subscription.[19] It seems likely that he was persuaded by his daughter, Susannah Saxon, as he attended the initial meetings with her alone. Saxon and Mrs Godsal were not included, presumably out of choice.

Charity fundraising in the eighteenth century and the Regency could be every bit as much a social event as it is for celebrities at the present day. Two, in particular, of Godsal's many charities, the Westminster Dispensary and the Foundling Hospital, were focussed on social entertainment. The Dispensary, of which he was a Governor by virtue of paying two guineas a year, held frequent fundraising dinners which were widely reported in the newspapers where Godsal's name appears a number of times as a Steward.[20] His Diaries itemise the costs.

The Foundling Hospital had long been one of London's most fashionable charities when in 1802 Godsal gave £50 and became a Governor.[21] He attended the meetings in the splendid Governor's Hall, hung with Hogarth's pictures, and he attended their charity services and concerts and, of course, their charity dinners.

When he was appointed a Justice of the Peace in December 1806 it was the social occasions which were noted in his Diary. These were held in the Middlesex Sessions House, which was still called Hick's Hall, after the building it had replaced. The magistrates could pay a fee for dining rights and take their meals together there during sessions. Needless to say, Godsal was delighted to take advantage of this agreeable social facility.[22]

In 1810 he was also elected as a member of the Literary Club, that most famous of all literary clubs, which had been founded by Doctor Johnson, Sir Joshua Reynolds and their friends. The Club had ceased to meet in the 1790s but it was revived and Charles Hatchett, the chemist son of John Hatchett, the coachmaker became its secretary. Charles Hatchett and Philip Godsal had become friends and he arranged for Godsal's membership of the revived Literary Club, which met, talked and dined in Greenwich.[23] While the scientific lectures and practicals of the Royal Institution might perhaps have been intellectually beyond Godsal, he was nevertheless intelligent, well read, well travelled and a socially secure man who could contribute to discussions. His election to the Literary Club therefore need occasion no surprise.

On his retirement to Cheltenham in 1814 he left all these many London social groups. But he certainly did not retire from society. There was the Cheltenham Harmonic Society, lectures on astronomy, and the membership of all the Spas and the Reading Rooms. We shall follow this most sociable of men to Cheltenham in a later chapter.

'Fashions for 1809'

CHAPTER EIGHTEEN
Gentleman's Dress

That Philip Godsal was very much a man of his times is shown also in his dress and appearance. Throughout his lifetime fashion ruled and nowhere more visibly than in dress, when gentlemen paid almost as much attention to their appearance as did ladies. But, as Diana Donald has pointed out, it would be 'misleading to see fashion as an irresistible force, dragging the public in its wake…most buyers were careful and discriminating'.[1] Philip Godsal was most certainly both.

In *The Analysis of Beauty* Hogarth wrote 'We know the very minds of people by their dress'. One is tempted to say, like Lord Copper's aide, 'Up to a point', for businessmen like Philip Godsal, have always dressed as their customers might expect to see them, rather than indulging themselves by revealing quite what may be in their minds. They want to look smart but not to be avid followers of the latest fashion.

For example, when Philip Godsal took over the coachmaking business in Long Acre in 1768 , his customers, aristocrats and gentlemen, would not have expected to see the young coachmaster dress like a macaroni (high wig, high heels, and silk embroidered fabrics), the latest fashion for young men, and for others who should have known better. He dressed smartly in the typical eighteenth century fashion, wig, full skirted coat, wide cuffs, unstarched neckcloth, long waistcoat, breeches tied at the knee. The tricorn hat was still worn but gave way by the 1780s to the round hat which got taller by the 1790s.[2]

Godsal doubtless eschewed the fads of the macaronis and later, by the 1790s, those of their idiosyncratic successors, the crops and the jessamies. He followed the universal trends of the time where the full skirted coat was gradually replaced by the cut away coat, dark breeches often became buff and were tied lower on the calf. Because, like all gentlemen, Godsal's clothes were bespoke, we can be assured that his tailor would have kept him up to, but not ahead of, the fashion, while still dressing suitably.

By 1800 Godsal was at the pinnacle of his business and social success and it is at this time that his Diaries and bills give us much greater detail of his clothes. It was a period characterised by Beau Brummell who eschewed the brighter colours of earlier days, and the exaggerated appearance of the dandies' predecessors the macaronis, thirty years earlier and the jessamies of the 1790s. Brummell made fashionable the starched neckcloth, darker clothes, including pantaloons and boots. Restrained elegance was the aim. This made it easier for middle aged gentlemen, like Godsal, to be fashionable without requiring them to have ostentatious and eye catching clothes which their characters and fuller figures would find unappealing and inappropriate. From 1800 it was the cut, and, it may be added, the cleanliness of the garments, which made a man well dressed.

Philip Godsal's Diaries and his tailors' bills reveal him to have taken a great deal of trouble in presenting himself before the world as smartly, elegantly and appropriately dressed. Not only was there an appropriate dress for business but for the theatre and opera house, for the freemasons' meetings, the Hampstead clubs, the Volunteer messes, the magistrates' courts, and the dividend and charitable dinners which he attended, there was a recognised dress code which all gentlemen felt obliged to observe. Though, like all gentlemen, he expressed some individuality in his waistcoats, Godsal seems always to have worn either black or dark blue coats. In 1810 Ackermann's *Repository of Arts* declared that this season's colours for gentlemens' coats were blue, black or plum,[3] but Godsal never seems to have taken such a drastic step as plum, and blue or black they remained.

An analysis of all his expenditure on clothes over a twenty year period between 1799 and 1818 shows that he spent a total of £1,036.1s.5d, an average of £51.16s.1d per year. Of this almost exactly ten per cent was spent on boots and shoes and another ten per cent on hats. The remaining £40 was spent on clothes and included blue and black coats, black, buff or brown breeches and pantaloons, satin, linen, flannel and twill waistcoats, silk and woollen stockings, white shirts and stocks, flannel drawers, gloves, silk handkerchieves, dressing gowns, long and short gaiters and braces. All these items are mentioned in his papers.

A bill from one of his tailors, Thomas Barber of 5 Haymarket, is a typical example and by itemising costs helps to put the annual average expenditure of £52 into context.[4]

Jan 17	To 2 fine stripe Marcella Waistcoats lined & interlined	£3.3s.0d
Feb 23	To a Superfine Black Cloth Coat	£5.5s.0d
	To a pair of superfine breeches lined with swansdown	£2.12s.6d
May 6	To a pair of mixed Stocking Breeches, lined with drab stocking	£2.16s.6d
	To altering a pair of breeches not made here	£3.6s.0d
Aug 3	To a Superfine Blue Cloth Coat	£5.5s.0d
	To Best Gilt Buttons	£7.6s.0d
	To a White Diamond Marcella Waistcoat	£1.8s.0d
	To a Blue stripe ditto	£1.8s.0d
	To a pair of drab Ribbed Stocking Breeches	£2.16s.6d
Dec 7	To a pair of Black Milled Breeches lined with leather	£2.16s.6d
	Total	**£28.2s.0d**

For other items of costume not recorded here Godsal paid between £1.8s.0d and £4 for pantaloons; 12s 6d for shirts; 10s 6d a pair for his silk stockings; 9s for silk handkerchieves; 4s 6d for woollen stockings; £1.6s.0d for a dressing gown; 6s to 7s for gaiters; £1.1s.0d for braces; and 2s 6d for a pair of gloves. Shoes ranged from only 10s 6d a pair to £2 for boots; most of his hats cost around £1.8s.0d, the exception being a black silk hat which cost him £5.19s.0d in 1808.

It is evident that a gentleman could dress extremely well on £52 a year. For the last twenty-five years of his life, as he moved from Hampstead back into London and then to retirement in Cheltenham he patronised several tailors, Otley of Bond Street, Barber of 5, Haymarket and Reeve being the London principals and Bastin or Bishop in Cheltenham. No doubt all considered him a good customer because the evidence is that, unlike the stereotype Regency gentleman, he paid his tailor's bills on time. On one occasion Barber even presented him with a hare and a brace of partridges.[5]

It may be added that he spent almost as much again with his tailors on liveries for his servants and there was a period of about five years when his son was at or after

Oxford when he spent more on the young man's clothes than on his own.

He bought his hats (his Diary always always spells them 'hatts') from Lock's, Jupps, Morris, and Tremans, who was a regular advertiser in *The Times* newspaper. His shoes came from Hay or Saunders. Only between 1799 and 1810 did he buy boots.

In 1801 when he received his King's Commission as a Captain in the Loyal Hampstead Volunteers, Philip was delighted to pay Sheriff the tailor £45 for his uniform of a Military Coat, military waistcoat, breeches, boots, a helmet and plume. For several years, like other Volunteer officers, he delighted in wearing his uniform when the opportunity offered itself, on social rather than strictly military occasions .

He travelled in cold weather in the practical coat with the heavy cape, worn by coachmen and called by the French a 'Carrick' [sic] under the mistaken impression that it was David Garrick who had popularised it.[6] Godsal carried a cane or an umbrella, surprisingly an item in a fashionable gentleman's accoutrements. Until around 1780 they had been carried in London only by women and Frenchmen. Godsal bought a number of them including a silk one designed perhaps more obviously as a fashion accessory than a practical protection from rain.

Confirmation of his essentially conservative approach to his appearance was that he continued to wear a wig after most had abandoned it by 1800. His last recorded purchase of a wig was in 1796 but he paid Vane, his hairdresser, an annual sum of £2.12s.6d to have it powdered and dressed until 1806. Powder was one of those luxury items which became subject to tax in 1795 during the French Wars. Godsal paid £1.3s.6d per year for a licence which he had to present each time he bought powder, which also carried a tax. He continued to pay for the licence for the rest of his life for even when he ceased to wear a wig he had his hair powdered. From 1806 his Diary entries start to record 'haircutt'.

He was clean shaven, as was the universal practise of his times, and there are occasional entries in his Diaries for razors, patent razors and razor strops. Throughout the Diary there are records of the purchase of four rings, a Nelson ring in 1805, two mourning rings for friends, one an amythyst, and a 'double diamond ring' so that it seems probable that he wore a ring, at least on some occasions.

CHAPTER NINETEEN

Regency Interiors

Nothing confirms Philip Godsal's wealth, status and social aspirations more clearly than the way in which he decorated and furnished his various houses. He employed the painters, carvers, gilders, plate glass mirror and wallpaper manufacturers commissioned by the Prince of Wales to decorate both Carlton House and the Royal Pavilion at Brighton. Godsal bought clocks, items of silver, and even decorative pistols, from other of the Prince's suppliers and paintings from artists favoured by the Prince.

He also bought fine furniture and china, glassware, engraved prints and a gentleman's library of volumes of the classics in translation and books by modern travellers. Busts of Roman Emperors and contemporary statesmen, scientific instruments and his collection of coins itself adds to the image of the owner as collector and a man of intellectual curiosity as well as possessing the nicest judgement of elegance and good taste. And of course the 'Romantic Interior', as this style of decoration is now known, demonstrated the house owner as a man possessing the wealth to be able to afford and display his evident fine discrimination.[1]

When Philip Godsal bought the lease of 84 Piccadilly from the actress Frances Abington in 1788 he called in the decorative painter, John Crace who was undertaking work at that time for the Prince of Wales in Carlton House and whom Godsal had known as a coach painter whose rococo designs had led the fashions in the exterior decoration of carriages from 1760 to 1780. Since receiving his first commissions to decorate the interiors of fine houses, Crace had abandoned coach decoration for house decoration. 'Houses' became 'palaces' when the Prince of Wales commissioned him to decorate rooms in Carlton House in Pall Mall, of which the Prince took possession in 1783.[2]

The details of the work which Crace undertook for Godsal at 84 Piccadilly is not known, and, as the house was demolished in the nineteenth century, it will not be serendipitously discovered behind later papering. What is known, is that it cost Godsal £74.18s.6d and that when Godsal renovated the house as a wedding gift to his son in

1816 the Craces (Frederick Crace had by now for some time been his father's partner) were paid a further £153.13s.0d.[3]

It is likely that at the latter date the style was amended to reflect current fashions. If this is the case then the 1790 version, contemporaneous with the Craces' work on Carlton House, would probably have featured a form of highly refined neo-classical style.[4] The 1816 version, contemporaneous with their work on Nash's new Brighton Royal Pavilion, would probably be based on Chinese textile or porcelain design.

Undoubtedly Crace's interiors, in whatever state of stylistic evolution, provided a visually striking backdrop for Godsal's frequent entertaining in the drawing room, his main reception room. The dining room, library, parlour, bedrooms and corridors were stained or wall-papered by Robson and Hale, whom he also commissioned for his next door property, 83 Piccadilly, which he let out to Lady Euphemia Stewart, sister of the Earl of Galloway, after having it papered at a cost of £45.5s.0d.[5]

Robson and Hale also provided the wallpaper for Godsal's country house in Hampstead, for which he paid them three bills amounting to £181.15s.3d.[6] He called on their services once again when he moved into 243 Oxford street in 1805 and which they repapered for £168.6s.5d.[7] They also papered Godsal's Albany 'sett' in 1808 which he was renting out.[8] Again, we do not know the designs specified by Godsal. The bamboo designs employed by Robson and Hale for the Prince of Wales were for a specific overall chinese scheme. It seems more likely that Godsal's papers were drawn from their floral range, or the Regency stripes which enjoyed posthumous popularity in the 1960s and 70s.

Godsal also fitted flamboyant chimney piece plate glass mirrors by Ashlin and Colling in four of his houses, in Hampstead, 243 Oxford Street, Albany and Cheltenham. Such mirrors were costly. That at Cheltenham, measuring fifty inches × forty inches, cost £54;[9] the sizes of the others are not known, but their scale and opulence can perhaps be calculated by noting their costs, no less than £265 for Hampstead and £370 for Oxford Street.[10] The specific designs are not known but examples by Ashlin and Colling can be seen in the Royal Pavilion in Brighton.

Such decorative wall painting, wallpapers and large mirrors by the Prince's craftsmen formed the sumptuous backdrop for Godsal's pictures, furniture, carpets, clocks, silver and porcelain. Some of his paintings even had frames made by Fricker & Henderson, carvers and gilders to the Prince. The bill for three of these was for no less than £44.[11]

The pictures themselves were many and various, in both style and quality. The family portraits included some outstanding works. The delightful portrait of his three children, painted by John Hoppner in 1789 for £45 hangs to-day in The Huntington in San Marino, California.[12] On completion it was immediately reproduced as a mezzotint published by J. Young and Godsal bought ten of them for gifts to his family and friends.[13] At the time Hoppner was not yet a member of the Royal Academy although he had been appointed Portrait Painter to the Prince of Wales in this same year. It is entirely characteristic of Godsal that he should choose the Prince's painter to portray his own children.

A possible engagement picture of Godsal's daughter, Maria by John Opie, R.A. has only recently been re-discovered. The portrait, which is beautifully painted and utterly captivating, is presently the subject of further academic research.[14] The full length portrait of Philip Lake Godsal was painted by Isaac Pocock, immediately after Philip Lake graduated from Oxford.[15] At the date of the portrait, Pocock was only two years older than the sitter, and still a pupil of Sir William Beechey, R.A. Competently painted, with the subject, in classic contemporary style, leaning nonchalantly against a plinth, the painting later suffered from having the legs cut off to make the three-quarter length portrait which survives to-day (see page 111).

No such indignity has been suffered by the portrait of Philip Lake's wife, Grace Anne Best, painted by Samuel Woodforde, R.A. on the occasion of their wedding in 1814.[16] This handsome portrait has a strong resemblance in pose and in dress to the unfinished portrait of Princess Charlotte, the daughter of the Prince Regent, painted by Sir Thomas Lawrence in the same year as Woodforde's portrait of Grace. It was to be one of the last of Woodforde's portraits before his own marriage the following year and his early death from an infection caught on a visit to Rome shortly afterwards.

Godsal's own portrait was painted, as a miniature, by Alexander Pope, the Irish artist and actor of whose theatrical benefits he was a regular patron (see frontispiece). Godsal had this too engraved as a print to be given to family and friends. Other family portraits, of a different sort, were added when Philip bought a job lot of portraits at auction in 1813 for the sum of £2.7s.0d.[17] Perhaps he felt they would impress his guests.

His collection of paintings was by no means limited to family portraits, his own and others. Francis Wheatley, R.A. was an artist much favoured by him and, in 1791, he bought three of his characteristic rural studies with figures for a total of £72.15s.1d.[18] 'Children with cat' is a beautiful image of women and children before a cottage door in a development of a theme first broached by Gainsborough which expresses powerful emotions through the contemplation of domesticity amongst human beings close to nature. 'The Pedlar' is another facinating variation on the theme of the cottage door. Both will feature in a major exhibition to be shown in 2005/6 at the Yale Centre for British Art and The Huntington in San Marino, California. Godsal also bought a set of eight prints of Wheatley's well known 'Cries of London' to decorate his new home at 243 Oxford Street in 1805.[19]

Wheatley's paintings were bought from the artist himself as were three maritime scenes, for a total of fifteen guineas, by Thomas Luny, with whom Godsal had become personally acquainted while staying at Teignmouth in Devon. He also bought an important cattle painting from Charles Towne, with whose early work as a coach painter he had been familiar.

Like many gentlemen he commissioned an imaginative classical Italian Mediterranean coastline scene, completed in 1806, from Robert Freebairn, a regular exhibitor at the Royal Academy[20] as was William Burgess, from whom Godsal commissioned two views of Green Park taken from his house at 84 Piccadilly.[21] This was in 1789 when Burgess was teaching drawing to Godsal's daughter, Susannah. When he visited his son in Oxford in 1803 he bought for £52 three studies of Rome, of which he became particularly fond, executed in bistre by the Reverend Doctor George Nott of All Souls.[22]

Godsal also bought other paintings from dealers and at Christie's and at Phillip's auction houses. These included two large pastoral landscapes by Francesco Zuccarelli, R.A., whose work remained fashionable in grand houses at the turn of the eighteenth century, and a colourful pair, contrasting English wealth and Indian poverty, by Henry Singleton, a regular Academy exhibitor. He also bought works by painters of the Dutch School including Griffiers, Berchem, Wouvermans, Neefs, Teniers and Vandervelde and a pair by a member of the French School of 'Christ before Caiaphas' and 'The Flagellation of Christ'.

The Cottage Door. Godsal bought several paintings from Francis Wheatley

He continued to buy paintings, in 1822 buying two from Henry Room,[23] still only twenty and an unknown, recently arrived in London from Birmingham, and a splendid trio of biblical subjects in watercolour by R.H. Guitabard.[24]

Paintings were for the main reception rooms, the drawing room, parlour, dining room, and library. The bedroom and corridor walls were covered by decorative prints, often proofs. Royal portraits were favourites. The kings, of course, in their turn, George III and George IV

who also featured in his previous apotheoses as Prince of Wales and as Prince Regent. Curiously it might seem, they were joined on the walls by his unpopular brother the Duke of Cumberland. Less curious perhaps, when it is known that the Duke was a customer of Philip Godsal. And, not curious at all, a print of Princess Charlotte, the popular favourite of all who did not know her. There was a print of another monarch, 'poor Louis' as Godsal called him,[25] executed by the artist before the guillotine did its work.

In addition to the 'Cries of London' set, Godsal's walls featured the equally popular Thompson's 'Seasons' and a pair of aquatints after the classical coastal scenes of Robert Freebairn. He also had twenty aquatints after Thomas Girtin's own soft ground etchings, 'Views of Paris'. Surprisingly, because Godsal had no known connections with the city, he had a set of Banner's 'Views of Glasgow'. Like most households in the years after 1805 he had a print of the 'Death of Nelson' and he also displayed panoramas of 'The Siege of Seringapatam' and 'St Petersburg'.

Many of his prints were not displayed on his walls but were held in a mahogany portfolio case for viewing on the display easel in his library. These included the celebrated 'Shakespeare Gallery' line engravings which made John and Josiah Boydell famous, but whose expense ultimately ruined their business. Godsal bought proof sets of the two sizes.

He also subscribed to the lovely soft coloured aquatints of Daniell's views of India and to Miller's 'British Gallery' which contained a hundred uncoloured reproductions of Old Master paintings.[26]

The purchase of many pieces of furniture are recorded throughout his papers and some of the pieces survive in the family, including a cabinet with ebony and brass inlay which is possibly by Blades or John McLean; four mahogany hall chairs by or in the style of Hepplewhite with decorative central lozenge, twelve drawing room chairs in black and gold with cane bottoms and a pair of terrestrial and celestial globes with mahogany feet. Godsal's papers, *passim*, mention a number of mahogany pieces, a secretaire, a round writing table, a library table, a pair of dining tables, a breakfast table, a sideboard and a number of book cases in both his library and two for 'the back drawing room' in 243 Oxford street for which he paid the large sum of £28.

By the beginning of the nineteenth century rosewood from Brazil had joined mahogany in providing the wood for much of the finest furniture. Godsal seemed to be particularly fond of it and the pieces recorded include a sofa table, a loo table, two card tables, an inlaid round table, two chiffoniers and a pillar stand with claw feet. In January 1813 he paid a bill of £20.16s.0d to Gillows[27] but most of his furniture was made by Thomas Whitby.

This cabinet, thought to be by Blades or John McLean, was one of Godsal's many fine pieces of furniture

Until his retirement to Cheltenham he had always had a piano in his drawing room. In 1806 this became a piano forte when he bought a 1797 Stothards at a cost of £38.17s.0d.[28] In Cheltenham he would rent one for visits by his daughter Susannah.

Other items in the drawing room and parlour included a leather screen, an India [silk] screen, and a patent foot stool. There was a Grecian couch, but otherwise nowhere is there a mention of any easy chairs, and it must be presumed that he still had furniture inherited from his mother, or that he had bought these before 1789 when his Diaries begin to list his purchases of furniture.

The houses were lit by wax candles and oyle [sic] lamps, possibly whale oil, although the frequent purchases of 'oyle' are never specific. He appeared to have a contract with an outside firm to light, and presumably douse, these oil lamps. It was a time when new patent lamps were being introduced, and in 1806 the Diary records what was such a one, with the purchase of 'a lamp at a cost of £5.9s.6d from Kay, late Fowler'.[29] He took out a contract with James Smethurst 'Patent Lamp Warehouse 138 New Bond Street' to have his 'private lamp carefully lighted by the month at a cost of £5.8s.0d for three years'.[30] When he retired to Cheltenham he had a gas light installed in front of the house in 1816.[31]

The houses were heated by coal, and with fireplaces in all rooms and the kitchens using coal stoves and ranges, the consumption of coal was large and costly. An analysis of Godsal's coal purchases over ten years between 1800 and 1809 shows that he bought an average of no less than thirty-four tons a year at around £2.10s.0d per ton, often specifying the coals as 'Meadow', 'Park End', 'Bilson kneblings', 'Wednesbury', 'Staffordshire', or 'Kitchen' or 'Best'.

Clocks and watches seem to have been a particular interest of Philip Godsal. A principal feature was the black and gilt long cased Equation clock made by Thomas Tompion, one of the most celebrated of English clock makers in 1710. Philip gave the clock to his son when Philip Lake moved into 84 Piccadilly and paid the bill for its servicing and repair in 1818 by Vulliamy and Sons of 74 Pall Mall, whose invoice survives.[32]

Cleaning a striking regulator name Tompion London, unrusted all the steel work which was very rusty, and polished it like new and polished all the brass work, polished the pallets, the teeth of the 'scape wheel & all the pivots & made a new hook & mended the chain of the Equation work & generally put the clock in good

order as when new £ 2.2s.0d
    To new silvering & lacquering the dial & circles 12s
    To sending the clock home and fixing it up and coach hire 5s.

It is a reminder of comparative values that, in the week in which the present author wrote this chapter, he paid £120 for the cleaning and servicing of a modest clock.

Godsal also bought a 'turrit clock', with ormolu casing by Benjamin Vulliamy himself, for £92.15s.6d,[33] another clock from his equally celebrated contemporary James Tregent,[34] a 'French clock' from the silversmith, Hamlet for £47.5s.0d[35] and a 'kitchen dial' by Thomas Iles.[36] His collection of watches included items by Vulliamy, and a 'silver seconds' watch by the great Thomas Earnshaw, 'made on the Timekeeper principle, capped & jewelled-five ports with compensation slide for the effect of heat & cold. This goes whilst winding up'.[37] This cost £31.10s.0d plus 12s for a gold key. These and other watches were displayed on a mahogany watch stand which itself had so impressed the Spanish Ambassador during a visit that he ordered one for himself.[38]

The dining room or dining parlour, as he sometimes called it, had a turkey carpet measuring sixteen feet by thirteen feet, for which he paid £21.10s.0d.[39] His pair of mahogany dining room tables, the scene of so much entertaining throughout his life, had a pair of silver branch candlesticks made by Makepeace, supplier of many silver items to the Prince of Wales. The table centrepiece was a silver epergne with five crystal serving dishes. In 1805 he bought two plated dishes with covers, and the following year bought four plated tureens and covers for £21. The argyle or cylindrical gravy container was silver and the splendour of the dining table was completed by his armorial china, made in Canton, and ordered through Mortlocks; cutlery including the newly fashionable four prong forks and crystal glass bought from James Blades' dazzling showroom on Ludgate Hill.

The mahogany sideboard formed part of the dining room furniture as did the dining room chairs, which were a set of eight black horsehair. There was a pair of wine coolers. The thirty piece breakfast set was Coalbrookedale china with a gold lace border design and the forty-five piece tea service was French (unfortunately his Diary does not record the manufacturer). The cake basket and cake forks were silver as were the two tea pots, and the cream ewer. At various times Godsal had a plated tea urn and case and a bronze and gilt tea urn.

Towards the end of his life he bought a pair of solid

Godsal's armorial service was shipped by the East India Company from China

silver caddies, weighing sixty ounces and costing the correspondingly heavy price of £42. His other silver items included a bandeau, more caddies and waiters, those small trays for handing letters, or, more usually in Godsal's household, for the footman handing wine glasses to the host and his guests. Most silver pieces were bought from Makepeace or from Thomas Hamlet, the royal goldsmith, to whom Godsal paid £115.2s.6d in the year 1806 alone.[40]

His library writing table had bronze candlesticks and three plated ink wells, and he had a separate reading table, and it was in this room that he displayed busts of the Roman Emperors and of Pitt, Fox and Nelson, and also his matched pair of travelling flintlock pistols, made by Durs Egg which he bought in 1793.[41] It will by now occasion the reader little surprise that the Prince of Wales's travelling pistols were made by the same maker and displayed in Carlton House.[42]

It seems likely that it was in his library that he displayed the model of the State Coach which he had made for the

Lord Lieutenant of Ireland in 1790 and of which he was so justly proud. This is the model discussed on pages 50-51. His telescope, 'lunar microscope', barometer and *camera obscura* also stood in the library, which had some panels of painted glass as a decorative feature.

Godsal bought books throughout his life and in some years his bills for bookbinding exceeded the cost of the books. In 1805 for example he spent £59 on bindings and he spent an average of £34 over a period of ten years. The books in a gentleman's library were of course also a decorative feature, and a part of the picture forming the 'Romantic Interior'. But it would be quite misguided to believe that Godsal bought books simply for show. He was an extremely intelligent, practical and well informed man with good taste. It was from this combination of personal qualities that he made himself one of the richest men in England. There can be no doubt that he made himself familiar with the insides as well as the outsides of his books.

So what sort of books did he buy?[43] There were works of reference of course, the *Annual Register*, the *European Magazine* and the *Asiatic Review*, to which he was a founder subscriber; atlases and maps (he subscribed to Chauchard's Maps from Paris); thirteen volumes bound in red morocco of *The Spectator* and *Tatler*; Ackermann's *Microcosm of London* and *Loyal Volunteers* (as an enthusiastic Volunteer soldier he also bought Henry Angelo's book of *Light Horse Exercise*); and a multi-volumed edition of the British Poets beginning with Chaucer and ending with Thompson. Contemporary poets, Wordsworth, Coleridge and Keats do not feature, although he bought the collected works of Lord Byron, one of the few contemporary poets much spoken of in the fashionable world and clubs which Godsal frequented. The provincial poetics of Wordsworth and Coleridge were less to metropolitan taste.

A magistrate, as Philip Godsal was, might be expected to concern himself with the law and his library included Williams *On the Law*. As a man of affairs concerned with contemporary issues, he bought the complete works of Lord Orford (Horace Walpole), Wraxall's *Memoirs of the Courts of Berlin, Dresden, Warsaw and Vienna* and biographies of Frederick the Great, Pitt, and Nelson

He bought few novels, not a popular genre in the age in which he formed his taste. No doubt the sentiment of Rousseau's *Emile* did not appeal and the novels of Richardson and Fielding, much less of Jane Austen did not find a way on to his shelves. Of course it is possible that he borrowed and read novels, although nowhere does he record the books he borrowed from the several libraries of which he was a member.

There are several books of sermons by Dr Eveleigh, Provost of Oriel, his son's Oxford College and by Francis Close, the up and coming curate of Holy Trinity, Cheltenham, who became rector of the parish church of St Mary's shortly before Godsal's death.

Godsal bought the complete works of the orientalist William Jones and a number of works of foreign travel, a strong contemporary genre. These included Bruce's *Travels*;

Both Philip Godsal and Miss Godsal were subscribers to Macklin's celebrated edition of the Bible

Stolberg's *Travels*; *Views of Mysore*, Cary's *Baltic and Ireland*; and Valentia's *Travels in the Far East and Persia*. This last was of particular personal interest to Godsal for he had entertained the author in his home (see page 76).

His practical interest in gardening is reflected in Thomas Hill's *Eden: or a complete body of gardening* and Godsal's close attention to it is discussed on pages 189-191. As a regular theatregoer it is no surprise that he bought Bell's edition of Shakespeare and the same author's *British Theatre*. He had all thirty-four volumes of Bell bound for £6.16s.0d. As a dog owner he bought Brydon's *Book of Dogs*, an expensive purchase at two guineas.

Confirming the fact that Philip Godsal was on the whole a serious minded man there was no light reading in his library unless one counts Aesop's *Fables* and Lavater's *Physiognomy*, which popularised the idea that a person's character could be discerned from their looks, and thirteen volumes of *The Wonders of Nature*.

. In total his library extended to close on one thousand volumes, many of them leather bound and for all their role in the education and entertainment of his household they also played an undoubted role in the household decor.

Other *objets d'art* taking their place in Philip Godsal's homes were glass and bronze lustres, Meissen figures, a bronze figure of a vestal, and plaster figures by John Flaxman, who sold them at his shops in Covent Garden and the Strand, and was the father of the celebrated sculptor of the same name. There were a pair of large open vases by Piranesi, with 'beautiful, broad, perforated and bold enrichments, entwined serpent handles, on a pedestal, 24 inches high'.[44]

The item which above all suggests that there was in part a conscious intent by Philip Godsal to follow contemporary fashions in the 'Romantic Interior' was a collection of historical coins and medals which he bought at one sale at Phillip's in 1808 for a total of £32. Such collections were entirely characteristic of the 'Romantic' interior and Godsal's decision to purchase a ready made collection suggests his awareness that fashion should play its part in the interior decoration of a gentleman's home.[45]

He displayed his instant collection in the approved place, in a drawing room cabinet, for the interest of family, friends and visitors. His coins and medals bore the heads of Charles I, Oliver Cromwell, Charles II, William and Mary, Queen Anne, and George II. Only George I was missing from this chronology, his absence being compensated by

the inclusion in the cabinet of three gold twenty franc coins bearing the head of the Emperor Napoleon, an object of horrified fascination to many Englishmen but undoubtedly a Romantic icon.

The move to Cheltenham, to a smaller house in 1814 at the age of sixty-seven, did not bring an end to his interest and expenditure on his interior decoration. He had two new grates installed and the floors re-laid in both the drawing room and dining parlour. As noted earlier, he installed yet another ornate Ashlin and Colling mirrored chimney piece and Fricker and Henderson papered his walls and also provided new carved and gilded frames for the three bistre drawings of Rome by Nott of which he was so fond. Quite how elaborate these particular frames were, may be estimated by their cost of £44.14s.0d. He also took the opportunity to have nine other frames re-gilded. He bought new carpets for both drawing room and dining parlour and also for the stairs.

He sold the Grecian couch, but he had an extension added to the mahogany sideboard. He bought more furniture, including two more rosewood chiffoniers, a rosewood inlaid table, two inlaid cabinets for the drawing room, a Pembroke table, a dumb waiter, an inlaid commode, a bagatelle table and a mahogany wardrobe with five drawers. He had the library shelved, and installed mahogany book shelves in the upper sitting room, normally his wife's domain, but his retreat when afflicted by the pains of the kidney stone. He bought new fire screens for all rooms.

He continued to add items of silver including a pair of caddies in a black shagreen case, a tea set stand, a tea sieve and six oyster forks, and he bought twelve large and twelve small marble handled knives and forks. Other late purchases included a musical box, a Bramah patent pen and a silver and gold pen.

He continued to buy royal prints, most notably a proof print published by Bowyer of 'The Trial of Queen Caroline', although he noted in his Diary 'this is the last folly I shall ever incur to Subscription prints'.[46] It was not.

Perhaps if one characterises Philip Godsal in terms of his choice of household interiors it could be said that here was a man with high social aspirations, himself a fashion leader in his own field, who had visited many of the great houses, who had the good taste to recognise the best in quality and design, and who had the money to buy it.

CHAPTER TWENTY
Investment Portfolio

As one of the wealthiest men of his time, Philip Godsal had an extensive portfolio of investments. Those in property, the theatre and in personal bonds for money lent, are discussed elsewhere, and this chapter concerns itself with his investments in joint stock companies, insurance companies, government stock and sundries. As is the way of investments, some were particularly successful, others less so, and some caused particular disappointment.

The Sierra Leone Company was founded in 1791 by a consortium of thirteen directors including William Wilberforce, and it was intended as both a commercial investment and a humanitarian gesture. It was enshrined in the articles of agreement that in Sierra Leone all would live 'free and equal, regardless of colour' (a quite startling aspiration at that date), and that there would be free education for all (almost as startling).[1]

Wilberforce and his fellow promoters hoped to persuade the Government to grant them the same exclusive rights and privileges in the Africa trade as the East India Company had in the Far East trade. Parliament passed a bill in June 1791 setting up a joint stock company, entirely dependent on its own capital, and receiving by Charter some rather ill-defined and not exclusive territorial rights. It was not required to make any financial grant to the Government but in return it was given no monopoly or financial support. Philip Godsal invested in four shares of £50 each on 30 April 1792, paying the money to the Treasurer, Henry Thornton, a close associate of Wilberforce in the campaign to abolish slavery. It may reasonably be assumed that Godsal too sympathised with the cause, as the commercial potential of the Sierra Leone Company was by no means assured.

There is no evidence in the Diary or bank accounts that Godsal received any dividends, nor that he disposed of his shares, although the gap in the Diaries between 1797/98 suggests that if he did so, then it would have been at this time. However the shares were of little value at this time and this investment of £200 would seem to have been a total loss.

Godsal's only previous shares purchases were in the Polbreen Tin Mine in St Ann's, near Truro, in Cornwall, in December 1791, when he bought eight shares of £40 each from his wife's brother-in-law, Charles Cole. At the time Cornwall, with its known deposits of tin, copper and kaolin was widely held to be the source of great potential for investors.[2] Twenty years later, with the benefit of hindsight Godsal recalled that 'my too credulous late brother-in-law received information or pretended information from a Mr Oates, a Cornishman, who was the first to allure him by hopes of great gain & from Mr Cole's kindness I received this good seeming property'.[3]

Godsal paid Cole the £320 in two instalments the following year. He was now the owner of eight of the fifty-three shares issued, but this was an open ended investment in so far as the shareholders, or adventurers, as they were very accurately called, had to agree to bear their share of the operational expenses for exploiting the mine. In the first four months Godsal was called on to pay a further £21.17s.4d for the operational expenses.[4]

His fellow shareholders included Charles Cole himself, Cole's brother Henry, Godsal's friend Thomas Courtenay Devenish, (to whom Charles Cole sold his shares 'having grown so weary of the concern that he got rid of it') and, surprisingly, Joseph Stuteley, a bricklayer who was undertaking extensive work for Godsal in Long Acre at that time. All were resident in London, and not able to keep an eye on matters in Cornwall, which may have contributed to some of the problems which arose.

The most obvious problem was that the expenses continued to exceed the returns for many years. The tin mine produced virtually no tin. No dividends were paid, and as the years passed by the mine ceased to operate, although the original adventurers still held their unwanted and clearly useless shares.

In 1813 Godsal asked his solicitor, William Seymour, to have a look at the investment and advise whether it had any value.[5] Seymour was very strongly of the view that it did not, but Godsal could not get rid of his responsibilities unless he could find a private buyer to buy his share, which for obvious reasons was very unlikely.

Then in 1816 meetings of the adventurers were held in both Truro and in London, neither of which Godsal attended, to decide whether the mine should be finally abandoned. Godsal certainly wished to do so, and his lawyer William Seymour agreed vehemently, but the problem seemed to be that some of the adventurers wanted to continue, and it was not possible for the others to assign their shares and evade any subsequent commitments. However it was agreed not to make any further payments and there the matter stood for a further seven years.

But the *ignis fatuus* of future profit would not go away. It was in 1823 that one of his fellow adventurers, John Aldridge, reminding Godsal that they were fellow masons, members of Somerset House Lodge, wrote to say that he had been to the mine and now had realistic hopes of finding that hidden treasure by agreeing to re-open the Polbreen Mine as otherwise 'the lords and bound owners of the land' would withdraw the mining rights. He reported that Captain Henry Peters would establish a new company, the Wheel Coit Tin Mine which would secure the shares of the adventurers and exploit Polbreen by building 'Adit shafts, working shafts, drifts and levels'. There was of course a snag. Captain Peters required an immediate £50 per share.[6]

Peters himself wrote directly to Godsal saying 'We have specimens of the white tin melted which is proof of the quality'.[7] But faced now with the prospect of throwing another £400 of good money after bad, Godsal refused his fellow freemason's promptings and the carrot dangled by the Captain. Instead he offered to sell his own shares for £20, and it appears that the Captain took him up on the offer, as there is no record of the share holding in Godsal's executors' accounts on his death little more than two years later.

In 1793, two years after his investment in Polbreen Mine, Godsal had agreed to invest in another Cornish company, this time the Trevanaunce Pier and Harbour, in which he took three shares of £100 each out of a total of sixty-four shares. This company formation required an Act of Parliament which cost £311.12s. shared between the proprietors in proportion to their shareholding.[8] In 1797 eight of the proprietors, but not Godsal, invested a further £50 each towards the cost of a vessel carrying coal, timber, slate and lime. By an oversight, Godsal was paid a share of the profits of the vessel and thereby later deemed to have given his 'tacit consent' and required to pay in his £50.[9]

Like the Polbreen Mine, the Trevenaunce Pier necessarily incurred operational costs to which the shareholders had bound themselves. Godsal was relieved to think that he had reached an agreement to assign his

shares to Mr Robert Hall in 1799 for a cost of only £5 per each £50 share, but Hall withdrew at the last minute. Godsal issued a writ against him but failed to obtain a verdict in his favour, and, hard as he tried, could not get rid of the shares and the responsibilities.[10] In 1818 he tried again, but the Secretary pointed out that 'there is no market price as such — the business is known only to the proprietors'.[11] Alas, it was known too well.

There had been many false dawns. At a dinner with the proprietors at the George and Vulture in April 1804 they were informed that the prospects were now favourable,[12] yet for the following two years no dividends were paid. Then in 1806 Godsal had been required to pay a further £111.10s.0d on his three shares for trading capital.[13] But from that date, the pier, unlike the mine, at least paid some dividends. These fluctuated, but over a period of twenty years from 1806 averaged approximately £15 per year or approximately five per cent on the original purchase price of the shares, less the costs of setting up the company and the dreaded operating costs. The Company Secretary's reports tell the story. The highest dividend was in 1818 when Godsal received £30. Between 1812/14 no dividends were paid due to 'Mr Maze's failure' (unexplained). In 1816 there was no dividend due to a 'blow-up at the pier' and in 1821 the dividend was only £12 due to a 'universal diminution of trade'. The Secretary's report for this year was unusually detailed.

> It has been a very violent stormy winter which took away some of the solid rocks near the Pier Head. There was a need to hire a boat to weigh in some large rocks and we need more rocks to turn the current that brings in the sand. We have tried to bring in some Norwegian vessels but a Captain who visited the Pier said this would not be possible.[14]

Godsal still held these shares at the time of his death and the attempts of his son and heir to dispose of them is another story.

Lest it would seem that all Godsal's investments were ill fated 'turkies' the story of the Grand Junction Canal shares offer a very different story. The first boom in canal building had been in the midlands and the north of England between 1768 and 1776. The American Revolutionary Wars had brought a temporary end to investment in new canals but a second boom began in the late 1790s and the canals had now moved to the south.

The Grand Junction Canal was begun in the last year of the eighteenth century to connect the midland canals to

London and the first section between Paddington and Uxbridge was opened in July 1801. Philip Godsal was there at the opening ceremony, and recorded in his Diary for 10 July 'The Grand Junction Canal opened for trade – went up the canal in a procession of barges, bands of music &c &c – went to Bull Bridge – 14 miles & returned to dinner at the Yorkshire Stingo- expenses for water excursion £2.9s.6d.

Three weeks earlier he had bought four original shares at £250 each which were discounted so that he was required to pay only £873. Then over a fifteen month period he bought further optional shares to the value of £1,250. The first dividends were paid out in July 1803 and he received £17.10s.0d on his original shares and £22.3s.4d on his optional shares.

The Canal was the hoped for commercial success, and over the coming years Godsal received regular dividends, and both bought and sold shares in an active market. The optional shares were bringing in yearly dividends of around £62.10s.0d or approximately five per cent on which, in the first years, he had to pay income tax of £3.3s.4d. The original shares however paid consolidated dividends in the first seven years of only approx £10 per year or little over one per cent.

In 1809 Godsal decided to sell his five optional shares of £250 each at their face value of £1,250 less broker's commission, but then changed his mind and instead bought a further five shares at between £180 and £220. By 1818 he calculated that he had paid £1,945.16s.6d for shares which had a value of £2,300[15] and in that year he received £70 in dividends, an annual return of approximately three-and-a-half per cent interest. In modern terms this does not appear a great return but it was during a period of minimal inflation and it was a safe and secure investment. At his death in 1826 his executors calculated their value as £2,580.[16]

Another long term investment was in the new bridge over the Thames designed by Sir John Rennie, which was to become known as Waterloo Bridge. When the proposals were issued in 1811 of course the great battle of Waterloo had not been fought, and it was known as the New Bridge, or the Strand Bridge. It was to be a toll bridge and the investors' dividends were therefore to come from this source. Godsal invested £544 in ten original shares and £600 in ten annuity shares, and he paid in instalments over the five years until the Bridge was opened by the Prince Regent on 18 June 1817 to mark the second anniversary of the battle of Waterloo.

The initial dividend was £77.10s.0d providing annual interest on his investment of 6.7 per cent and this had increased until it reached £110 by 1825, a return of 6.5 per cent. It seems surprising that a year later his executors sold the ten original and the ten annuity shares for only £340.[17]

Godsal invested £100 in another bridge, the Tewkesbury Iron Bridge across the Severn.[18] This was in part of course, a sentimental investment, in so far as Tewkesbury was always thought of as the original Godsal family home and the new bridge was likely to contribute materially to the prosperity of the whole area. He made the last of ten equal payments of £10 only a year before his death and, as it does not appear in the executors' accounts, it appears possible he transferred these shares before his death to his son, Philip Lake.

His other investment in Tewkesbury was the Market House in which he had bought a share for £70 with other members of the Godsal and Webb families in 1789. This had paid him an annual return of between four and five per cent per annum and appears in the executors' account, still at the original value of £70.[19]

Godsal of course had the money to take up any local investment opportunity which occurred. On his seventieth birthday he bought for £32 the assignment of a bond given by the trustees of the Cleeve road from Cheltenham who were bound to pay annual interest from money received from tolls.[20]

He had also made a small investment in 'the intended Western Canal' in 1810.[21] Other than noting his financial contribution to the necessary Act of Parliament and a premium of £18.6s.0d for three shares there is no further record to be found in his papers. Another investment which was certainly aborted was his investment of £50 also in 1810 for the British Herring Fishery.[22] This promotion was abandoned shortly afterwards and Godsal made a loss of £37.10s.0d.

More significant investments were the purchase of shares in several of the insurance companies. In 1798 he bought five shares in the Pelican Life Insurance office at £27.10s.0d a share.[23] It proved an excellent investment. By 1818 he noted that these shares were now valued at £140 each, and his annual dividend in that year was £32, representing a return of twenty-four per cent.[24] In 1825 the dividend was a very healthy £45 or thirty-three per cent. Unsurprisingly, he retained the shares, and of course the dividends, until his death .

Between 1799 and 1801 he bought £500 of shares in the British Fire Office. This was paying annual dividends of five per cent when he decided to sell in 1806 to realise capital for the purchase of the lieutenancy in the Gentlemen Pensioners for his son. His investment in the Rock Life Assurance office was longer term. Godsal bought fifty shares at £2 each in 1806. No dividend was paid until 1812 but subsequently the Rock paid a five per cent dividend and by the date of Godsal's death the value of the shares had risen from £100 to £331.10s.0d.[25]

Godsal's investments in East India cargo, and in the highly profitable transferrable lieutenancy in the Honourable Company of Gentlemen Pensioners, are discussed elsewhere. His regular purchases of lottery tickets are perhaps strictly outside classification as portfolio investments but it should be noted that he regularly bought tickets in the national lottery, on one occasion winning £10. He also bought tickets in two lotteries for the disposal of stock by bankrupt publishers; Bowyer's Historic Gallery in 1807[26] and Boydell's Shakespeare Gallery in 1805.[27] In neither was he successful.

For the last thirty years of his life however his principal investments were in Government gilt-edged stock. He was therefore a Government Stockholder or Fundholder, that essential though often criticised figure. Government Stock consisted of five, four, three, three-an-a-half per cent Reduced Consolidated Stock ('Consols'), and Navy Bonds. India Bonds and South Sea Stock, guaranteeing fixed interest by companies supported by Government monopolies, were also effectually gilt-edged. Godsal was a man of his age, a time when those with money to invest beyond the immediate needs of their business did not look first to buy land, until then widely considered as the symbol and reality of wealth. Government stock was secure, and it was easy to buy and to sell, although its profits were not exempt from the new Income tax, or Property and Income tax as it was later re-named.

The Government required to borrow money to fund the National Debt, which Godsal recorded in his 1801 Diary, had increased from £88 million in 1760, when George III came to the throne, to £451 million in 1800. It had almost doubled in the eight years since the Wars with France began in 1793. Government borrowings from the Fundholders were paying for the prosecution of this expensive war. The Government, of course, had to pay interest to attract investment by the fundholders. Ever increasing tax burdens, of both direct and indirect taxes, were required to raise the revenue to pay this interest.

It was this rather simple explanation which made radicals, and many members of the general public, accuse the fundholders of being profiteers from the war, and of living off the backs of the poor. What these critics chose to forget, was that, without the fundholders lending their money, the war could not be fought without raising taxes to a totally unsustainable, even unobtainable level. And,

like many fundholders, Godsal usually re-invested the interest he received straight back into Government stock. Godsal certainly saw his investments in government stock as both a patriotic duty and as a sound investment.

From 1800 it became his principal form of investment. He was no longer in need of significant new investment in his coachmaking business, whose continuing profits made money available for investment. He had, moreover, sold half his business to Messrs Baxter and Macklew, and had paid off the principal mortgages he had raised on his properties in 1789/90. He had a portfolio of property investments, but the new income taxes were biting into the rental income, and property requires management supervision. He continued to lend money to individuals but this was restricted to customers of his coachmaking business, and he did not choose to extend his clientèle. Besides, the Usury Act limited returns on this activity to five per cent, and there were the attendant risks of bad debts and court costs.

Contemplating his investment options at this time, he no doubt reflected that his investments in joint stock companies, the Sierra Leone Company, the Polbreen Mine, the Trevanaunce Pier had proved unsatisfactory, if not disastrous. Furthermore he was approaching a period in his life when he would have significant family calls on his savings. Daughters' marriage settlements had to be paid, a son educated and established. Government stock could be immediately disposed of, unlike property or commercial shares. That guaranteed fixed return offered by Government stock, and its immediate availability, must have looked ever more attractive .

His mother had left a sum of money to his daughter Susannah which he had invested for her in three per cent Consols. His own first record of interest payable was in January 1801 on £300 of four per cent stock. From that date he seemed to get a taste for gilt-edged. By 1803 he had £7,300 of three per cent Consols, and the following year he bought another £5,700. The next year he invested no less than £10,000. From that date he bought and sold, and transferred between individual funds, and by the time of his death in 1826, his executors broke down his holdings of £34,128 value as follows[28]

£		£
10,000	New Four per cents @ 94	9,400
19,500	South Sea Stock 3½% @ 87	16,968
4,000	3½ Reduced @ 84	3,364
4,550	Three per cent Consols @ 78	3,549
1,100	Three per cent Reduced @ 77	847

The annual income which these produced in the last year of his life was £1,454, this at a time when the annual salary of a country rector, a middle ranking army officer or a London solicitor rarely exceeded £200.

To this figure of £1,454 can be added the dividends from his insurance shares, from the Grand Junction canal and the Waterloo Bridge, from the share of tolls on the Market House, Tewkesbury and Cleeve Road, Cheltenham, from the interest received from personal bonds on money he had loaned to individuals and from the net profits on the London property portfolio. The figure of £1,454 can be more than doubled to reveal an annual income from his investment portfolio of some £3,000.

'Godsal made significant contributions to Tewkesbury Abbey'

CHAPTER TWENTY-ONE
Charities and Taxes

Charitable donations, and taxation in the form of excise duties, local taxes and Government or 'King's taxes were the ways in which individuals made their financial contributions towards society. They represent the voluntary, and so to say, the involuntary way in which money was raised. Any reader who supposes the present day is more charitable, and also more overtaxed, than our predecessors is likely to be surprised at the details and the volume of Godsal's contribution under both headings. There is no *prima facie* reason to assume that the contributions made by Philip Godsal were unusual for a man of his wealth and position in society, but the comprehensive detail of these contributions, recorded in his Diaries, makes it possible to provide an unusually informative case history.

Charities

The many and various charitable donations given by Godsal will be described under a number of heads

Religious
Sons of the Clergy
Hampstead Sunday School
Cheltenham Sunday School
New Church of Holy Trinty
New Church of St James
Easter Offerings to Clergy
New Parsonage, Tewkesbury
Vestry fireplace, Tewkesbury
Burial fund for Rev Grant
Bible Society
Sacramental plate, St Mary's
Pews for St Mary's
Curtain for Holy Trinity
New bells for Holy Trinty

Personal
Old Master at Soho Academy
Clerk's widow
Boy joining navy
Band master's benefit
Workman's father's funeral
Victims of fire
Servant's brother
Friend's house-moving expenses
Employee's sick wife
Distressed family
Servants to theatre

Poverty
Mercers' Company Poor Box
Poor of St Martin's
Poor of Hampstead
School of Industry
Matthison Fund for Poor
St George's Soup Kitchen
Hampstead Society fee
Hampstead Soup Kitchen
Re-building Workhouse, Hampstead
Coals for the Poor
Blanket Fund, Cheltenham
Poor Man, Hampstead

Other
Philanthropic Society
Widows and orphans of Waterloo
Widow of Bow Street officer
Cenotaph Memorial for Princess Charlotte
Russian Manufacturers
Irish Peasantry
Gloucester Female Penitentiary
Literary fund
Dog Kennel at Cheltenham
Jewels for new Masonic Lodge
Friendly Society

Medical
St George's Hospital
Middlesex Hospital
Westminster Dispensary
Cheltenham Dispensary

Education
Marylebone Charity School
National School, Cheltenham

Children
Charity Children
Foundling Hospital
Freemasons' Concerts

He was also a generous tipper and gave regular Christmas boxes to tradesmen

Religious

Although the ministry of the Established Church of England was an educated profession, and to some degree a gentleman's profession, most ministers had modest livings. A house was usually provided for the rector or vicar and for the curate but a living of £200 was unusual, and many earned less. It was only bishops and the senior cathederal clergy who enjoyed higher financial rewards. Wealthy parishioners understood, much more clearly than to-day, that their ministers needed some financial contribution to give them and their families a degree of civilised comfort. Godsal, like most gentleman, included the rector, less often the curate, in his regular domestic entertainment and gave generously, usually £1, to the Easter offering which was traditionally for the benefit of the clergy. In Hampstead, Godsal gave gifts from time to time to the curate. On the death of the Reverend Mr Grant, Rector of Hampstead Parish Church and Chaplain to the Loyal Hampstead Association, Godsal joined with others members of the Hampstead Society to pay the funeral expenses.[1]

He made regular donations to the Sunday schools wherever he was living, and he made occasional contributions to such established charities as The Sons of the Clergy and The Bible Society. In his retirement he made significant contributions to three Cheltenham Churches and Tewkesbury Abbey.[2]

Poverty

The poor were a constant preoccupation, both of the Government and the wealthier members of society. A humanitarian element combined with self interest, for there was the belief that the poor represented a possible threat to established order and thereby to the property and security of the rich. There was a Poor Rate, a local tax which served to finance the provisions of the Poor Law, an aspect of Government legislation which was periodically reviewed. The Poor Rate is discussed later dealing with Taxation but there was a proliferation of private charities aimed at ameliorating the privations of the poor.

Each member of the Hampstead Society, of which Godsal was a member from 1796 to 1814, paid 1s levy at each meeting for the support of the poor, and after he had left Hampstead Godsal continued to pay 1s week, paid in occasional lump sums for this purpose. He contributed to other Hampstead initiatives in the years when he resided there, to the Philanthropic Society, the Coals for the Poor and he paid for the rebuilding, at his own entire expense, of the wall of the workhouse which had collapsed. He received a warm letter of thanks from the trustees.[3]

Both the local authorities in Hampstead and Cheltenham organised 'Schools for the Industrious Poor' to which he contributed, and his local churches of St George's, Hanover Square and Hampstead promoted soup kitchens, an interesting early use of the term.

Medical

In Godsal's lifetime only the Chelsea Hospital for soldiers and the Greenwich Hospital for sailors were state funded. Other hospitals and dispensaries were paid for by the private donations of the wealthy or by individual contributions for treatment. The wealthy members of society, including most emphatically Philip Godsal, were not treated in these public hospitals, but at home, by doctors and apothecaries, and even when operations were necessary, as for Godsal's stone, these operations took place in the rich patient's home.

From 1790 to 1814 Godsal contributed an annual subscription of three guineas to St George's Hospital which had been founded in 1734 and which had three large and three small wards for both men and women. John Hunter, the father of scientific surgery, had been employed there since 1768.[4] In Godsal's day St George's was sited just beyond the turnpike toll on what is now the Bayswater Road, backing on to Hyde Park. From Godsal's Oxford Street house, where he lived from 1805 to 1814, it was but a stone's throw distant. Philip Godsal became a Governor in 1807.

Godsal also paid an annual subscription of three guineas to the Middlesex Hospital, located in Marylebone Fields, just north of Oxford Street. The Middlesex had been founded in 1745 'for the relief of the poor of St Giles and Soho'[5] and it was therefore the place of treatment for any of Godsal's employees and their families. In 1791 the private subscriptions were used to open the first cancer ward in a London hospital. In 1811 Godsal subscribed to a separate appeal to install iron railings on the frontage.

The Westminster Dispensary in Garrard Street, Soho was opened in 1774 'to afford Medicine *gratis*, or at a cheap rate, together with medical advice, and where necessary, attendance at the habitations of patients on gratuitous terms'. It had no residential wards.[6] Godsal paid an annual subscription of two guineas a year from 1799 until his retirement to Cheltenham in 1814 but his contribution was much greater than this because the Westminster Dispensary organised a number of Subscription Dinners each year, at which Godsal was an assiduous attender, serving several times as a Steward. He also contributed 10s a year to the annual Charity Sermon.

On his retirement to Cheltenham Godsal gave two guineas a year to the Cheltenham Dispensary.

Children

Childrens' charities were of course closely related both to those for education and those for the poor but may be treated here as distinct from either. As with benefactions to the poor, there was perhaps a mixture of motives amongst the wealthy contributing to childrens' charities but no doubt the humanitarian concern greatly predominated.

Godsal had contributed to the Marylebone Charity Childrens' fund for many years before being appointed Steward to organise the Charity Childrens' Service in St Paul's Cathedral to be attended by the greatest of all social lions, the Emperor of Russia. The Tsar was in London in June 1814 to celebrate the imprisonment of Napoleon on Elba, and he was the object of the greatest possible curiosity. Godsal and his committee could not have found a more important Guest of Honour and the Cathedral was packed.

The charity children had been zealously rehearsed, and joined the Gentlemen of the Choir in singing the Coronation anthem, 'Zadok the Priest' and in chanting the 'Gloria patri' to each of two Psalms. The Bishop of London preached the sermon and the occasion should have been one of the highlights of Philip Godsal's life and worth every penny of the heavy cost of his expenses as Steward of £13.8s.6d. Sadly, poor Godsal was unable to take his place in the cathderal as he had torn his Achilles tendon and he was forced to watch outside from his carriage. It was some consolation when the committee presented him with the Tsar's personal copy of the Order of Service which his Imperial Majesty had left behind.[7]

The undoubted social cachet offered by the position of Steward at this service was matched by his role as a Governor of the Foundling Hospital which, since its foundation in 1724 by Captain Thomas Coram with '21 ladies of Nobility & distinction', had been the most fashionable of all London charities. Then as now fashionable charities look for large contributions and Philip Godsal had to pay no less than £50 before he took his place as a Governor in January 1802.[8] His induction was in the splendid Governors' Room, famously decorated with paintings by William Hogarth.

Like the Westminster Dispensary, the Foundling Hospital constantly raised money with its Charity Dinners and Charity Sermons, preached in its Chapel with the celebrated organ donated by Handel himself.

The Freemasons' Concerts held in Great Queen Street, and which Godsal attended, were always in aid of childrens' charities.

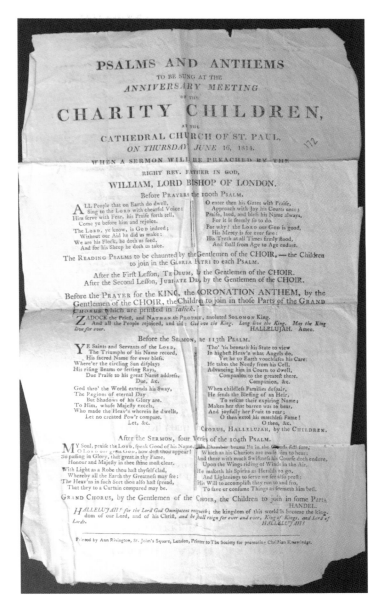

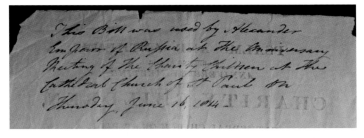

The Tsar's Order of Service at the occasion orgnised by Philip Godsal in St Paul's Cathedral

Education

Children and education are natural if sometimes reluctant bed-fellows. Godsal had subscribed to the Marylebone Charity School for many years and on his retirement to Cheltenham both he and Ann Godsal took a great interest in the National School, established there in 1815. At this date there were no schools in England funded by central or local government. There were fee paying grammar schools in a number of larger towns and a number of public, i.e. private schools, also fee paying. For the most part however the poor remained un-educated. A Parliamentary Bill of 1807 to make education state funded was defeated, and there was no compulsory education for children until 1870.

There were some church and parish schools, and some private schoolmasters offering a form of primary education, but the new National Schools were a popular and exciting development. They were established on the initiative of the Church of England Commissioners who, in 1811, embraced the monitor system developed earlier, and separately, by a Quaker, Joseph Lancaster and an Anglican, Andrew Bell. This method involved the teaching of younger children by older children, or monitors, and did not therefore require trained and paid teachers in every class. They proved successful, not least because they provided the only opportunity for many of having any form of secondary education. Philip and Ann paid separate subscriptions, and Philip made a special payment in 1819 for a clock in the Cheltenham National School.[9]

Personal and Other

Philip gave money to a number of individuals with whom he had some personal connection, including a generous gift of £10 to James Goode, his old master at Soho Academy to assist him in his old age. He gave his servants occasional gifts of money with their annual salary, in the case of his cook and laundry maid, or their quarterly payments for others. He gave his coachmaker's yard employees gifts of money from time to time to bury a relative or if a member of the family was ill. And he gave free beer and money when celebrating a wedding, or when Philip Lake went up to Oxford. This was the normal small change of master servant relationships.

There were many national charities, promoted then as now to alleviate sudden emergencies. To the 'Irish Peasantry in time of starvation' he gave in both 1821 and 1822. To the widows and orphans of the Battle of Waterloo, a most popular charity, he gave generously. When a Bow Street runner was killed apprehending the Cato Street conspirators only days after the accession of George IV, he promptly despatched £1 to the relict, Mrs Smithers.[10]

When the Prince Regent's daughter and heir, Princess Charlotte died in childbirth in 1818 he supported the fund to erect a cenotaph for her monument.[11] He sent money to the fund for the relief of the 'Russian manufacturers' but quite whether this was for what it says or whether for the relief of those trading with Russia is not clear.

Law and order was as close to his heart as it was to anyone with property to safeguard. He contributed to a fund to apprehend felons in Cheltenham and to build kennels to impound the many stray dogs roaming the streets of Cheltenham and fouling the fashionable promenades. During his last years he contributed to the 'Magdalene', the female Penitentiary in Gloucester.

Philip Godsal's charitable gifts were evidently many and various, but perhaps no more than any man of his station in society. They were a matter of choice, but his lifetime coincided with the first serious effort by the state to overhaul the taxation system and give its citizens, and in particular its wealthy citizens no choice in much of what they paid.

Taxes

Taxes on the individual were of three kinds: Government or 'King's' taxes' or 'Assessed taxes'; Indirect Taxes in the form of Excise Duties; and local taxes, levied by the Town vestry or Parish Council.

Assessed or King's Taxes

Before William Pitt introduced the first of a new raft of taxes to finance the French Wars the taxes had been made up as follows

Window Tax was the oldest extant assessed tax and it continued throughout Godsal's lifetime. It was based, as its name suggests, on the number of windows in a residential dwelling. There is still evidence of walled up windows in period dwellings, which no doubt is evidence of efforts to reduce tax commitments. At various times Godsal's annual bill was[12]

£14.9s.4d on 28 windows at 83 Piccadilly in 1795

£35.9s.0d on 61 windows at Grove House, Hampstead in 1803

£25.15s.0d on 40 windows at 243 Oxford Street in 1806

£28.6s.6d on 40 windows at 243 Oxford Street in 1807

£21.6s.6d on 32 windows at Montpelier Place, Cheltenham in 1818

House Tax was somewhat similar in its method of

CHAPTER TWENTY-TWO
Maiden Aunt

As the novels, and indeed the personal experience, of Jane Austen make clear, the position of unmarried women in the late eighteenth century was greatly dependent on the goodwill or otherwise, of their families. As Jane herself said, 'Single women have a dreadful propensity for being poor'. There were few career opportunities open to a woman of genteel family. She could perhaps remain at home and look after her parents. If there were other brothers and sisters the problem of where she might live and what she might do after their deaths, remained to be answered.

She could perhaps be a governess or a companion. Both placed her in the role of a servant, albeit possibly a higher grade of servant. The first required some smattering at least of an education and sufficient intelligence to pass on that education to the next generation. If fiction may be used in evidence few governesses seemed content with their mistress and their lot. The role of companion, usually to an elderly lady, required the subsuming of the companion's personality in the service of her employer.

If the unmarried lady had been given an adequate allowance or inheritance then, of course, she might choose to live alone with her own modest household. Less well endowed sisters often chose to live together to pool their limited resources. But much the best career opportunity for a genteel woman was to marry. For all its problems, marriage gave a woman her own household and a place in society. If she were fortunate, she might be freed from money worries, might enjoy the love of her children, and even the love of her husband.

Marriage was most definitely the career aspiration of most girls, an aspiration in which they were encouraged by their parents. Marriage in the eighteenth century, however, was not only the consequence of a girl having a pretty face, lady-like accomplishments and a modest grace, but also having, at the least, a modest dowry. For a father of relatively modest means, and with a large family of girls, the youngest girls might be handicapped in this regard, and might suffer the fate of eternal spinsterhood.

The Webb girls of Tewkesbury were just such a family.

There were six of them, and a brother, who died young. Their father, John Webb, an ironmonger, died at the age of only forty-seven as a result of a fall from his horse in 1766. At the time of his death his eldest two daughters, Elizabeth and Frances, had been married off and four years later the next oldest, Ann Webb married her cousin Philip Godsal, the recent inheritor of a coachmaking yard in London. At that time the three younger sisters, Mary, Sarah and Susannah were only thirteen, twelve and seven. Mary later married and was to be twice widowed, but the two youngest girls, Sarah and Susannah, were to remain unmarried.

They continued to live at home in Tewkesbury with their widowed mother, Anne Webb who, shortly before her death in 1795, bought two tontine shares for £201 to provide the two girls with a shared annuity which the survivor would inherit.[1] This produced only £10 per year and with both parents dead, and with no brothers, the two unmarried sisters had to look to their brothers-in-law for financial support for the rest of their lives. In this they were fortunate, for the four brothers-in-law were all successful men. Elizabeth's husband, Charles Cole, was a man of private means; Frances's husband, Thomas Brown, was a mercer of Tewkesbury; and Mary's first husband, Michael Procter, also of Tewkesbury, was a maltster. Ann's husband, Philip Godsal, was a prosperous London coachmaker.

Sarah and Susannah left Tewkesbury after their mother's death, and were established in lodgings in Bath, still at the height of its fashionable reputation. Little is known of the detail of their lives, but they appear from time to time in Philip Godsal's Diaries, as visitors to the Godsal homes in Piccadilly and Hampstead. They are also recorded as guests when the Godsals visited other members of the family. In 1806, the eldest Webb sister, Elizabeth Cole, left the significant sum of £600 in her will to her spinster sisters.[2] Philip Godsal, as executor, invested this on their behalf in government stock, and subsequently paid them the annual interest .

Understandably, the two maiden ladies otherwise made few waves in the great and glittering ocean of Philip

Godsal's dazzling business and social life. However he did his duty by them by assigning to them a debt incurred to him by the Right Honourable John Foster, then Chancellor of the Irish Exchequer in the English Parliament. Foster agreed to re-pay the debt in the form of an annuity to the two sisters of £200 per year, of which Godsal gave them £100 cash and used the other £100 to buy a life insurance on Foster's life (in 1806 he was then aged sixty-six) of which the spinsters were the beneficiaries.[3]

Two years later Sarah, the elder of the two maiden ladies, died at the age of fifty, leaving Susannah, now aged forty-one, with her lodgings in Bath to be paid for, but with the not unreasonable income of £100 per annum from the annuity, plus £45 annual interest from the government stock and £10 from the tontine and as the beneficiary of a life insurance on the life of John Foster, for which Godsal paid the premiums.

In 1811 their brother-in-law, Thomas Brown, died. Charles Cole and Michael Procter were already dead. This left Philip Godsal as the only man to whom Susannah, now aged forty-eight, could look for financial support and advice, should she need it. The evidence during the coming years is that she was to need it, and that he was prepared to give it. In 1812 Philip and his wife Ann invited Susannah to join them on their summer holiday in Teignmouth[4] and Philip's later letters to Susannah throw light on some of the intimacies of family life amongst the Godsals and provide some interesting details of day to day existence in Regency England.

In 1813 Philip wrote to say that he had decided to send her half yearly interest via her bank instead of by bank note enclosed in a letter as before, because 'there has been so many robberies and breaking open letters of late that I thought it safest to send it this way'.[5] Referring to his house in Oxford Street, he writes 'We are certainly most comfortably lodged & in the best air of Town & at this moment the Guards in martial array with a magnificent Band are marching past my windows'.[6] In the first of many later references to an elderly valetudinarian male friend of Susannah Webb, he wrote to her 'Keep up your spirits which must certainly be affected by the sufferings of your excellent friend and we never read your letters upon that subject but our hearts bleed for poor Mr Wright'.[7]

Philip was still living in London and Susannah was in Bath, but in 1814 the Godsals moved to Cheltenham, which made visits a little easier. In a letter dated 21 April 1816, Susannah thanked her sister Ann for generously giving her the rent on the Market House in Tewkesbury which gave her another £15 a year, but she intimated that her interest

on the three per cent Consols was not enough to support her expenses as the £600 was producing only £45 per annum, and perhaps Philip could make it more profitable. She unashamedly played her 'helpless female' card 'I am not young, I am ashamed to say and will remain the Old Maid'.[8]

Philip took the hint and wrote back 'I am glad you desire that I should take the Bank Stock & grant you the Annuity & which, but from delicacy, I had long meant to propose to you – not from any selfish motive but that I have ever felt reluctant that the principal should go out of the Family'.[9]

In return he paid in another £1,450, making a total of £3,050 and gave her his Bond for an annuity for her lifetime of £88.10s.0d. He wrote, 'You may be assured that my Security is as good as that of the Government. And please assure yourself that our source of happiness is never so greatly gratified as in the hopes that those we so much love and regard may outlive us and that the Old Maid may live these Thousand Years'.[10]

A delighted Susannah replied, 'It will certainly prolong my life in doing what you have done. I shall be an everlasting old maid but I shall have money and laugh about it'.[11]

Susannah still retained the £100 per year from John Foster's annuity, the £10 annuity on the tontine, and she remained the beneficiary of the life insurance on Foster for which Philip paid the annual premium of £100.

By now there were children and babies of her niece and nephew for her to take an interest in. On a visit back to London from Cheltenham in May 1816 Philip wrote

> Our children Saxons & Haslewoods are all well, & so are all our Grand Children – My son's darling is one of the liveliest Babies I ever saw – & promises a delightful temper. She is never known to cry, or whimper but is always laughing & crowing & will come to any one. Of course we are not a little fond of it.[12]

He added the latest London gossip on the Royal Wedding – no doubt of great interest to the old maid – between the Prince Regent's daughter, Princess Charlotte and the handsome but impoverished Prince Leopold of Saxe-Coburg

> London was yesterday in a great bustle for the Royal Wedding – I have not seen the Prince, but those who have say he is a very personable & fine man & of a kind & good temper & very amiable. This is certain, he is a

most fortunate one, to marry the Royal Heiress of England's future hope – a Queen in expectancy – & £60,000 a year & as much to begin the World with – I hope he will make her a good & kind husband & that she may prove a good wife – she will be his Sovereign & that then she will recollect that he is her husband.

In the same letter, which Susannah will have read with much pleasure, Philip happily name drops that he has been talking with Admiral Sir William Hotham, now attached to the Court, who tells him he will be entertaining Philip's friends, the Edwards, in Bath. The long and chatty letter ends with an interesting P.S. 'The postman is ringing his bell – so must conclude'.

Susannah responded, 'I do not wonder at you and my dear sister being a littel fond of that sweet baby'.[13]

In the same letter she told them that sister Martin had been hindered in writing because of the seventeen leeches used to bleed her.

Although Philip Lake and Grace visited Susannah in Bath to show off their children, Maria Haslewood did not find herself able to do likewise, and Susannah had to make do with learning something of them in letters from her brother in law. (It seems always to be he, rather than her sister, who was the correspondent). Philip wrote her cheerful letters, and even when he was suffering greatly from the stone, he seems to have had a penchant for teasing the old maid. When she enquired about his illness he wrote, 'You are not quite in the knowledge of my complaint as they are in parts not explored by maidens'[14]

Poor Susannah might not understand the illness, although she probably did, but she was properly concerned. Grace, Philip Lake's wife, took over the role of family correspondent in a letter to her in October 1818, when Philip's continuing pain made it impossible for him to write. Grace wrote to her about Philip's illness, about her children and about her sister-in-law, 'my dear little girls are quite well and the baby begins to speak and runs alone. The Saxons are gone to Paris & we have not heard of them since their departure'.[15]

Grace's next letter, dated 3 January 1819, was able to reassure Miss Webb of the good recovery Philip was making from the operation and that the Saxons are well and back in Town after their enjoyable visit to Paris. She gave much news of her own family. Her father, Serjeant Best, has just been appointed a Judge, her sailor brother has just returned from a three year tour of duty in Crete, but there is sadness as well. Her younger brother has died of a fever at Eton.[16]

Then, out of the blue, in October 1819, came a letter which greatly agitated Miss Webb's vulnerable temperament. She had been the sole executrix of her sister Sarah's will in 1808 and now, eleven years later, the Legacy Office wrote to say that they could not trace having been paid the Death Duty. A flurry of letters followed between Miss Webb, her Tewkesbury solicitor and, of course, Philip Godsal.[17]

For Susannah it brought back memories that when she had proved the will, she had been required to explain why legacies of £50 to each of the married sisters had been crossed out in Sarah's will. It was entirely understandable to the family that Sarah should have done this, as she had little to leave and the married sisters were all comfortably off, but the matter had naturally embarassed Susannah as the sole benefactor, the sole executrix and the person who had found the will. The memory of these events, so long forgotten and the worry that she would be required to make a payment with interest naturally brought on an attack of the vapours.

It was evident to Philip that the solicitor who had helped her at the time, and who was now dead, should have ensured that any necessary payment of death duties was made, and the receipt kept. The solicitor's successors were a little embarassed, and assured both Philip and Susannah that the matter was in reality 'very trifling'. Indeed it was and they satisfied the requirements of the Legacy Office.[18]

Susannah Webb's letters in 1820 and 1821 reveal the Best family taking a kindly interest in her. Judge Best, no less, calls on her and her friend, Mr Wright. Grace takes her children to see her. But Susannah's letters, while recording these pleasantries, are preoccupied with her own miseries and those of the unfortunate Mr Wright.

I am not free from the gout in my hand. I am obliged to keep it rap'd [sic] up. I cannot put my hand behind me to lace my stays if you would give me the World...I have been to see my friend Mr Wright. It is but next door and I went about 5 o'clock and staid two hours...he is much altered in health...he is shut up and cannot see anybody very often for three or four hours together...[19]

In October 1821 she had taken new and cheaper lodgings, although still in Bath's fashionable North Parade, at No 11, with a Mr and Mrs Willsher. The rent was now £80 per annum (against the former rent of £100), but the accommodation was still ample: 'Front parlour, two bedrooms adjoining furnished, with use of kitchen fire, china, glass & linen together with the use of the servant'.[20]

But the following year all was clearly not well. The trivial gripes about the state of her health, and that of the unfortunate Mr Wright, which had characterised the tone of all of her letters, changed to one of desperation in a hysterical unpunctuated letter of 13 June 1822.

My dear brother
I must die or my mind and senses will be quite gone if I do not open my mind to you as the only hope left to me to be myself again if it is in your power to advance to me one hundred pounds I shall be able to pay it to you a little at a time if I can get into lodgings that is lower do not ask me any question It is to clear me so that if I could leave Bath I can get no sleep now I go out no more I am almost lost I am so weak of my inside it is impossible for me to live in this state of mind It will be the death of me to tell my sister Martin for God sake do not tell my sister Godsal by your lending me this one hundred pounds…[21]

The effect on the seventy-five year old Philip reading this hysterical letter from his sixty-four year old sister-in-law may be imagined. He responded immediately,

My dear sister
Your letter greatly distresses me. You enjoin me not to inform my wife or Mrs Martin – surely they have ever been most kind and affectionate to you & you add further, do not ask me any questions. In me and your sisters you may rely on every possible comfort & assistance. Therefore explain for what you want this loan of £100. If I read your letter aright it is to clear you so as to leave Bath. As such I am led to think you have incautiously incurred some debts – if so be most explicit & inform me the amount & they shall be paid…[22]

This prompted a response from poor Miss Webb that was, if anything, more hysterical than the first, 'For God sake do not let my sister Martin know it. It must kill me'. The principal problem was clearly her debts, but she also wrote, 'I do not know how I can go on their is this very hautey [sic] lady in the Drawing Room with servants who notices every thing'.[23]

Philip Godsal's response was to assure her that all her debts would be paid, that she should move nearby to a Mrs Hiscox, that she should tell her, and her present landlord that he, Philip Godsal, would pay anything due, that she should 'never mind the haughty lady' and that he himself might be able to come to Bath. He immediately summoned

their sister, Mary Martin, from Tewkesbury for a family conference at which it was decided that she should travel with her companion, Miss Procter, to Bath and sort out the mess. Exactly one week from the date of Miss Webb's first letter the two arrived at Mrs Hiscox's home at Number 13 Norfolk Buildings, Bath.

With Miss Procter as her amanuensis, Mrs Martin reported back that her sister's debts were much greater than they had feared. She had interviewed first Mrs Hiscox, who was owed £40 which she lent to Miss Webb a year ago; then she spoke with Miss Webb's doctor, Mr Soper, who said that he had not been paid. Only then did she speak to the unfortunate Miss Webb herself of whom she wrote, 'none would have supposed Miss W would ever have deceived her friends in so cruel a way'.[24]

One can see why Miss Webb was so keen that Mrs Martin should not get involved.

Mrs Martin however asked Philip to send £100 immediately so that she could ensure the known debts should be paid before she left Bath, and also any more debts which might come to light before that time. No sooner had Philip despatched the money than Mrs Martin had discovered further debts. They amounted in all to £128. 2s.9d, sixty-five per cent of Miss Webb's annual income of £200. How serious this was, can be imagined by relating it to the present day where a maiden aunt with an income of some £10,000 is suddenly found to be owing £6,500 and expects the family to bail her out.

How on earth had Susannah Webb got herself into this desperate position? The answer would be almost laughable if it had not had such serious repercussions. The sixty-four year old spinster had an irrisistible weakness for ribbons and frippery. Mrs Martin discovered that not only did she owe her doctor three years fees (she was, as we know, something of a hypochondriac), but she owed significant sums to a series of mercers, drapers and milliners. They delivered over to the infuriated sister, Mary Martin, their detailed accounts.

Those of J. Cole at the 'Haberdashery, Hosiery, Lace & Fur Warehouse', No 2 Bath Street and of Carlisle Wardle & Co, 'Haberdashers, Hosiers, Glovers, Lacemen & Silk Mercers' of 21 Union Street were relatively modest in amount. But there were others that revealed a positive spending spree. From J. Spornberg, 'Milliner, Dressmaker, Straw & Leghorn, & Bonnet Manufacturer to the late Queen Charlotte & her daughters' of No 41 Milsom Street, Miss Webb had bought recently two dresses for £3.13s.6d each, a sarsenet petticoat for two guineas, a fine leghorn bonnet for £2.12s.6d, silk handkerchieves, caps and yard after yard of

Sussex. With that over, his way to completing the purchase was made even easier by the receipt of £3,225 as a part payment for his coachmaking business, and a loan of £4,000 negotiated with his bank. But it was now that Philip Godsal got cold feet.

In a conversation with his solicitor, William Seymour, he happened to mention that Thomas Smith was a Government contractor for the supply of post horses. Seymour knew that such contractors had to give a bond to the Government against failure to fulfill their commitment and that Montpelier Place might conceivably be part of the security, thus invalidating the title.

When Seymour passed on the doubt to Smith's solicitor, Theodore Gwinnett, perhaps not surprisingly, Smith wrote a most indignant letter, dated 21 December 1813, and with much underlining, to Godsal in London,

> I have considerable capital locked up in the Concern and it does therefore appear to me very strange that such an objection should be taken to my title by the solicitor of one whom I have known for so long…you will recollect the last thing you said to me was 'you would come down in a fortnight and settle everything'. As you had purchased before under the same title I had not the most distant idea that anything could arise to procrastinate the business…[16]

Before a reply could be received, Smith's solicitor followed up with an offer that Smith would give his bond to Godsal for twice the purchase price, confirming, with the signature of a 'gentleman of large property exceedingly well known to Mr Godsal', that the bond to the Government expires before the date agreed for Godsal's final payment.[17]

Seymour advised Godsal against proceeding along that line, and poor Godsal, feeling he might be impugning the honesty of a man he had come to know well, and also worried that Smith, in Cheltenham, would be giving his version of Godsal's conduct to their mutual friends, wrote an emotional letter to Smith assuring him that 'verily I think you as Honourable a man as ever existed, and as a Gentleman, one whom I shall always be happy to be on the best terms with'. He assured him that his hesitation was only because he could not go ahead without the approval of his solicitor.[18]

As the weeks turned into months the interchange of letters between the two principals continued. Smith reminded Godsal that he had said, 'Any written paper is unnecessary between us'. For a moment Smith appeared to weaken saying, 'I allow that the objection may be a legal one' but then he added, 'but to make it a just one you must suppose that I and my sureties are not able to pay the Government rent as it becomes due, and that the Premises in question will be seized under an Extent'.[19] This was deeply embarrassing to Godsal for Smith's sureties were two of his own personal friends, Captain Morris and Mr Turner, head of the leading Cheltenham bank.

Godsal now began to come up with other reasons which look rather weak on paper. He had been ill; his son had become engaged to be married in a very advantageous match and it would take every guinea he had; his wife had decided she did not like the location of Montpelier Place and 'stands fearful of my returning home after dark in the Autumnal nights'.[20]

Reading the correspondence, it is Smith who assumes the moral high ground and Godsal who squirms and wriggles, and he would perhaps have been better advised just to stick with his inability to complete without his solicitor's satisfaction of clean title.

In the event it appears that Smith and his friends bought out the bond with the Government and William Seymour, Godsal's friend and solicitor, announced that all objections to title were now clear.[21] At the end of April 1814 Smith and Godsal met in Seymour's chambers in Margaret Street, Cavendish Square, London to complete the purchase whose copyhold had already, on 25 April, been registered in the Court Baron of the Manor of Cheltenham.[22]

Godsal invited Smith to stay with him in Oxford Street, and it would have been an opportunity to build bridges to restore their former intimacy after the unfortunate correspondence. Smith refused the invitation, albeit in gracious terms.[23]

In the spring and early summer Godsal had many commitments in London which prevented him being free to take up residence in Cheltenham until the end of July. He wanted nevertheless to have many alterations and improvements made to Montpelier Place before moving in and wrote to Smith for his assistance. In reply, he received a warm letter,

> …Pray do not hesitate to give me your commands and I shall execute them with the greatest pleasure. I wish to forget all that is passed & hope we shall never revert to it again, except as to the interest at Christmas! But I remember your observation, and I will dismiss the subject from my mind.[24]

It must be said that Mr Smith did write extraordinarily

good letters and he certainly proved as good as his word, undertaking the supervision of the builders under Godsal's directions until Godsal's arrival, which for various reasons, was not until the end of August.

The principal reason for this delay was that on 19 May, while walking in Rathbone Place, Philip Godsal collapsed when he 'broke the muscle that leads from the calf to the Achilles tendon…the sensation as if my leg had been hit by a cannon shot.[25]

The metaphor was particularly appropriate because soldiers were the toast of London with the recent capture of Napoleon and his exile on Elba. Godsal suffered his own unwilling exile for he was confined to his room for eight weeks.

In June London was *en fête* to welcome the state visit of the Tsar of Russia and the Allied Sovereigns. Poor Philip was confined to his room just at the time when he had an important role to play in this visit. He had been appointed as Steward responsible for organising the Service for the Charity Children in St Paul's which the Tsar would attend. He was also the organiser for the Charity Dinner which was to be held the day before.

It was one of the great disappointments of his life that he was unable to attend either the Dinner or the Service although he was allowed out in his coach to go to St Paul's and at least was able to witness the Tsar coming out of the Cathedral. On the following day there was a celebration of another kind with the arrival of another grandchild when Maria was safely delivered of a girl.

Despite missing much of the fun at first hand, Godsal was fortunate at least that his house at 243 Oxford Street looked across into Hyde Park and he had a grandstand view from his balcony to sample the excitement of the two occasions when the Allied Sovereigns appeared in Hyde Park. In his Diary, which of course he had plenty of unwelcome leisure to complete, he wrote on 12 June 1814

The Prince Regent, the Emperor of Russia, King of Prussia, Prince of Orange, Princes of Prussia, Marshalls Blucher & Platoff & many other illustrious Princes of Russia, Prussia, & Austria & the Royal Dukes rode on horseback in Hyde Park on Sunday. The Park covered with thousands and thousands of persons of all ranks & carriages innumerable. Day very fine.

He was at last up and about for his son's wedding at St Giles's Parish Church on 23 July and in this summer of celebration, on 1 August, he looked down Park Lane to the

fireworks celebrating one hundred years of the Hanoverian accession.

It was now time to supervise the packing up of his possessions at number 243 Oxford Street where he had lived for the past ten years. Packing cases had been made by the furniture manufacturers, Whitby & Co, and some items were sent by river up to Lechlade. The first waggon load with furniture and wine went off to Cheltenham by Dawes, the carrier on 1 August, two more following on 15 and 22 August.

The Godsals themselves set off on 25 August, staying overnight at Wycombe and then at Witney, and on 27 August 1814 Godsal was at last able to write in his Diary 'came into my new house at Montpellier Row (sic), Cheltenham'. One trusts Mrs Godsal's fears of her husband's safety on those dark autumn nights had now been allayed.

Now that he had finally taken possession of the house, Philip threw himself into the improvement of the house and development of the estate with the same vigour he had shown when moving into Grove House, Hampstead twenty-two years before. Only a fortnight after his arrival he bought yet more land from Thomas Smith, this time 'a piece of copyhold land, known as the Upper Paddock facing my house and ground on the Bath Road, contents 1 acre & 2 roods for £1,050'.[26] (see Plan, plot 4). This too was part of the old Red Acre Field which spanned what was now the new Bath Road.

The frontage of this new piece of land was 275 feet, and Smith and Godsal agreed to build, at their joint expense, a party fence between the Upper Paddock and the Lower Paddock which Smith still owned. They also agreed 'that no building shall ever be erected within 100 feet of the said party fence'.

Godsal's estate now comprised three and a half acres but there was neither coachhouse nor stables at Montpelier Place, and on his arrival he rented facilities from Colonel Lennon immediately across the Bath Road in what was called the Lower Paddock. The first major building work undertaken at Montpelier Place after Godsal's arrival was a coachhouse for his two carriages and stabling for three horses and a coachman's room above. Together with the cobbled yard the cost was £567.4s.9d.

Although no pictures of the house survive and what was left of Montpelier Place, by then part of the Langton Hotel, was pulled down when the thirteen storey Eagle Star Tower was built in 1967/8, some detail of the Godsal's Cheltenham residence is known.

Philip Godsal was a great list maker and he jotted down

the detail of how the window tax was assessed. His note reads[27]

Attick (sic)	Front Bed rooms	2 windows
	Passage & store room	2 windows
Bed Chamber Floor	Large Front Bed Room	2 windows
	Small Front Bed Room	1 window
	Sitting Room	1 window
	Stair case	1 window
	Back Bed Rooms & closet	3 windows
	Gentleman's Dressing Room	1 window
Ground Floor	Drawing Room	3 windows
	Dining Room	2 windows
	Library	1 window
	China & Water Closets	2 windows
	Garden Door & Fanlight	2 windows
Basement	Kitchen & Scullery	3 windows
	Servants' Hall	1 window
	Butler's Pantry & Meat Store	2 windows

Total = 31 windows

The frontage was only forty-seven feet from the Bath Road, and the main gardens were to the rear of the house. The size of the rooms is not known, but Thomas Smith had written to Godsal before his arrival confirming that the height of the 'Best Bedrooms' was eight feet eight inches, the 'Landing Bedroom' seven feet eight inches and even the attic rooms were seven feet four inches.[28]

In the exchange of correspondence between Godsal and Smith in the three months after the purchase was completed, it is clear that there was a conservatory, that new shutters were installed, that a door was knocked through connecting the kitchen and the scullery, and that new marble fireplaces were ordered for the principal reception rooms on the ground floor. There was also a laundry, and Godsal's bill shows that he installed two water closets immediately on his arrival. Two years later he had the floors re-laid in the drawing room and dining room.

It was a gentleman's house of medium size, much smaller than his previous residences, 84 Piccadilly with its forty-eight windows, Grove House, Hampstead with sixty and 243 Oxford Street with forty windows. But the Godsals were now in retirement. There were just the two of them, looked after by five living-in servants.

Some of the servants were old faithfuls, the cook, Sarah Davis, the laundry maid Mary Chapman, and the footman, Thomas Parkin, together with a maid and a coachman. There was also a gardener and a garden labourer who lived out.

The house was heated principally by coal, with fireplaces in almost all the rooms. A gas light was fixed in the front garden shortly after their arrival, but the interior was lit by whale oil. The interior decoration of the house is described in a separate chapter (see page 152).

On 31 October 1816 Godsal extended his estate still further by buying for £280 from Thomas Jones, a builder, yet another piece of land, one hundred feet by eighty feet, on the corner of the new Bath Road and the road leading from it to Thompson's Montpelier Spa. To its south was the Sandford – Westall Road and just beyond that was Sandford Place.[29] (see Plan, plot 5). He followed this up on 24 June 1817 by buying from Thomas Smith the Lower Paddock, (see Plan, plot 6), immediately to the north of the Upper Paddock which he had bought in October 1814. The Lower Paddock had a frontage of 226 feet along the new Bath Road and Godsal again paid Smith £1,050.[30]

Godsal now decided to sell on the piece of land he had bought from Jones in 1816, (see Plan, plot 5) and it was bought for £300 by one Edmund Carr, 'a most respectable neighbour. That he is a man of taste is testified by his being captivated with the situation of my land, for I do not think Cheltenham, or its environs, has its fellow'.[31] Carr agreed to build 'a substantial dwelling house with stone, covered with stucco, fit in every respect for the reception and residence of a family of distinction. To face the Bath Road and to be painted white'.

Godsal also insisted that Carr sign an agreement that the property was not to be used as School Room, Meeting Room, Church or Synagogue, Burial ground, Cricket ground, or an alley for skittles and quoits. Carr said that this was quite unnecessary, but agreed to sign.[32]

It was shortly after this, in 1818, that Godsal drew up one of his memoranda relating to his property, heading it

Cost of Land , House &c &c at Cheltenham

Bought of Thomas Smith 17 Oct 1810	£725.00s.0d
Paid for inclosing above	£375.00s.0d
Bought of Smith house & garden with paddock behind 28 April 1814	£3,150.00s.0d
Bought Upper Paddock 14 September 1814	£1,050.00s.0d
Bought Lower Paddock 24 June 1817	£1,050.00s.0d
Stables & sundries	£567.04s.9d
Lawyers' bills	£82.15s.3d
Total	= £7,000.0s.0d

The memorandum[33] was drawn up at a time when Godsal was suffering dreadfully from the stone in his bladder and awaiting the operation which he could not expect to survive. In the event he recovered well from the operation, but now seventy-one, he ceased adding to his estate, although it is clear from his accounts that he maintained his buildings in good order and devoted much of his time to the supervision of his garden, the making of which is described elsewhere.

In September 1819 he had considered selling the Lower paddock, or that part of it which was to the south and next to Colonel William Cranford Lennon. He had noted 'This ground has become most valuable, as it is the only spot of any consideration or size on the Cheltenham side of the Bath turnpike without probable interruption'.[34]

He thought of putting it on the market for one thousand guineas, but then changed his mind as it would be clearly even more desirable if Colonel Lennon could be persuaded to sell him his land first. He instructed Theodore Gwinnett to make enquiries as to whether it might be for sale, and if so, at what price. Lennon showed some interest but nothing came of it.[35]

Then on Christmas Eve 1819 Philip Godsal had a very nasty shock indeed. A solicitor's letter was delivered from a Mr Dorant, stating that he had been instructed by Mr John Smith to commence proceedings against Philip Godsal and others, for the restitution of lands and properties on the field formerly known as Red Acre in the Manor of Cheltenham.[36] This was a bombshell, for the properties claimed were all those properties which Godsal had bought from Thomas Smith (no relation to John Smith), and from Thomas Jones between 1810 and 1817.

It was an extraordinary case in which John Smith claimed to be the rightful heir of his grandfather, the owner of Red Acre Field, but on whose deathbed his second wife, Jane Ireland, had brought undue pressure on him to leave the land to her, instead of his children by his first marriage. She then sold to John Delabere, attorney to the Manor of Cheltenham, who sold it to Henry Thompson, who sold it to Thomas Smith and Thomas Jones who sold it to Philip Godsal. All these persons, with the exception of Henry Thompson, were still alive, including the indicted wicked widow of the claimant's grandfather, now known as Jane Russell, and in her eighties. All were included as defendants in the claim.[37]

The claim went to the Chancery Court but was not called until November 1821, and the intervening two years gave plenty of opportunity for the defendants to quarrel amongst themselves as to how best it might be defended.

In particular, Pearson Thompson, the heir of Henry Thompson, disagreed strongly with Philip Godsal, who believed that the best professional advice should be sought, paid for and the costs shared between all the defendants.

Thompson persuaded Mrs Russell that he could represent her and himself, and Godsal wrote 'I think him incapable & were our success to depend on his abilities it would be lost as he would mar the lot to save a farthing'.[38]

All the defendants agreed that John Smith was a vexatious litigant, but knew little about him until the Lord Chancellor called upon him to identify himself. He said he had left Cheltenham to become a midshipman in the Royal Navy, afterwards purchasing an Ensigncy in the 72nd Regiment of Foot, but was allowed to serve as a Lieutenant in the Worcestershire Militia until 1806 when he went to London and became engaged as a clerk to a law firm in the City. Twelve years later, quite by accident, he came across 'divers Abstracts, Title Deeds and other Papers' by which he learned for the first time that he was the rightful heir to Red Acre Field.

There was a further delay as the Lord Chancellor reserved his judgement. It finally came in August 1823, almost four years after the claim first surfaced. The Lord Chancellor found against the claimant John Smith. The immense relief to Godsal was tempered only by the lawyer's bill for £141.14s.6d.[39]

While this protracted business was dragging on, and possibly even expecting the worst and the seizure of his Montpelier estate, Godsal instructed the same lawyer, Theodore Gwinnett, to look for an Estate for his son, Philip Lake, costing £20,000 which would yield four per cent. Gwinnett drew up an advertisement for the local papers and received three responses from owners of properties in the Worcester area. One of these owners, a Mr Madocks, was particularly keen to sell and pestered the lawyers to arrange an interview with the anonymous advertiser, but Godsal decided to postpone his plans and it seems that Philip Lake was not as enamoured of the idea, or more likely the location, as his father.[40]

In May 1824, with the wretched Smith claim behind him, Godsal began to make the final adjustments to the disposition of his estate and, at last following up his earlier thoughts, sold the Lower Paddock for £2,000 and not the one thousand guineas which he valued it five years earlier. The purchasers were William Jay, an architect, and Thomas Hall, a toyman. The Deed of Covenant is retained in the Iscoyd Papers.[41]

The Diary for 14 May records 'Signed the Agreement for the sale of the ground in the Paddock joining Colonel

Lennon's stables to Will'm Jay & – Hall. The above ground is part of the paddock I bought of Mr T.Smith on 24 June 1817 – see Court Roll memorandum –' This is quite clearly only a part of the Upper Paddock (see Plan, plot 4).

Godsal wrote himself an *aide-memoire* of the proposals entered into by the purchasers of his land. It is undated, and is preserved in the Iscoyd papers.[42] This makes it clear that the frontage of the part of the paddock sold was only of 150 feet frontage on the Bath road. (N.B. The Upper Paddock itself had a frontage of 275 feet). The plot sold was 200 feet in depth, and the proposals were for 'six houses of 25 feet each with uniform fronts to face the new Bath Road & only handsome gentlemanly residences will be erected agreeable to the Plan exhibited'. These houses, when built, were to become known as Paragon Buildings.

By June of the the following year only one of the houses had been built and it was occupied by Dr Dixon of Worcester.[43] At this point Jay and Hall had paid Godsal £1,200 of the agreed £2,000, leaving £800 to be paid. It was now that Godsal agreed to sell to Jay and Hall the remainder of the Upper Paddock for a further £3,200. The Diary entry for 28 June 1825 reads

> Sold to W. Jay & T. Hall a plot of ground adjoining the ground sold to them in May 1824 being 138 feet front 118 feet behind widths [sic] & likewise a joint right of road adjoining the same of 42 feet width. See Deed signed 28 June 1825 for the sum of £3,200, interest on above to commence at 5% from 28 June 1825. Gwinnett & Newman, attornies, Mr Bubb, attorney for Jay & Hall.

The total frontage on the Bath Road of the two pieces of land purchased by Jay and Hall was therefore 330 feet – i.e. 150 feet plus 138 feet plus 42 feet.[44]

Given the current interest in the work of the architect William Jay, it is interesting to note that in March 1825 he produced for Philip Godsal a detailed specification for a villa at an estimated price of £3,800.[45] This was before the sale by Godsal of the second plot of the Upper Paddock, and possibly was meant as a property speculation by Godsal himself on the other half of the Upper Paddock, or on the Lower Paddock, to the north, which Godsal still retained. In either event Godsal did not proceed with the plan.

There is a final curious tailpiece to the story of Philip Godsal's property dealings in Cheltenham. On 13 April 1825 before selling the second piece of land to Jay and Hall, Godsal records in his Diary that he 'purchased from Pearson Thompson, Esq his claim for a guinea a year for ever for every house built, or to be built on the ground opposite my present dwelling house, being & lying on the east side of the turnpike road leading to Bath, being assured by the attornies Gwinnett & Newman and further by H.W. Harris, Esq of Cambrai, Cheltenham, who practises as counsel, for the sum of £200 paid this day to Mr Thompson'.

This had been a great irritant to Godsal, for once the sales to Jay and Hall had gone through and the proposals to build on the Upper and Lower Paddocks had been announced, Pearson Thompson came up with his claim. Essentially it was that his father had sold the land to Godsal but reserved this claim to a future benefit should any houses be built on the land.

Godsal said there was no record of this in his purchase documents but was shown evidence in Thompson's copies. He was particularly annoyed with his solicitors, for if this had been made clear earlier, he could have passed on this claim in his sale to Jay and Hall who would then have been required to settle with Thompson. After much grumbling Godsal reluctantly paid the very high one off sum of £200 to be free of Thompson's claims.[46]

The reputation of Godsal's coach making manufactory was evidently widely known

CHAPTER TWENTY-FOUR
Life in Regency Cheltenham

When Philip Godsal moved to Cheltenham in 1814 his name was well known to members of Cheltenham society as one of the most celebrated of London coachmakers. The point is well made by noting the trade card of a local Cheltenham coachmaker, Powell, who proudly boasted his own pedigree as being 'from Godsal's of London'. Powell assumed, no doubt rightly, that anyone with an interest in coachmaking would know of the reputation of Philip Godsal as maker of the finest carriages. Amongst the well-to-do, his was a famous name. Of course his money was made from trade and no doubt there were those who would have held that against him, although even they would certainly have known who he was.

But there were trades and trades and coachmaking was near the top of the list in terms of respectability, providing as it did fashionable and expensive items for the nobility and gentry. It is probably not too fanciful to imagine that there were many denizens of Cheltenham who would have

been interested to meet the man behind the name, and his arrival would have attracted the same interest in the relatively small community as that of say, Josiah Wedgwood or Benjamin Vulliamy, other manufacturers of widely known luxury items.

Indeed, even before his arrival in Cheltenham, rumours were circulating of his son's engagement. Local solicitor Robert Hughes wrote to him in London on 22 March 1814.[1] 'I have heard from my friends in Town of the near prospect of Mr Philip Godsal forming a most desirable connection – I hope it will not be premature to offer my sincere congratulations on the expected event'.

A connection, with the Prince Regent's Attorney no less, was probably a good enough recommendation of social standing, even in status conscious Cheltenham. Within days of his arrival at Montpelier Place on 27 August 1814 Philip presented himself to Mr King, Cheltenham's Master of the Ceremonies [sic] to request membership of the Rooms for himself and his wife. The Rules of the Assembly Rooms

Philip Godsal and his wife became members of the Cheltenham Assembly Rooms immediately on their arrival

were rigid. It was prohibited 'to wear boots, undress trousers or coloured pantaloons. No clerk, hired or otherwise, no person in retail trade nor theatrical or other performers by profession' were admitted.[2] Mr King, who was the ultimate arbiter of social acceptibility, deemed Mr and Mrs Godsal qualified to join the select group of members and levied a first annual subscription of two guineas.[3]

Mr King's reign was coming to an end but not before the Waterloo Ball was held in the Assembly Rooms on 2 August 1815. The Godsals attended, paying one guinea for their patriotic privilege.[3]

The following year the Rooms were re-built and opened by none other than the victor of Waterloo himself, the Duke of Wellington. Philip and Ann attended, and Philip described the occasion to his sister-in-law, Susannah Webb, a sixty-year old maiden lady, in a style she no doubt enjoyed

Now for the Noble Duke of Wellington – Monday was a gay day but an even more brilliant night. Our new Ball Room, so long in the building, was open for the occasion. You may suppose that all the Belles from every part shot forth their laughter lustred eyes to attract the notice of the immortal Man. To speak of him as a Man I should say that he is all that Nature in her kindest moments could delineate – the front of Jove himself – an eye to threaten and command, a form indeed to give the World assurance of a Man. Such is the Hero and joined to this a playfulness that must win even with the Softer Sex. I never faced a combination so powerfully attractive.[4]

One can imagine Miss Webb's maiden heart fluttering as she read the letter. She herself was a member of the Assembly Rooms in Bath and Philip wrote 'Although we cannot vie with Bath, our New Room is magnificent & when quite finished and furnished will scarce give place to any'.

Mr King was succeeded as Master of the Ceremonies by Mr Fotheringham, but his reign was to be short. Basil Blackmantle, the pseudonymous author of *The English Spy*, published in 1826, although not necessarily of course the most reliable witness, notes that Mr Fotheringham was imprisoned for debt, was relieved by a former lover, now a widow, who forthwith died, leaving Fotheringham 'the victim of powerful emotions' to follow her immediately to the grave.

Whatever the full facts, he was succeeded in 1820 by

Charles Marshall who was the director of Cheltenham's fashionable world for the next sixteen years. Blackmantle, again, called him 'The Grand Marshall, a very gentlemanly, jovial and witty fellow; just such a man as should fill the office of the Master of Ceremonies, having both seen and experienced enough of the World to know how to estimate character at first interview; he is highly and deservedly respected.'

Philip Godsal paid these successive Masters his annual subscription until the time of his death in 1826. He also made a practice of inviting them to dine at his home when he had important or fashionable guests from London. Credit was thus reflected on all parties, including of course the host.

Philip had always been a notably sociable and 'clubbable' man, a member of the Hampstead Society, the Union Club and the Hampstead Assembly Rooms, of the fashionable Light Horse Volunteers Mess and three Masonic Lodges. The Assembly Rooms in Cheltenham provided him with the social life he most enjoyed, cards, billiards, conversation, wining and dining, assemblies, routs and balls. There were also concerts and in 1821 Godsal attended a recital by Angelica Catalani, the leading *prima donna* of the day, still aged only forty-one.[5] Philip had always enjoyed hearing a good voice and he was again a member of the audience when she returned to Cheltenham in 1825.[6]

Many of the fashionable people who came to Cheltenham swore by the benefits of the mineral waters. The Spas also made it their business to supply genteel amusement in the form of walks, rides and music. Philip told Susannah Webb that both he and Ann believed the waters to be good for their health and they were members of all the various Spas.

The Old Well was the earliest Spa but named, not for its age, but because it was in the grounds of Old Farm, home of Henry Skillicorne, who had blazed the trail which brought fashionable valtetudinarians to Cheltenham. His successors claimed the title 'The Royal Spa', as it was here that King George III had taken the waters in 1788 and helped Cheltenham on its fashionable way. When Philip Godsal became a member in 1814 he paid an annual subscription of one guinea for the waters and 12s for the walks.

Philip's neighbour Henry Thompson had opened his Montpelier Spa in 1809. The original Pump Room where Philip first took the waters and listened to the musical entertainment, is well illustrated in Ackermann's Views of Cheltenham by the artist Thomas Hulley. This building was

Godsal attended two concerts in Cheltenham given by the celebrated soprano, Angelica Catalani

The Godsals were regular visitors to the Montpelier Pump Rooms which were very near their home

extended in 1817 and, shortly before Philip's death, it was given the magnificent dome which still graces the Rotunda to-day (it is now a bank). The splendid gardens of Montpelier Spa backed on to Philip's own estate. Montpelier Spa's facilities were much superior to the older Royal Spa and Philip had to pay a correspondingly higher subscription of two guineas a year plus 10s 6d for the rides and walks, 5s for the music and 15s 6d for the pump woman and man.

Philip and Henry Thompson were much of an age and they became friends exchanging social visits between Montpelier Place and Hygeia House, Thompson's splendid house in nearby Vittoria Walk. Philip noted Henry's death in his Diary in 1820 adding 'the Gentleman to whom Cheltenham is much indebted for its celebrity, having opened many wells'.[7]

When Pearson Thompson inherited his father's business Philip agreed to make an annual contribution of £1 to maintain the Montpelier Spa Road although, as noted in the previous chapter, there were to be disagreements between Pearson Thompson and Philip Godsal.

The Gardens became a particularly popular feature of Montpelier Spa and Basil Blackmantle provided his readers with the following doggerel

> Where Thompson's supreme and immaculate taste
> Has a paradise formed from a wilderness waste
> With walks rectilineous, all sheltered with trees
> That shut off the sunshine and baffle the breeze.

In 1818 the Sherborne, or Imperial Spa, was established on what is now the site of the Queen's Hotel. Philip, an inveterate joiner, was one of the first to sign up for an annual subscription.[8] He was also present in May 1825 when the key stone was laid, 'in the Masonic manner' for the Pittville Pump Room, but he died before he could enjoy their splendid facilities.[9]

Philip and Ann were members of all the Cheltenham Subscription Libraries. Most of the libraries had other strings to their bow. Heynes' Regent Library (subscription one guinea per year) also hosted concerts by the Harmonic Society (subscription four guineas per year) which Philip attended. Heynes also sold garden plants which Philip bought. Bettison's Library (subscription £1.5s.0d per year) was also a bookshop and bookbinder whose services Philip utilised. Williams's Library, near the Old Spa (subscription £1.5s.0d) also sold books and lottery tickets on which Philip had always been a regular gambler. The largest of the libraries was Duffield and Weller's Literary Saloon which opened in a rather grand former ballroom on the north of the High Street, to the east of Cambray Place in 1822. Philip, of course, joined immediately and also bought books there; a number of the books in the library at Iscoyd Park have the Duffield and Weller book mark.

There were other entertainments to be had in Cheltenham. Philip attended Lloyd's lectures on astronomy in 1815. It was a subject which had interested him for some years. And there was the theatre. Philip had seen the great tragedienne, Sarah Siddons, play there in two of her most celebrated roles, Euphrasia in *The Grecian Daughter* and Zara in *The Mourning Bride*. He noted in his Diary that he enjoyed the rope dancers (tight-rope walkers) who performed in an *entr'act* there in 1816, and he contributed to theatrical benefits. But after 1816 it seems that his bladder problems prevented him attending the theatre and, even when he had recovered, he appears to have stopped his theatre going.

Another of his great interests was put aside in his last years. He had been a leading freemason in London, a Grand Steward of the Somerset House Lodge, a member of the Blue Apron Lodge and Grand Master of Carmarthenshire. He resigned from these Lodges when he retired to Cheltenham and joined the Cheltenham Lodge which met in Sheldon's Hotel in the High Street. His fellow members there included his doctor and former tenant, Doctor Henry Boisragon. Godsal decided to resign from the Lodge in 1819 when he was seventy-two[10] but he contributed to the purchase of Masonic Jewels when the new Masonic Hall was built in Portland Street in 1823.[11]

Philip attended Cheltenham Races from time to time but surprisingly for one who had a professional and private interest in carriage horses, the sport of thorougbred racing had little appeal. The Races however usually attracted a number of old friends from London whom he was always delighted to entertain at what one friend called his 'hospitable mansion'.[12] Charles Hatchett, son of the Royal Coachmaker, and himself a leading chemist, paid a number of visits as did Godsal's old partner, Charles Baxter, and Ann Godsal's niece Elizabeth Bourdillon and her husband.

Cheltenham Races have always had a special appeal for the Irish, and Regency Cheltenham had many Irish residents as well as Irish visitors. Philip knew more stories about the Irish aristocracy than most and he was kept up-dated by a number of visits to Cheltenham by his old friend and lawyer John De Courcy from Dublin.

Philip had always entertained a great deal at home and for the last ten years of his life this was his preferred social activity. His childless daughter, Susannah Saxon and her solicitor husband were frequent visitors to Montpelier Place, staying in the house and, on these occasions, Philip would hire a piano forte for Susannah to play. His other daughter Maria and her large family could not be accommodated at Montpelier Place and were seen in Cheltenham less often. Philip Lake and his young family on the other hand paid three or four extended visits to Cheltenham each year, taking a house for their stay, at nearby Montpelier House or Tynte Villa, Sandford Place, Rathbone House, Grove Cottage, Keynsham Bank, Bath Villas or Berkeley Place.

Philip Lake's father-in-law, Serjeant Best (later Lord Wynford) dined with the Godsals during his annual Circuit to the Western Assizes at Gloucester. Local solicitors Hughes and Gwinnett were delighted to accept an invitation to dine with an establishment lawyer (Best was Attorney to the Prince Regent until he was appointed Lord Chief Justice of the Common Pleas in 1818). The social cachet was sometimes reinforced on these occasions by the presence of the Master of the Ceremonies. On one of Lady Best's visits Philip hired a ventriloquist to entertain them after the meal.[13]

Best's Marshall on the Western Assizes was William Nettleship with whom Philip had been friendly since Hampstead days. Nettleship bought No 1 Sandford Place, just south of Montpelier Place and the two men exchanged regular visits even before the friendship was cemented by a family alliance when Nettleship married Best's niece.[14]

Among the many guests who dined at Montpelier Place were Admiral Sir Edward Thornborough, who had married the daughter of Philip's close friend Sir Edwin Jeynes, the Lord Mayor of Gloucester. Thornborough had been promoted to the rank of Admiral after distinguished service in the naval wars against Napoleon. Other military guests were Captain Ricketts, Colonel Ollney, Colonel Lennon, Colonel Herries, Colonel of the Light Horse Volunteers of which Philip had been a member, and Major Haines, brother of the Member of Parliament for Tewkesbury.

Local landowners who dined with Godsal included Sir Gerard Noel, a relation of Arabella Milbanke, the ill fated bride of Lord Byron, Henry Thompson, proprietor of Montpelier Spa, Henry Bromfield of Sandford Place and Thomas Smith from whom Philip had bought much of his estate.

In his retirement the number of guests at Philip's table were rarely more than eight or ten. They were always well catered for. The lamb, veal, pork or chicken was often from his home 'farm' and the vegetables and much of the fruit was home grown. Philip's cellars were still well stocked with sherry, port, Madeira, Portuguese calcavalla and claret. Champagne was bought in for many important occasions. His cook, Sarah Davis and his footman, Thomas Parkin had been with him for many years now and the service must have run on oiled wheels.

Philip maintained his carriages until his death although he ceased to employ a coachman and to keep his own horses for the last four years of his life. During that time he hired horses and a coachman from the Plough Inn and he continued to have his carriages serviced by Powell, whom he had employed in Long Acre.

The agreeable life which the wealthy inhabitants of Cheltenham enjoyed would not have been possible of course without the support of the professionals, the tradesmen and the shopkeepers, who provided essential services and made good livings from the lifestyle of the wealthy. They were the surgeons, doctors and apothecaries; the lawyers, the bankers, the surveyors; the various building tradesmen, the ironmongers, blacksmiths and carpenters; the spa and library proprietors and the bookbinders; the nurserymen, the newspaper dealers, the brewers and licensed dealers in wines and spirits; the tailors, hatters, and the shoemakers. And keeping the wealthy provincials in touch with London manufacturers and suppliers were the two carriers, Dawes London Fly waggons and Hearne's London Flying Waggons.

Every increase in the population of this most popular and stylish of provincial towns was geared inevitably to a growth in the providers of facilities. That they sometimes looked to take advantage of their predominantly wealthy clientèle is evidenced in 1815 when Philip Godsal paid 10s 6d 'towards the fund for lowering the price of provisions and other abuses in Cheltenham'.[15]

Although Philip's life in retirement remained highly sociable, indeed self indulgent, he did not neglect his civic responsibilities, and he gave generously to a number of local charities. Both he and Ann gave annual donations to the School for Industry, the orphan asylum for girls, where they were trained for domestic service. Both also gave donations to the Church of England's new National School which provided free education, and to the 'climbing boys', those unfortunate chimney sweeps employed in the houses of the wealthy, including of course of Philip himself. He also subscribed to the Cheltenham Dispensary which provided medical care for the poor.

From the date of their arrival in 1814 Philip and Ann worshipped at the Parish Church of St Mary's, in the centre of the town. Dating from the twelfth and fourteenth centuries its tower and elegant spire made it the principal landmark as well as the religious heart of Cheltenham. Because attendance at church was an almost universal duty, St Mary's witnessed the most regular congregation of the town's inhabitants. As in most assemblies in a society which remained conscious of a hierarchy of rank, the wealthy were not expected to share their seating with the lower classes, and the Godsals paid Wilcox, the church warden, for a private pew, the rent of which was raised to £6.6s.0d by 1818. Philip paid to have his pew quilted to provide some comfort for the services which were longer than those of to-day.[16] The pews enjoyed the services of a pew opener to whom an annual gift was given.

In 1814 the minister was the Reverend Mr Foulkes, who retired two years later to be replaced by the Reverend Mr Jervis. Under an unusual condition at St Mary's the ministers were appointed as perpetual curates and had to buy the living as rector. Their income from the living was augmented, according to the usual practice, by the Easter collections which went to them rather than to the Church. Godsal began by giving a generous £2.2s.0d for his Easter gift, but from 1818, when the rector began to visit him in his home to administer the sacrament prior to his operation, Philip increased the gift to £4.4s.0d and he subsequently gave £7.7s.0d for the sacramental silver and a contribution towards the re-hanging of the seventeenth century bells.[17]

With the rapid growth in Cheltenham's population, St Mary's could no longer accommodate all those who wished to worship in the town and plans were put forward in 1819 for a new Church in Portland Street. It was to be a proprietary chapel of St Mary's, with shares being sold and the shareholders being granted the use of a pew. Before the building began Philip paid a deposit of £20 on a five seater pew.[18] He paid the balance of £80 when the church was completed in 1822 and he and his daughter Susannah Saxon occupied the pew for the first time when the church was consecrated by the Bishop of Gloucester as Holy Trinity on 11 April 1823.[19]

Each Sunday however Philip continued to attend St Mary's where he now paid £60 for pew number 25 in the north aisle.[20] He rented his Holy Trinity pew at first to one of his neighbours, Mr Pickering, and then to another, Mr Bettison, the bookseller, who lived at Tynte Villa. In 1825 however Philip decided to worship in Holy Trinity and arranged with H.W. Harris, the agent of the Lord of the Manor, Lord Sherborne, for the purchase of another pew, this one a three seater on the ground floor at a cost of £37.10s.0d, plus an annual rent of £1.17s.6d.[21] It seems probable that his switch from St Mary's to Holy Trinity was

a result of the growing reputation of the young curate, Francis Close, a book of whose sermons he bought in June 1825.[22] In March 1826, a month before his death, by which time Close had been appointed rector of St Mary's, he bought another book of Close's sermons.[23]

As Cheltenham's population continued its exponential rise yet another church was planned. This was to be completed in Suffolk Square, close to Godsal's home in Montpelier, though only after his death. Philip had already subscribed the first £26.5s.0d of an agreed subscription of £100 towards what became the church of St James.[24]

It was to be in the church of St Mary's that Philip's funeral service was to be conducted by the Reverend Mr Francis Close. The funeral arrangements were to confirm the retired coachmaker as one of Cheltenham's wealthiest inhabitants.

Godsal's garden achieved something of the effects illustrated by Humphrey Repton

CHAPTER TWENTY-FIVE
The Making of a Regency Garden

On his retirement in 1810 Philip Godsal began to buy land in the Montpelier area of Cheltenham to which he was to add in the coming years to create a small estate of around five acres. When he completed his move to Cheltenham in 1814 he set about creating a garden or 'pleasure ground' at his house Montpelier Place.[1]

For the remaining twelve years of his life the creation of the garden became one of his greatest interests and he recorded the details in his Diary. He recorded the employment and dismissal of gardeners and garden labourers; the layout of the garden with its walls, terraces and walks; the purchase and planting of trees, shrubs and flowers from nurserymen in London and locally; the building of a greenhouse; the making of a well and reservoir with pumping equipment; and the purchase of features such as chairs and sundials.

It was not the first garden he had created. Between 1792 and 1804 he had created a garden on a part of his twenty acres at Hampstead, and this provided an obvious template of example and experience for the garden he was to create in his retirement in Cheltenham.[2]

He had some claim to have assisted in the creation of another garden, this certainly one of the most celebrated of private gardens to have been created in the first years of the nineteenth century. He had lent the Marquess of Blandford over £10,000 between 1802 and 1810 when he had made his gardens at Whiteknights, Reading. Godsal's loan had played a major part in the extension of the lake, the building of a grotto and the purchase of the rarest and most expensive of plants.[3] Godsal had visited the Whiteknights gardens on several occasion and he had also visited the great Blenheim estate which the Marquess was to inherit in 1817.

When he came to create his retirement garden, Godsal had the examples of Whiteknights and Blenheim, and of the many gardens of the nobility and gentry which he had visited in his travels around England and Wales. He had an immediate inspiration in the gardens being created by his new neighbour, Henry Thompson at the Montpelier Spa, and he had his own experience in Hampstead to draw on.

There was one other inspiration which, in practical terms, may have been of even more significance.

Immediately on his arrival in Cheltenham in 1814 Godsal recorded in his Diary the purchase of a gardening book by Thomas Hill, *Eden: or a complete body of Gardening*, first published in 1757.[4] It was expensive, Godsal paying £1.12s.0d for his copy, and its price reflected its seven hundred large quarto pages, and its magnificent hand coloured illustrations of some three hundred species of flowers. (The only copy currently advertised for sale on the Internet is offered for £35,000.)

It is a remarkable book and it played an important part in Godsal's transformation of his estate. To explain how this happened requires a description of the book and an understanding of Philip Godsal's character. It also requires a brief recapitualtion of the styles of garden design which influenced Regency England.

The immemorial cottage garden of the poor had been purely practical, providing fruit and vegetables for the cottager, with the accommodation of a pig and chickens, if there was room. There were few flowers and no lawns. Gentlemen's gardens confined the practical aspects of fruit and vegetables to a walled kitchen garden or orchard. For them too flowers were of less importance than beds of ornamental hedges in walled areas near the house and, by the eighteenth century, in landscapes of grass, trees, water and classical features.

The eighteenth century was the great age of the English landscape garden, a fashion which had spread into Europe in the last years of the century. A recent garden historian describes the landscape style as

a pastoral scene of rolling lawns and water which replaced beds as a means of organising the precincts of a country house. Tree introductions were compatible with the landscape garden but flowers were to a great extent irrelevent and flower gardens were kept away from the principal views. Many of the popular introductions of the eighteenth century were confined to the glasshouse and flowers fell out of fashion. The fashion for the landscape garden spread throughout Europe in the 1770s and remained dominant in the early nineteenth century when English gardeners had begun to bring the flower bed closer to the house.[5]

It might be added that deer, horses, cows and sheep could be admitted to provide what 'Capability' Brown called 'living landscape'.

This then was very much the prevailing fashion when Thomas Hill published his book in 1757, and it was remarkable, not least, in being unconcerned with landscape gardening but awarding the primacy in gardens to flowers, grown outside the glasshouse. The book therefore was ahead of its time, looking forward half a century. When Philip Godsal bought it in 1814, its ideas were very much in fashion, for flowers were now at the centre of the new smaller villa gardens that were springing up around all the major towns and cities of England in the wake of the industrial revolution and the wider distribution of wealth.

Hill's *Eden* was also ahead of its time in that it had been published in weekly parts, which on completion were bound together in book form, which was the form in which Godsal bought it. The format of part publications is a familiar style for present day gardening and D.I.Y. manuals which offer a binder to house these monthly or weekly parts. Indeed the function of the publication as a working manual is exactly what Thomas Hill had in mind for he wrote 'The reader's eye should recur from the garden to the book, and again from that to the garden, confirming the one by the other'.[6]

It appears that Philip Godsal used it in precisely this way, reading it in his library, stepping outside to instruct his gardeners, and returning to compare what he saw outside to what Hill told him he should be seeing.

In a gardening manual, the weekly parts themselves perform a function which is not necessarily the case in the D.I.Y. manual, for in gardening there is a time, there is a season, and Hill's parts, relating to each week of the year, provide a manual of exactly what to do in each particular week of the year.

Hill had written a manual but it was a gentleman's manual, designed primarily to instruct the gentleman, to enable him to instruct and inform his servants, the gardeners. It put the gentleman in control, and not the gardener. It suited Philip Godsal who in his forty-two years as a Master Coachmaker had not built the carriages with his own hands, but had known the in's and out's of the business, which allowed him to instruct the various craftsmen to produce the effect he wanted.

By providing instant practical and authoritative knowledge, Hill's book allowed Godsal to maintain a demonstrably informed authority over his gardeners. By following the detailed weekly instructions on feeding, planting, pruning etc, Godsal could pass on instructions that could be seen by the gardeners to work.

Thomas Barnes was Godsal's principal gardener during the initial period, and it is easy to imagine Godsal instructing him on the requirements for a soil feed which he had just read up in Hill's book.

Now then, Barnes, take a load of common mould plus a load of dry mud, ¾ load of rotted tree wood, ½ a load of sea sand and ½ a load of that rotted cow dung. Mix them together, break it every four days and you'll see that in two weeks it'll be ready for use. Very good for the hyacinths and tulips that'll be, Barnes, you'll see. Now I'll come back this afternoon and see how you're getting on.

No doubt he did come back to ensure the gardeners were carrying out the schedule of feeding, planting, pruning and watering which Hill's book so clearly laid out. And no doubt the gardeners were well aware that he would be watching their labours from his library at the back of Montpelier Place.

He could without doubt be a demanding master. Barnes stuck it out for five years and Michael Jackson for two, but there were others who came and went quickly, including James Ochiltree, a Scot whom Godsal had brought down from Hampstead with high recommendations.[7] He lasted twelve months and his successor, a female gardener called Mary Stokes, lasted only three months. Most of them probably left muttering, 'Thomas Hill this…Thomas Hill that'. The last surviving letter, written just before Philip's death in 1826, is a letter of complaint to his gardener, Cox.

Of course the gentleman and his gardeners were not equals and to think so is to misunderstand history. Thomas Hill was himself quite clear about the class distinctions of his day. Distinguishing between 'the useful and the pleasurable' he notes that 'the names of the flowers and curious plants being only the proper knowledge of gentlemen will be treated in the manner of a science'.[8]

A mere gardener could not be expected to understand or even be interested. And of course no one who had the land and the means to create and maintain a garden could be other than a gentleman, or wish to think of himself, and be thought, a gentleman. For Philip Godsal this aspiration

CHAPTER TWENTY-SIX
Food and Drink

In 1800 Philip Godsal purchased two of the new Rumford stoves, one for his Hampstead kitchen and one for his town house in Piccadilly.[1] They cost the not inconsiderable sum of £99, and were not only a clear indication of his wealth, but more significantly of his consuming interest in food, for this new invention, a closed top kitchen range, revolutionised cooking by providing a method of controlled heat.[2]

The inventor was the American born Benjamin Thompson who was first knighted by George III and subsequently nominated as a Count of the Holy Roman Empire by the Elector of Bavaria. On his return to England from Bavaria he was generally known as Count Rumford, and his celebrated stove was but one example of his fertile, practical brain. It was on his initiative that the Royal Institution was established in 1799, but his name remains most closely attached to the kitchen range.[3]

Looking remarkably like to-day's Aga, a system of flues, dampers and metal plates allowed the temperature of the Rumford stove to be adjusted so that it was not necessary to rake out coals, or let the heat die down. Food could now be sautéed; fine sauces could be produced and soufflés could be made. Meat could roast in the oven while one hot plate cooked vegetables and a second could be reduced in temperature to allow another course to simmer. A revolution, which we now take for granted, had taken place. The added bonus, that it was more economical on coal, was of less importance to those able to afford the new phenomenon.

Philip Godsal certainly did not buy two of these stoves because of their economy but because they enabled his cook, Sarah Davis, to produce better food for dining *en famille*, and for the frequent entertainment of his many guests. Sarah was his cook for almost thirty years and can be assumed to have given every satisfaction as Godsal did not continue to employ unsatisfactory servants. If the revolutionary new stoves caused her any early problems in their operation it is not recorded, but she was still a young woman when they were installed so not yet set in her ways.

Philip Godsal was undoubtedly a great trencherman, who loved his food and loved entertaining. Particularly during his Hampstead years often as many as twelve gentlemen would sit down to dine at his table. Mrs Godsal was not included in these men only affairs, but of course she joined him in hosting frequent family meals with their son and his wife and the Saxons and the Haslewoods.

The Godsals were particularly generous in entertaining their friends and family at home, much more often entertaining than accepting entertainment; more dined against than dining. Their housekeeping bills were consequently high. Beef, mutton, lamb and rabbit were the staple meats, and these were paid for in cash out of the weekly housekeeping allowance of £10. Only when he bought a large amount, for example a chine of mutton, did Godsal specify it in his Diary. Other meat was bought on account. 'Pig meat' (rarely called 'pork') appears as a regular purchase and occasionally ham, although it is likely that Sarah Davis salted her own ham and bacon from the pig meat.

Godsal was fond of venison and, like turtle, it often featured at his table when he entertained his male friends. Turtle was expensive and not always easy to obtain, and was reserved for entertaining. A haunch of venison in London cost around £3.3s.0d and for one gentlemens' dinner in Hampstead he paid £8.9s.0d for 'turtle, venison etc'. Other game included hare (another of Godsal's favourite meats), partridge, pheasant and grouse in season, and were bought on account from dealers when he lived in London and Hampstead. When he moved to Cheltenham he received frequent gifts of game and had little need to buy. These gifts from his friends and neighbours, always noted in his Diary, included hare, pheasant, partridge, widgeon, mallard, woodcock and snipe. During the shooting season he often despatched gifts of game from the country to his children in London.

Poultry featured regularly on his diet. Chicken, duck and turkey were much cheaper in Cheltenham than in London and for a time he was sending monthly supplies to all his three children, the unfortunate fowl being carried alive in baskets hung from the back of the stage coach on their fourteen or fifteen hour journey into London.

Fish included herring, cod, whiting and salmon, lobster and 'potted char' a lake fish from Windermere. He bought lampreys from Gloucester and Lady Best, his son's mother-in-law, took to sending to him a most acceptable annual gift of a barrel of oysters.

Vegetables were bought for cash in the weekly housekeeping and are unrecorded save for the 'Lancashire potatoes' which he bought in quantity. In both Hampstead and Cheltenham he grew his own vegetables and had large asparagus beds. His Diary records one purchase of 'vegetable syrup' for £6.10s.0d. He gave his family gifts of melon and cucumber, (still a rarity). His kitchen gardens produced grapes, gooseberries, strawberries, raspberries and black and red currants and his orchards contained peach, apple, pear, plum and cherry trees.

To place his eating in a contemporary context, it should be noted that Coleridge, who at the time (1814), was trying to spend no more than £2.10s.0d per week on household expenses, dined out and felt his appetite 'modestly returning' when he had 'Turbot, Lobster sauce, Boiled Fowl, Turtle, Ham, a quarter of Lamb, Tatas & cauliflower – then Duck. Green peas, a gooseberry & a current pie & a soft pudding'.[4] Had Coleridge ever dined at Godsal's table it seems that he would have enjoyed a similar feast.

Godsal's gourmand preoccupation with food was matched by his love of wine. Attention to his cellar was an attendant pre-occupation. Before the wars with France brought an end to the importation of French wine he had bought claret in barrel from Scott, a shipper in Boulogne. This became liable to duty when it was shipped to England, and in 1789 Godsal recorded paying £13.8s.1d on 'wine from Bordeaux of the 1784 vintage'.[5]

Wine, both still and fortified, was invariably shipped in barrels, or casks, and at some point therefore had to be bottled. Godsal paid £14.14s.0d for the bottles and bottling of one cask of six hundred bottles.[6] Glass was subject to an excise duty which made glass bottles of too great a value to be thrown away. They were returned and credited by the wine merchant against the next purchase. Frequent Diary entries record these transactions.

The French Wars brought a temporary end to the importation of the great favourites of champagne and of bordeaux and burgundy, both incidentally often 'Hermitaged' by the judicious addition of Rhone wine. Supplies remained available for some years from the wine merchants but as their stock reduced the price went up. In the absence of French wines, the English market turned to

Portuguese still wines to replace them. There was a flourishing market existing in Portuguese fortified wine, known of course as 'port', but the still wines had been less popular. But after 1793 Godsal, like many of his contemporaries, bought a great deal of 'Lisbon', as the unfortified reds were known, and Bucelas, the unfortified white which was the substitute for the Rhenish hock, which had also became unavailable during the course of the Wars.

But the unavailability of the great French still wines reinforced the already strong English taste for fortified wines. Godsal drank Carcavelos, which became popular in England for the first time from around 1800. But Godsal's principal purchases, in frankly incredible quantities, were the traditional fortified wines of port, sherry and Madeira.

His purchases make remarkable reading. In 1800 alone he records[7]

2 Jan	Paid Mr Johnson 12s for two bottles of Madeira
4 Jan	Had 6 doz of Madeira from Dunlop & Hughes @ £3.10s.0d per doz
13 Jan	Had pipe of wine [unspecified] for £90 & 1 doz Creme de Noyeau
11 Feb	Had into Piccadilly house pipe of port (52 doz) from Mr Chalie £101.6s.0d
7 Mar	Had 6 doz old port from Messrs Hollands
28 Mar	Had 2 doz old port from Hollands
1 May	Had pipe of port (52 doz) of Hollands laid in Hampstead house
17 May	Had ½ pipe (26 doz) old red port of Mr Knox for Hampstead house
7 Aug	Had ½ pipe port of Mr Knox £48.15s.0d

This quantity of alcoholic drink bought by Godsal in just one year is not unusual for him. There was no purchase in this year for example of sherry, of which Godsal or his wife was very fond, or of rum, shrub (fruit flavoured rum), brandy (the Spanish variety which Godsal bought four or five gallons a time), or raspberry and cherry brandy.

Gin, perhaps because it was a low class drink, was only bought occasionally, and whisky, not yet popular, never. Crème de Noyeau incidentally was hazlenut liqueur, known to be a favourite of the Prince of Wales.

It seemed right and proper for Godsal to buy each of his sons-in-law a pipe of port as a wedding present. No doubt they offered it to him when he visited them. Godsal regularly recorded the amounts stored in his cellars. When he transferred the contents of his Hampstead cellar to 243 Oxford Street in December 1804 he noted that there were

The butcher's shop

'144½ dozen of red Port; 7 doz & 7 bottles of Madeira; 5 doz of claret; 5 doz rum; 8½ doz sherry and 28 bottles of old hock. Between that date and 1808 he bought 10 doz Pale Sherry; 5 dozen Madeira; 2 doz port; 1 doz Vin de Graves and four gallons of brandy'.

By March 1808 the claret, hock, Madeira and sherry and brandy had all gone, and he had only forty-three dozen port left. In four years the domestic consumption at 243 Oxford Street was therefore 1,352 bottles of port; 151 bottles of Madeira; 222 bottles of sherry; sixty bottles of claret; 12 bottles Vin de Graves (probably a white Bordeaux); sixty bottles of rum; and twenty-eight bottles of old hock. He immediately ordered 127 doz port, 3 doz

bottles of sherry and 6 doz bottles of old Madeira, to restore the situation, and before the year was out he had bought another 20 doz sherry, 3 doz of red port and 4 gallons of brandy.

Of course Godsal did not drink all this amount of liquor himself. His wife and his family and friends were clearly willing to help him enjoy it, and as we have seen he did a great deal of entertaining. But he himself must have been what was known as a 'two bottle a day man'. If so, he was in good company. Only when under the doctor did Coleridge try 'to confine myself rigorously to the Pint of Madeira prescribed'.[8]

Prime Minister Pitt was well known as a big drinker and

the Lord Chancellor, Lord Eldon and his brother Lord Stowell, Chief Judge at the Admiralty were only two of the many noted 'two bottle men' in this period. Heavy drinking was the fashion amongst men of affairs and fashion. When Godsal entertained Colonel Boydell and forty-three officers and gentlemen of the Loyal Hampstead Volunteers he noted that they had consumed twenty-three bottles of sherry and thirty-five bottles of port and that it cost him £127.8s.0d.[9]

Godsal bought from a number of London wine merchants, all no doubt pleased to see him; from John Chalié of Mincing Lane, described by the *Gentleman's Magazine* as 'a very opulent wine merchant' and whose daughter married a Member of Parliament, William Garthshore, who was a customer of Godsal. Godsal always liked to make connections, as 'networking' was then described. He dined privately with Chalié and attended his tastings. Over the years he bought a great deal of port and sherry from Hollands (later Jones and Holland) of the Strand, attending their tastings and dining with them. The Light Horse Volunteers' principal mess was at the Crown and Anchor in the Strand. It was owned by Dunlop and Hughes and Godsal became their regular wholesale customer for wines and spirits.

It has to be added that it was not only at home that he wined and dined like a monarch. Fine food and wine invariably featured in his very active social life outside the home. In the twenty-five years from 1789 until his retirement to Cheltenham in 1814 he dined out two or three days a week. At various times there were his three Volunteer messes, his three Hampstead clubs, his two masonic lodges, his magistrates' dining club, his Old Boys' association, his livery company, the Foundling Hospital, and the Westminster Dispensary and the dinners on dividend days. Add to this the meals at his favourite inns and chop houses, at Dolly's in Paternoster Row, the Yorkshire Stingo in Marylebone, White Thatch Tavern in St James's, the George and Vulture in Cornhill, the Old Hatts, Slaughters, the Windmill at Salt Hill, the Greyhound at Enfield and Spaniards and the Bull and Bush in Hampstead.

On his many travels he wined and dined at the best inns and when, as often, he took a house for the duration of a holiday, he immediately opened an account with the local purveyor of fine wines, in Bath, Cheltenham, Teignmouth, Margate, Brighton or Malvern. Somewhere, one feels it had to end; surely the strongest constitution could not sustain

this level of conspicuous consumption for a long and healthy lifetime. Retirement to Cheltenham in 1814 at the age of sixty-seven inevitably marked a sea change for he left his clubs and old friends behind him in London.

But it was the bladder stone which, two years later, forced upon him the greater change in his lifestyle. For the next two years when the pain did not confine him to his room, he felt less inclined to pursue the non stop round of eating and drinking.

At the end of 1818 he finally decided to undergo the terrifying operation from which he expected to die. Miraculously, he believed, he was saved from death and his health restored. But the doctors had now got hold of him. He reduced his intake of his beloved fortified wines and the rich foods which put too many demands on his ageing kidneys. But it was not all bad news for a man who had drunk all his life. The doctors recommended drinking lots of tea but they also recommended drinking lots of small beer.

With his customary enthusiasm Godsal embraced this dual prescription. Suddenly purchases of green tea from Twinings start to appear regularly in the expenses listed in his Diary. One suspects that previously he had looked on it rather as a drink for old maids like his sister-in-law Susannah Webb to whom he had made a habit of sending supplies of this expensive beverage. But now he was clearly drinking it himself. He had never been a coffee drinker and chocolate too had only occasionally been bought although it was considered healthy.

But better still was beer. Initially he bought his beer from Gardener's Brewery on the High Street in Cheltenham, but then in 1820 he decided to brew his own. He bought two brewing coppers of fifty and twenty-one gallons and two wooden barrels of forty-five and twenty-six gallons. For the last six years of his life he kept an assiduous record of the hops and yeast and malt he utilised in making up to 1,350 gallons of beer per year.

Godsal never did anything by halves but 10,800 pints of beer for one household in one year is an awful lot of beer, almost thirty pints a day. Even taking into account beer he gave to his visitors, his servants, delivery men and his son Philip Lake when he took a house in Cheltenham, one has to believe that Godsal himself drank large amounts of small beer in his last years. Probably he drank rather more beer than the doctors ordered, but then he had never eaten or drunk moderately.

CHAPTER TWENTY-SEVEN
Sickness and Health

Philip Godsal possessed a vigorous constitution as his long life, and the manifest energy he put into his business and social life, bear witness. Certainly the amount he ate and drank would have seen off many a man, before or since. Inevitably, in that long life however, he had his share of sickness and accidents, and he suffered a prolonged time of trial for the three years before his operation for the removal of a kidney stone in his bladder at the end of 1818.

Until the time of his early symptoms for the stone, when he was already sixty-eight, he had relied on apothecaries rather than upon doctors. Apothecaries did not merely make up drugs to the prescriptions of doctors, they themselves sometimes prescribed them, having examined the patient. There was therefore a thin line between some apothecaries and some doctors although, in more serious cases, the opinion of a doctor would be sought, particularly by the rich. The problem of nomenclature immediately arises because 'doctor' is an honorary title and not a specific qualification. The title was most usually given of course to a physician, who diagnosed and treated illnesses through regimens (a popular term in medicine into the nineteenth century), or through the sort of drugs which the apothecary provided.

The apothecary often had a social position, probably the equivalent of to-day's general practitioner rather than of to-day's dispensing chemist. Of course there were apothecaries and apothecaries, and personal qualities counted for as much then as now, but Godsal was happy to number two apothecaries amongst his personal friends, Mr Winfield of St Martin's Lane and John Bliss, who was a member of the most exclusive clubs in Hampstead.

Those apothecaries providing a service for the rich could themselves become wealthy. The amounts they received may be surprising. Godsal himself notes paying Winfield £13.13s.0d for the year 1789.[1] His next payment was £63 for five years to 1795[2] and then £215 in 1808[3] (presumably for about twelve years, for much of which time he was living in Hampstead). Meanwhile in Hampstead he paid Bliss £20 in 1800, and in the same year

he paid Goodwin, another Hampstead apothecary ten guineas.[4] The very fact that these were accounts settled annually, or as we have seen, much less frequently, being perhaps evidence of the wealth of the apothecary.

Winfield retired in 1808, and Godsal later recorded the curious circumstances of his death on 1 May 1809 'My old friend, Mr Winfield of St Martin's Lane died at 71 years at a quarter before 11 o'clock p.m. Mr Winfield brought on his death by putting his feet in cold water when he had the gout which he was very subject to'.

One is tempted to say, 'Apothecary heal thyself'. But poor Winfield was probably just following the 'cooling regimen' recommended by his physician.

After Winfield's retirement Godsal consulted the apothecary Mr Smith when in London, paying him £60.15s.0d from 1808 until his departure to Cheltenham in 1814.

Partly because of the evident poor health of Mrs Godsal, Philip often made use of the services of local apothecaries when staying in Brighton (Mr Hall), Bath ('Bowen of Gay Street is a most excellent apothecary'), Cheltenham ('Paid Mr Newell, apothecary for advice & medicine £3.3s.0d), Margate and Teignmouth (Mr Cartwright).

For what then did these apothecaries advise and dispense? For colds of course, for bowel complaints, for piles and for lumbago. Godsal records all these illnesses in his diary. Piles and lumbago were re-occuring complaints. In 1816 Godsal suffered a 'dreadful pain with the piles' which cost him, incidentally, no less than £37 in doctor's and apothecary's fees. He perhaps suffered from high blood pressure, although this was not a contemporary diagnosis. He was bled from time to time, ('was cupped by Mr Watkins 9ozs one guinea'). His weight incidentally varied from 11 stone 8 lb in 1803[5] when he weighed himself at Fozard's Horse Repository in Park Lane, to 12 stone 7 lb when he weighed himself at Ruff's Library in Cheltenham in 1811.[6] The last time he recorded his weight was at the age of seventy-four when he weighed 12 stone 1½ lb.[7]

The cupping on more than one occasion was performed by Mr Watkin's who was also Godsal's optician. His first recorded pair of spectacles was in 1795 when he paid £2.12s.d including the case. He records purchasing other pairs from time to time and in 1805 he paid Watkins £6.7s.6d for his services as an optician. There is only one mention of having treatment for his teeth so he seems to have been fortunate in that regard.

Both he and Ann were convinced of the healthful effects of Cheltenham waters, although he did not make clear precisely what benefit they procured. C.M. Westmacott, writing as Basil Blackmantle in *The English Spy* was persuaded that they merely induced quick acting diarrhoea, and George Cruikshank provided a graphic illustration print, suggesting as much.

All these 'apothecaries' illnesses recorded above, are of course no more than any man might expect in the course of a long life. Others were more serious and unpleasant. Philip had three nasty accidents in his lifetime, all when he was getting older. In 1815, when he was sixty-eight, he fell down into the potato store in Cheltenham which he had had dug beneath his stables.[8] The result was a very painful broken shin which laid him up in bed for some time, and a doctor's bill for nine guineas. Another was when, at the age of seventy-four, he wrote in his Diary for 28 July 1821 'At about ½ past 3 o'clock myself, my son & his wife & eldest daughter were thrown out by being overturned of my pony phaeton opposite to Mr Delabere's house on the Prestbury road in consequence of the horse running away – by the goodness of Providence all escaped material injury'.

He was confined to the house for two weeks, but only his knee and his wallet suffered, for Mr Seager paid him six 'guinea visits' in the next four weeks. It would seem that the phaeton may have been overloaded for this local visit, but the pony, which he had bought only three days before, was sold forthwith at a loss of £5.

Even more painful was the occasion in May 1814 when Philip suffered an accident which 'broke the muscles that lead from the calf to the tendon Achilles of my left leg – cannot account how it happened – no exertion. This happened in Rathbone Place – Dr Hooper was wait [sic] and he was so good as to bring me home. The sensation as if my left leg had been struck by a cannon shot'.[9]

This accident kept him house bound for some six weeks, as we have seen causing him to miss the service in St Paul's attended by the Tsar. On this occasion he was attended not only by Dr Robert Hooper, who was well known in medical circles as the author of two standard text books and had been a licentiate of the exclusive Royal College of Physicians since 1805,[10] but also by Mr Cline, one of the leading surgeons of the day. Henry Cline had been lecturer in anatomy at St

Thomas's for thirty years and was now in private practise.[11] The cost of medical treatment was £17.15s.0d.

For the remaining twelve years of his life Philip looked to physicians and surgeons rather than apothecaries for his medical advice. In Cheltenham he consulted Mr Surgeon Seager, Doctor Newell and Doctor Boisragon, who had been consulted by King George III and by Lord Byron.[12] In London, as well as Hooper and Cline, he consulted three other celebrated surgeons, Sir Astley Cooper, William Wadd, and John Abernethy.

Throughout the eighteenth century, physicians, who had their own Royal Charter and College, were considered, and certainly considered themselves, superior to surgeons, a surprising anomaly in view of to-day's perception of relative status. But surgeons had, after all, inherited the role of the barber surgeon, and indeed anyone submitting to an operation, without anaesthetics and with rudimentary hygiene, was more than likely to die. The physician could be seen to be less lethal than the surgeon. But membership of the Royal College of Physicians was limited to fifty with another fifty as the lower grade of licentiate and most practising physicians, particularly in the provinces could not hope to become members, even though they had studied the medicine course at Oxford or Cambridge, or after 1800 in Dublin or the Scottish universities. Most practising physicians, many of whom had studied at the London or provincial hospitals, were not members.[13] The closed shop had the virtue of keeping up fees for those in the charmed circle.

In 1800 the status of surgeons was at last recognised by the granting of a Royal Charter, and the establishment of the Royal College of Surgeons, for which entrance was by examination. Subsequently, for a practitioner to use the title of surgeon, he had to be registered as a member of the Royal College of Surgeons of England. All Godsal's surgeons were in fact members and he had every reason to believe he was consulting the best. Certainly the fees, if not always the treatment, suggested that this was so.

Whereas the apothecaries had submitted accounts, often, as we have seen, long in arrears, physicians and surgeons were very prompt with requests for payments. The consultation invariably ended with a guinea being paid over. It was said of Dr Warren, physician to King George III, that as he examined his own tongue in the mirror each morning he involuntarily passed a guinea from one pocket to the other.[14]

Doctors had been the subject of caricature since the mid eighteenth century for this practice, being pictured with their pair of scales, with which they checked for false guineas.[15] A social historian of medicine has described physicians as 'turning from health to wealth and healing to dealing'.[16] It seems likely that Godsal's doctors, metaphorically at least, produced their scales from their bags to indicate that the consultation was at an end, for from 1814 onwards Philip's Diary is full of these guinea or two guinea payments.

Another practice, much favoured by medical men at the time, was joint consultations, a practice memorably re-created in the film *The Madness of King George*. This practice could have been an aspect of 'fee-grabbing', as the satirists claimed, or perhaps a sharing of responsibility, where the still limited scientific knowledge meant that recovery might be uncertain. Certainly on a number of occasions Philip Godsal's doctors called in one or two other medical men for their opinions.

The reasons for the increasingly frequent consultations for which Philip paid in the last years of his life derived principally from two painful ailments. The first was diagnosed by Mr Cline, after several joint consultations, as 'an abscess in the adipose membrane of the thick part of the buttock'.[17] This was in February 1816 and it flared up subsequently from time to time, most notably in August 1819. He was attending Cheltenham Races when 'the abscess was very bad, worse than I ever felt it'.[18]

More critical however was the problem that first made iteself felt early in 1816 when he started to experience 'leaking' and pain when passing water. At first it seemed as if the problem would be shortlived. He wrote in a letter to his sister-in-law in July 1816 'My Surgeon Attendant pronounces that a few weeks will render me as tight as any copper bottomed vessel that has ploughed the ocean'.[19]

Alas it was not to be, for in May of the following year, he noted in his Diary that he had paid Surgeon Home in London 'for his opinion on the red gravel'.[20] In Cheltenham he continued to take the waters hoping that their diuretic effects would help. Doctor Boisragon and Mr Seager attended him regularly and he was recommended opiates which he subsequently continued to take for the remainder of his life. He also resorted to any possible means of a cure, including 'Adam's Solvents', recommended 'and prepared' by yet another medical adviser, Surgeon Perry.[21] Probably his greatest solace however, was the sherry and Madeira which the medical advisers had not banned.

But by November 1817, when he experiencied the most dreadful pain in passing the red gravel, it was decided that he must go to London for further diagnostic consultations with Dr Hooper, Mr Cline, and two more of the leading surgeons of the day. Mr Surgeon William Wadd of St Bart's,

who had published standard works on surgery, and the celebrated Sir Astley Cooper, the brilliant pupil of Cline, and later to become physician to King George IV.[22] They agreed that it was 'the stone in the bladder'.[23] Godsal was by now a man of seventy and, if an operation was performed, without anaesthetics of course as there were none, it would be unlikely that he survive. Samuel Pepys, incidentally had been a vigorous young man of twenty-four when he submitted to 'the cutt'.

The hope clearly was that Godsal would pass out the stone naturally, albeit in the dreadfully painful red gravel. Surgeon Wadd inserted a catheter to see if that would facilitate the passage of the gravel and ease the pain. It did not, and Godsal was presented with a bill for twenty-eight guineas plus 10s 6d for the catheter and sponge. After two further joint consultations they recommended that he return home and keep quiet.

His immediate reaction was noted in his Diary on 25 April 'Received £105 of Mr Clarke for my pair of geldings – confess it heart rending that in consequence of my illness I sold my carriage & horses'. This dramatic, perhaps over dramatic reaction meant sacking the coachman George Best whom he had employed only three weeks earlier. He then returned to Cheltenham but in May 1818 he noted that 'my pains increased so much as to be beyond my power to support. My water came from me with much pain and deposited a most hideous quantity of thick mucus'.[24]

He resorted to a quack doctor, Mr Johnson of Tardebrigg, near Bromsgrove who actually stayed with him in his house to administer 'Constitution Water', which he claimed would dissolve the stone.[25] The result alas was recorded in the Diary 'so bad a night – sent for Seager – stoppage of water'.[26]

It could not go on, and after further consultations between his various medical advisers, and a new one, Mr Surgeon Abernethy, the greatest anatomy lecturer of the day,[27] 'Abernethy, Seager & Boisragon determined that my constitution was strong enough to enable me to be cutt & which they recommended'[28]

He agreed to undergo the dreadful operation, the doctors recommending that it be performed in winter when it was cooler. (Pepys's doctors had recommended the operation in the spring when it was warmer[29]).

In that terrible interval, in periodic acute pain and, no doubt in dreadful anticpation of the operation, he continued to receive almost daily 'guinea visits' from Dr Boisragon and Mr Seager, although they could do little. He bought a three wheel invalid chair for £14.9s.0d and a hip bath for £2.5s.6d.

He resorted to the opiates, and in desperation, to a quack doctor's remedy 'Johnson's Constitution Water', which had made him ill when he had taken it earlier. He wrote his Will, paid his attorney's fees in full, and took private communion in his house with the Rector of St Mary's. 'Rev Mr Jervis administered to myself & Mrs G the most comforting sacrament'.[30]

Queen Charlotte, widow of King George III, died a month before Godsal's operation and perhaps mindful of his own probable death, he gave £5 to his three female servants to buy black gowns. Then in a sudden surge of perhaps unaccountable optimism, he ordered a new chariot which Philip Lake brought to Cheltenham at the end of October.[31]

His daughter-in-law, Grace Anne Godsal, described life in the Godsal household at this time in a letter to his sister-in-law Susannah Webb to whom she made things seem a little better than they could have been, and she made it seem almost as if the real sufferer were his wife, rather than Philip himself

He generally confines himself to the small sitting room upstairs but has been a few times in the garden. His appetite is good & excepting the severe pain he labors under at times the general state of his health is improved. Mrs Godsal is as well as can be expected from the unremitted attention and close confinement.[32]

Just how Philip was suffering mentally as well as physically is shown in a poignant prayer which he composed at this time,

Almighty and most merciful Father, I most humbly implore the blessing to the means about to be taken for my recovery from the painful complaint Thou has been pleased to afflict me with. As the preservation of Life is in thy hands alone & as the operation resorted to is of a very hazardous nature, grant O Lord to my Surgical Friend sufficient skill and strength of mind to accomplish it. I beseech thee also O God to give me strength of body to support these sufferings…Butt if it should please thee O Lord that what is done in the hope of cure should be the means of Death, I most humbly pray that having been desirous of applying to such a remedy to ease my pain, which only Thou, O God knowest to be, but for thy gracious aid, beyond the strength of man to bear, it may not be imputed to me that I have, by my want of confidence in Thy mercy, been the cause of accelerating my Death.[32a]

The operation was performed in Philip's Cheltenham home on 28 December by Mr Seager with Surgeon Fletcher of Gloucester and two male nurses in attendance. The operation was without anaesthetic, although he was given a dose of opium. The principal roles of the nurses were to bind him, tie him to the table and hold him down.

Patients submitting to 'the cutt' sometimes died from shock, and Godsal's surgeons had examined him (at a further cost of four guineas) and certified that his constitution was sound enough to undergo the operation. For a separate fee he was 'sounded' six days before.[33]

The first report on the operation came six days later in a letter from Grace Anne again written to Susannah Webb

His pains having increased very considerably, he determined to submit to the operation which was performed last Monday most skilfully and successfully by Mr Seager, the surgeon of this place. For the first 24 hours every appearance was most favourable but an inflammation of his bowels then came on & his life was despaired of for a night and day. Happily this has subsided and we trust he is on his way to a perfect recovery. Mr Seager assures us that he never saw anyone at any age better than he is after a similar operation. He is free from pain, his pulse is good and he is now pronounced out of danger. Mr Seager was not more than 9 minutes in extracting the stone which is about the size of a small walnut.[34]

Philip Godsal himself noted in his Diary 'On 28 December Mr Surgeon Seager attended with Mr Surgeon Fletcher cutt me for the stone – I write this on 14 January 1819, the Almighty having given me the power. To Him be all thanks from the innermost recesses of my heart for preserving me so far'.[35]

He later noted that he paid fifty guineas to Mr Seager who had 'performed the operation in the most masterly manner and slept afterwards four nights at my house for which I gave him my chronometer made by Mr Earnshaw'.[36]

During his convalescence Philip carefully listed his medical expenses for the year 1818. They amounted to £276s.1.0d, a sum incidentally, greater than the annual salary of many lawyers, clergymen or army officers, but not of course of the wealthy guinea an hour doctors.[37]

Philip Godsal lived for another seven years after the operation, and suffered episodic pains with the abscess. He noted in his Diary on 27 November 1819 'Mr Seager undertook to cure my abscess' and in a letter dated 21 December Susannah Webb wrote to him 'My sister Martin told me you had been undergoing another operation and thank God you was better'.[38]

But for the most part he was in good health and heart, once again travelling regularly from Cheltenham to London to see his children and grandchildren, and going on many excursions, to exhibitions, concerts, the theatre and sight-seeing.

He reduced his consumption of his favourite fortified wines. It appears that the doctors had recomended plenty of liquid for his kidneys' benefit and, as we have noted he began to brew his own small beer which he appears to have drunk in large quantities. He also appears to have drunk much more tea than ever before (see page 198).

Such a long life was a tribute to his strong constitution, but perhaps some credit can be given to his doctors, those guinea a visit men, of whose profession so many contemporaries had so low an opinion. At the time Godsal underwent his terrible operation no physician had ever been admitted to the Upper House, while many members of the other professions had long sat on the red benches. Because of this lower social ranking one physician wrote 'The office of physician can never be supported but as a lucrative one'. Philip Godsal, for one, had always been grateful enough to pay their price.

The Godsal-Best coat of arms

CHAPTER TWENTY-EIGHT
Death and Legacy

Philip had first made a will in July 1803 at the age of fifty-six. It was drawn up for him by his Hampstead friend George Bogg, the Proctor of Doctors Commons. He could scarcely have gone to a better man for Doctors Commons, the colloquial name for the College of Advocates and Doctors of Law, near St Paul's Cathederal, was responsible for the Prerogative (probate) court. The charge of fifteen guineas reflects perhaps that it was just about the most authoritative will that money could buy.[1]

It was fifteen years later in 1818 that Philip, diagnosed as having a potentially fatal kidney stone, had a new will drawn up. George Bogg had been dead for some years and Evan Foulkes, his regular solictor was the same age as Godsal and had already retired. He turned to Foulkes's successors, Walford & Walford. It was this second will, with two later codicils added in 1821 and 1824, that his executors administered after his death seven years later.

Meanwhile Philip had made other arrangements to be put in place after his death. While awaiting the operation his thoughts also turned to the melancholy but important question of what arrangements should be made for his burial. His father had been buried in the crypt of St Martin in the Fields in London and his mother had been buried in a vault in Wokingham Parish Church in Berkshire. The large vault stone for his mother suggests that when this vault was created Philip had it in mind that this might be his own future resting place. But this was thirty-four years ago, and he had always looked on Tewkesbury as the original family home of the Godsals. His grandparents and other relations had been buried in the great Abbey Church there, and he decided that was where he would wish to lie. In August 1818, through the medium of his nephew Edward Brown, he opened negotiations with the church wardens for permission to be buried in a new vault in the Abbey.[2]

In a temporary interregnum between vicars, the church wardens granted permission, and Godsal went into the ordeal of the operation with his mind easy at least on this point. As we know, he survived the operation but within two weeks he received a letter from his nephew saying that the new vicar, the Reverend Mr White, had stopped proceedings as he wanted to redraw the agreement, made 'without vicarial authority', and specifically he required a 'vicar's fee' for an 'alien burial'. He declared that permission would be granted only if Philip agreed 'to expend twenty guineas on the repairs, ornamentation, or lighting of the Abbey in the time of afternoon service' and to agree to ten guineas 'vicar's fee' at the time of burial.[3]

At the time he received this communication, Philip was perhaps so relieved at his survival that it caused him no more than a slight irritation, for he immediately paid the £21 to Messrs Butt and Bannister, the church wardens, and said he would also wish to ornament the church. Perhaps he felt that the new vicar had not fully appreciated what an important figure this 'alien' was. After discussions with the vicar and the wardens he commissioned a gothic fireplace and chimney piece for the vestry. The vicar liked the design[4] and it was executed and installed by Gardener, a Tewksbury mason, at the remarkably low cost of £12.7s.4d.[5]

Meanwhile, Godsal's nephew, Edward Brown, wrote to say that Tewkesbury had been innundated in one of the periodic floods, but that he had examined the proposed vault area and it remained perfectly dry.[6]

By the end of April 1819 the vault itself had been built, also by Gardener, the mason. This cost a total of £74.11s.0d., and it was no doubt a job requiring great care, for Tewksbury Abbey has some of the finest medieval tombs in England, and the Godsal vault was sited near the magnificent Warwick Chantry, immediately next to the vaults of the Duke of Clarence and of Sir Guy de Brouhin, Standard bearer to the Black Prince at the Battle of Crècy. The Godsal Vault stone measures nine feet by seven and is the largest stone on the floor of the Abbey. There can be no doubt that Philip Godsal was making a statement about his own wealth, achievements and social position. Happily, of course the vault was to remain unoccupied for a further seven years.

After the operation in December 1818 Godsal, as we have noted, remained in apparently good health, save only for the abscess, which gave him pain periodically, and the fall from the phaeton which was a short lived inconvenience. He was able to resume a full social life, to travel regularly and to supervise his garden. On 5 January 1826 however he noted in his Diary 'very ill – bile'. This continued for almost two weeks but then cleared up. There is no further mention of illness but the final entry in his Diary is dated 13 March when he noted 'Mr PLG came'. It appears likely that Philip had by now taken to his bed for the last time, for on the 26 March a special delivery was made from London by Dawes's Fly Waggon of a 'Night Covenience in excellent mahogany with patent casters and large enamelware pan'.[7]

Philip died on 12 April 1826 at the age of seventy-eight years and five months. The cause of death is not known, probably it was recorded as 'old age', which then sufficed on a Death Certificate.

It is curious, astonishing even, that neither his father's death nor the funeral is mentioned in the Diary of his son Philip Lake Godsal.[8] He records only travelling to and from London and Montpelier Place twice between 13 March and 8 April and he was at Montpelier Place when his father died. The only entries for that day however read

| 12 April | Paid for paper & wax | 4s 2d |
| | Paid for Visiting Cards | 1s 6d |

The funeral was certainly a spectacular affair as is evident in the four page bill from the undertaker Thomas Jones amounting to the enormous sum of £207.7s.1d.[9] It seems that Philip had made the arrangements with the same care as he had arranged for the creation of the vault.

His body, dressed in superfine flannel robe and cap, was laid upon a mattress and pillow of flock in an inside coffin lined with flannel. This was placed in a 'very stout' lead coffin, which, in its turn, was placed inside a 'very stout oak coffin with brass handles and a burnished brass breast plate elegantly engraved covered with a richly ornamented black Saxony cloth'.

The procession from Montpelier Place for the half mile journey to the Parish Church of St Mary's Cheltenham, stetched back for much of that distance. It was lead by the featherman with black ostrich plumes followed by two assistants. Eight underbearers followed with truncheons tipped with brass. The hearse followed, drawn by four black horses with 'the richest ostrich feathers & velvets', followed by two mutes bearing poles draped with black ribbons. They were followed by trestles, covered in black silk, borne by eight pages and bearing the wreathes.

Next came the chief mourners' chariot, containing Ann Godsal and Philip Lake and Grace Anne. This too was

drawn by four black horses with ostrich feathers and velvets. Three family coaches followed, the horses again with black ostrich plumes, and then came the private coaches, for six of which the undertaker provided the coachman and the footman, who lead the horses.

These six coaches contained Philip's old friends, Mr Bromfield, Mr Nettleship, Mr Roebuck, Captain Ricketts, Colonel Ollney and Mr Seager, the surgeon. All these gentlemen were given 'best French kid gloves' costing £2.11s.6d per pair and other gentlemen known to have attended, including Doctors Newell and Boisragon, also received these expensive mementoes as did the four officiating clergymen. The undertaker's men were given black gloves costing only two shillingss but the undertaker and his assistant, the underbearers, the mutes and the vault maker all had hatbands of black 'Gros de Naple', an improbable two-and-a-quarter yards in length which were wound around the hat and then served as a scarf. Philip's three female servants, Mary Chapman, Sarah Davis and the young maid were given black silk gloves.

The funeral service was conducted in St Mary's by the up and coming new rector, the Reverend Francis Close, two books of whose sermons Philip had bought in his last years. At its conclusion the procession re-assembled for the nine mile journey to the great Abbey at Tewkesbury for the internment. For this journey the undertaker, the underbearers and the footmen rode saddle horses and the pages and mutes were taken by mule carts.

On their arrival at Tewkesbury the muffled bells tolled and the Reverend Mr Charles White and the church wardens met the coffin at the church door where it was placed on a bier and conducted to the vault, already opened to receive it. Prayers were said and the coffin was placed in the vault which was then sealed by Mr Gardener, the mason.

The Reverend Mr White received from the undertaker the 'vicar's fee for an alien burial' of ten guineas on which he had insisted when the arrangements for the vault had been made. The church wardens, perhaps mindful of their embarrasment of being over-ruled in their initial agreement at that time, advised the undertaker that they would relinquish their fees and they were credited on the undertaker's account to Mr P.L. Godsal as executor.[10]

The vault stone read simply

In a vault beneath this stone
are deposited the remains of PHILIP GODSAL, Esq
who died at Cheltenham on 12th April 1826
in the 79th year of his age

Glossary

'Carriages'

This is the generic term for the variety of individual styles and models of vehicles. The term 'carriage' is also used to mean the framing which supports the body of the vehicle The styles of carriages which Philip Godsal manufactured are listed below:

Cabriolet A two-wheel owner driven one horse two Seater carriage of weighty construction with a retractable hood and having a rear platform for an attendant.

Chaise An alternative usage of **gig**, a two-wheel uncovered and owner driven one horse carriage quite distinct from post-chaise (q v).

Chariot Stylish four-wheel carriage, driven by coachman and pair, and attended by footman; covered 'half-body' (i.e. the front part of the body of a coach being cut-away in the chariot). One forward facing bench seat. Could be converted to travelling post chaise by removal of coachman seat and footman's platform.

Coach The largest and usually grandest of four-wheel carriages for private travel, driven by coachman with pair, four, or even six horses. Covered body with central door and two facing seats. Footmans platform. For travelling out of town, the footman's platform could carry a trunk or could be replaced by rumble seat for servants.

Curricle Similar to **chaise** and **gig** but drawn by pair of horses.

Fly Philip Godsal designed and built an unusual 'Military Fly' to carry the infantry troops of a cavalry regiment.

Gig *See* **chaise**

Landau Grand four-wheel coach style with facing bench seats but with retractable hoods. Driven by coachman and pair or four, and attended by footman.

Landaulet A smaller version of landau, with only one forward facing passenger seat and hood. The landau is to the landaulet as the coach is to the chariot.

Phaeton Four-wheeled owner driven stylish carriage with pair of horses; body with open top and retractable hood. There were both high and low wheel versions.

Post Chaise Not driven by coachman but by horses ridden by post-boys or postillions, hired for individual stages. Usually of chariot shape, one bench seat facing forward only. Usually employed for out of town travel when it would carry imperials, budgets etc.

Sociable A phaeton with a double or occasionally triple body. Open top with retractable hood to rear and umbrella pole at front. Principal uses were as pleasure carriages for very local travel for family etcc or to convey servants on longer journeys. Driver in carriage sitting back to back with one of the two other bench seats.

Vis-à-vis Literally 'face to face', a small fashionable lightweight version of the **coach** for short town journeys.

Whiskey, or **tim-whiskey** One horse two-wheel gigs of the lightest construction, employed in parks and very local journeys, often driven by ladies.

Parts and Accessories

Body loops Iron loops secured to bottom corners of the body of the carriage by means of which it hangs.

Boodge Parcel receptacle in form of protruberance to rear of body accessible from inside.

Boot Leather travelling case

Box The coachman's seat [box seat or coach box].

Braces The leather straps by which the body is secured.

Budget Leather travelling case.

Canterbury boot Large receptacle carried below the coachman's seat.

Crane [neck] A style of design for the central longitudinal support in the undercarriage whose front part [less frequently also rear] bent upwards to allow larger turning circle for wheels.

Drag chain Carried below the carriage and employed by footman to anchor or slow the carriage on hills.

Futchells The timbers of the under-carriage to which the pole is fixed.

Hammer cloth The covering on the box or coachman's seat – often highly decorative.

Head plates Decorative items on upper body of coach or chariot.

Holders Tassels of lace or webbing fixed to outside rear for footman to hold.

Imperial Leather travelling case carried on roof of carriage.

Lanthorn Lantern.

Perch Form of [usually] straight central longitudinal support in the undercarriage – cf crane.

Platform The footman's stand at rear of coach; it carried budgets, trunks etc when travelling out of town or supported a rumble seat to convey servants.

Pole Horizontal pole from carriage to which horses are secured.

Splinter board The fore-bar to which the horses are harnessed to the pole.

Standard Decorative vertical item on footman's platform.

Sword case Similar to boodge, slightly smaller.

Tub-bottom Roundish shape to body base.

Wainscot Provides additional storage capacity under the seats inside carriage.

Well Deeper body providing additional space for luggage.

Appendices

1. Apprentices of Thomas Godsal, Susannah Godsal (née Lake) and Philip Godsal

Thomas Godsal

19 Nov 1747 – 20 Nov 1754	Mitchace Smith
9 Aug 1750 – 10 Aug 1757	Edward Roberts
26 Oct 1752 – 27 Oct 1759	John Dowsbory
17 Oct 1754 – 10 Oct 1764	Thomas Brandroth
6 Feb 1762 – 22 Oct 1769	Joseph Iles

Susannah Godsal (widow)

31 May 1764 – 1 Jun 1771	Henry Bell

Philip Godsal

12 Jan 1770 – 13 Jan 1777	Joseph White
25 Aug 1772 – 26 Aug 1779	Richard Hooper
17 Jun 1773 – 18 Jun 1780	Henry Hamnett
28 Nov 1774 – 29 Oct 1781	John Wilson
26 Oct 1775 – 29 Oct 1782	James Furnell
24 Apr 1777 – 25 Apr 1784	Richard Hatch
24 Oct 1782 – 25 Oct 1789	James Sidaway
1 Apr 1784 – 2 Apr 1791	Samuel Chase
27 Sep 1784 – 28 Sep 1791	James Wulbier
27 Mar 1806 – 26 Mar 1813	Philip Burgess

2. Coachmakers in Long Acre in 1791 listed in the *Universal British Directory*

No 6	John Molineux
No 8	Thomas Bromfield
No 13	John Brookes
No 16	Thomas Cox
No 23	Francis Stubbs
No 29	John Felton
	William Fenton
No 48	William Wright
No 58	Hankins & Hartley
No 61	West & Savours
No 80	Everett & Sutton
	John Randall
No 90	Marley & Barry
No 98	Houlditch & Benwell
	William Reeves
No 99	Owen O'Keefe
No 101	Lukin & Allen [successor to John Wright]
No 103	Philip Godsal
N0 120	Marriot & Markham
No 121	John Hatchett & Co
No 127	Thomas Nevitt

In addition to these twenty-one there are a further eighty London Coachmakers listed in the 1791 Directory.

3. List of Philip Godsal's residential properties

Prior to 1788 not known

1788 – 1793	84 Piccadilly
1793 – 1804	Grove House, Hampstead (Country House)
1793 – 1802	81 Piccadilly (Town House)
1803 – 1805	1 Clarges Street (Town House)
1805 – 1814	243 Oxford Street
1814 - 1826	2 Montpelier Place, Cheltenham

Godsal also owned or leased other residential properties but did not live there.

39 Gower Street was in his possession by 1788 and was given to daughter Susannah on her marriage to Nathaniel Saxon in 1802.

[?] Gower Street 'east side' was bought in 1786 and sold in 1788.

68 South Audley Street appears to have been inherited by PG and formed part of his marriage settlement to Anne Webb – it was rented out
Home Chapel Court, South Audley Street *ditto as with No 68 South Audley Street.*

Southgate House, Enfield Chase was bought in/or before 1791; Godsal acquired additional land by enclosure in 1801 and sold the property in 1802.

Ambrose's House, Hampstead was bought in 1793. Godsal pulled down the house and absorbed the land into Grove House.

Dingwall's House, Hampstead bought in 1795, sold the house the same year and aborbed part of land into Grove House.

40 Bedford Street, Covent Garden was leased from 1794 and rented out.

Albany, Piccadilly bought 'sett' on upper storey from original developer in 1803 and sold in 1809.

244 Oxford Street was leased from 1811 – 1819 and rented out throughout that period.

1 Addiscomb Place, Winchcomb Street, Cheltenham bought in 1809 and sold in 1811. It was leased back by Ann Godsal after Philip's death in 1826.

PG also owned a number of artisans' houses on and around his premises in Long Acre,

Cross Street, Castle Street etc. These are discussed in Chapter 9.

4. List of British customers of Philip Godsal

* = member of House of Commons/Lords

Angell, B.J.A.
Athynn, Mrs
*Audley, Hon George Touchet, Lord Audley
*Ailesbury, Thomas Bruce, Lord Ailesbury
*Bagot, Hon Charles (tenant)
Bayard, Colonel
*Beckford, William
*Bentincke, Hon Edward Charles
Birch, G
*Blandford, George Spencer, Marquess of Blandford, later 5th Duke of Marlborough
Bonaparte, Madame (French)
*Boyd, Sir John
Bradshaw, John
Brent, Robert
*Brooke, Thomas L.
Brydges, Reverend Mr Egerton
Brydges, Mrs Caroline
Buckley, William
Burgess, William (artist)
Burton, Sir Robert
Capel, Hon John Henry
*Cecil, Hon Henry, later 10th Earl of Exeter
Chamberlayne, Staines
Chase, H.A. of Barbados
Chatham, John, 2nd Earl of Chatham
Charlton, Colonel Lechmere
Chichester, 1st Earl, see Pelham
Chippendale, James
Clapton, Boothby
Coersmaker, Colonel George K.H. of Grenadier Guards
*Cooper, Sir Grey
Cooper, Mr (tenant)
*Courtenay, Viscount William, later Earl of Devon
Crane, J
*Cumberland, Duke of
Dalling, Sir John, Bart

*Delaval, John, Lord Delaval
*Dickinson, William
Dudley, Reverend Mr Henry Bate
Dymoke, Reverend Mr ('Champion')
*Eden, Sir John
*Edwards, Gerard Noel
*Elgin, Thomas Bruce, 7th Earl of Elgin
*Eliot, Edward St Germaine
*Elliot, Rt Hon H. Hugh
Exeter, Earl of see Cecil
Foster, Henry
*Garthshore, William
Glenville, Francis
Glyn, Sir George, Bart
*Greville, Hon Charles
Gould, Colonel Thoroton
*Hales, Sir John
Hamilton, Colonel J.
Harrison, James
Henderson, F
Hoare, Sir William
*Howard, Hon Bernard, later 12th Duke of Norfolk
*Jackson, Richard
*Jeffereyes, Nathaniel (tenant)
*Kemp, Thomas Read (tenant)
Knight, Mr
Lambert, William
Lister Kaye, John
Liston, Robert of Philadelphia
Lumley, Hon Frederick
Macdonnels, Colonel
Macleod, Colonel
Malden, Hon George Capel Coningsby, Viscount Malden, later 25th Earl of Essex
*Manners, Sir John
*Manners, Sir William
Marlborough, 5th Duke of see Blandford
*Melbourne, Penistone Lamb, Viscount Melbourne
Meares, Captain
*Milbanke, Sir Ralph, 5th Baronet
*Milbanke, Sir Ralph, 6th Baronet
Miller, William, publisher
Montelieu, Thomas
Nikel, John
Nutt, John
*Ossulton, Charles Augustus, later 5th Earl of Tankerville
*Oliver, Richard
Page, Richard
Parker, Thomas John
*Pelham, Thomas, later 1st Earl of Chichester
*Pennyman, Sir James, Baronet
*Perth, James Drummond, 7th Earl of Perth
Petrie, Borie
Phayre, Lieutenant Colonel Robert
Piere, Sir J.B.
Pitt, John see Chatham

*Pitt, William
Raikes, Thomas
Rawstorne, General of Madras
Robeck or Roebeck, Baron (tenant)
St George, Richard
*St John, Andrew, Lord St John of Bletsoe
Scott, Joseph
*Semphill, Hugh, Lord Semphill
Smythe Owen, C.
Somervile, Sir Marcus
Stevenson, Captain
Stewart, Lady Euphemia, sister of the Earl of Galloway (tenant)
*Strathmore, John Bowes, Lord Strathmore
*Stuart, Hon Frederick, bother of Marquess of Bute
Tankerville, Countess of, wife of 4th Earl of Tankerville
*Tarleton, Colonel Banastre
Tate, George
*Tatton, William
Taylor, General
Thomlinson, Mrs
Tickell, Richard
Tinker
*Trevanion, John
Treves, Mrs
Trotter, James
Trotter, John
Tyrwhitt, Thomas
Urmston, Captain James
*Watson, James
Wood, Colonel
Woodford, Colonel
Woodhouse, Francis
Wynch, Captain Charles
*Wyndham, Hon William
Wedderburn, Sir John
*Warwick, George Greville, Earl of Warwick

Includes a total of forty-seven members of the two Houses of the British Parliament.

5. Irish Customers of Philip Godsal

* = members of Irish Parliament (dissolved 1800) and/or British Parliament

Aldborough, 4th Earl see Stratford
Armstrong, Reverend Mr William
*Barry, J. Maxwell, later 5th Lord Farnham & Earl Mountmorris
*Butler, Sir Richard, 7th Baronet
Bruce, General Evan
*Caher, Richard Butler, Lord Caher, later Earl of Glengall
*Carbery, George Evans, 4th Baron
*Caulfeild, James, later Baron Kilmaine
*Cavendish, A.Bradshaw
Clare, Anne, Countess of Clare

Clare, 1st Earl of, John Fitzgibbon
*Concannon, Lord
Congreve, John
Craig, Captain Milikin
*Cremorne, Richard Thomas, 2nd Lord Cremorne
*Dillon, Henry Augustus, Viscount Dillon
*Donegal, 5th Earl of
*Dungannon, Arthur Hill-Treves, 5th Viscount Dungannon
Dwyer, John, private secretary to Fitzgibbon/Clare
Farnham, see Barry
*Foster, Rt Hon Sir John, later 1st Baron Oriel
Gawlor, John Bellenden
Glengall, see Caher
*Gort, Charles Vereker, Viscount Gort
Gould, Valentine
Heath
Inchiquin, Earl of, later also Marquis of Thormond
Jeffereyes, Arabella, sister of Fitzgibbon/Clare
Jeffereyes, George C., son of Arabella
*Kilmaine, James Caulfeild, 3rd Baron Kilmaine
*Kingston, George, Earl of Kingston
Kingston, Peter
*Lismore, Cornelius O'Callaghan, 1st Viscount Lismore
Lisburne, Lord see Vaughan
*Leslie, Sir Edward, Baronet
*Lucan, Richard Bingham, Earl of Lucan
*Massereene, Clothworthy Lumley Skeffington, 2nd Earl Massareene
Matthews, Hon Colonel
*Moore, Henry, Lord Moore
Mountmorris,Earl, see Barry
Mountnorris, Earl, see Valentia
*O'Brien, Sir Edward, 4th Baronet
Smith, Charles of Castle Park, Limerick
Smith Barry, James, younger son of 4th Earl Barrymore
*Stratford, Hon John, later 4th Earl Aldborough
Thormond, Marquis of see Inchiquin
*Tyrconnel, George Carpenter, Earl Tyrconnel
*Valentia, George Annesley,Viscount Valentia, later Earl Mountnorris
*Westmeath, George Frederick, Earl of Westmeath
*Vaughan, Hon John, later 3rd Earl of Lisburne
Whalley, Thomas ('Buck' or 'Jerusalem'), brother-in-law of Fitzgibbon/Clare and of Cremorne
Whyte, Francis, Red Hills, County Cavan

Includes a total of twenty-six Irish members of either Irish or British House of Parliament

6. Caroline Walkey

From 1823 until the time of his death in 1826 Philip Godsal was paying for the education of a young woman, Caroline Walkey. In 1823 Godsal began to pay £50 per year (rising to £60 in 1825) to a Mrs Martin of Chaple House, Twickenham for the education of the girl (extras in 1823 included £40 for Dancing and 6s for the extraction of two teeth). The girl was given sixpence a week for herself.

No evidence has been traced as to who she was and why Godsal chose to pay for her education. She does not appear to have been his ward and there is no mention of her in his will. Early on Godsal writes to say he is dealing with the matter 'in the absense of my son' which suggests that Philip Lake was involved, but in subsequent correspondence until the time of his death Philip makes no other mention of his son in this matter. Later it is clear that Philip Lake had been the girl's guardian.

Something is known of the girl's later career* and Philip Lake was certainly involved, to his evident irritation. On completing her education Caroline became a companion to 'dear Mrs Crapper' in West Brixton at a salary of twelve guineas per annum. She also received £50 per annum as settlement from Philip Lake.

In May 1832 she secured a more congenial position as nursery governess to a clergyman's family who moved to Bath shortly afterwards. Caroline Walkey immediately formed an attachment to a clergyman and she wrote to Philip Lake saying that the 'amiable clergyman' had asked about her history (which she herself evidently does not know the early detail) and was also asking why her money which her guardian managed had not been given to her on her majority. Philip Lake wrote an angry letter berating the impudent clergyman and by November 1832 Caroline wrote back 'The idea I had formed of marrying is quite at an end; indeed my friends here, having enquired the real character of the clergyman they really found an alliance with him would by no means add to my happiness or respectability. I have no further thought of him.'

Within six months Caroline was engaged to one William Humble, a chemist and druggist from Abergaveny. When she married in August 1833 Philip Lake paid her £1,000 as a marriage settlement. In November she wrote and asked Philip Lake for the interest payable on her money. Philip Lake wrote another angry letter pointing out that she was now married, had received her trust money and should not apply to him again.

There this intriguing matter rests until further information is discovered.

* Flintshire D/IP/246

7. Plays, operas, pantomimes and musical entertainments seen by Philip Godsal

Shakespeare
'Hamlet' with Master Betty
'Macbeth' with John Kemble & Sarah Siddons
'Macbeth' with George Cooke & Mrs Litchfield
'Othello' with George Cooke & Alexander Pope
'King John' with John Kemble
'King Lear' with John Kemble & Sarah Siddons
'Coriolanus' with John Kemble & Sarah Siddons
'A Winter's Tale' with John Kemble & Sarah Siddons
'The Merry Wives of Windsor' with George Cooke & John Kemble
'Antony and Cleopatra'
'As You Like It' with John Kemble & Mrs Jordan
'As You Like It' with John Kemble & Miss Biggs
'Richard III with John Kemble, Sarah Siddons & Charles Kemble
'Richard III' with Edmund Kean
'Measure for Measure' with Sarah Siddons

J.T. Allingham
''Tis all a farce'

Anon
The Ghost, or Dead Man alive', a farce
'The Rendezvous', an interlude

Margravine of Ansbach
'The Princess of Georgia' an operatical romance

Thomas Arne/Metastasio
'Artaxerxes', an opera

Henry Bate
'The Woodman' a comic opera

Bianchi
'Alzira' a Grand Serious opera

Isaac Bickerstaff
'The Spoil'd Child', a farce
'The Absent Man' a farce

J.Byrne
'Leander and Leonore'

James Cobb
'Paul and Virginia', a farce
'The Seige of Belgrade', an opera
'The Haunted Tower' music by Stephen Storace, an opera

Charles Coffey
'The Devil to pay, or the Wives metamorphosed', a ballad opera

George Colman, Junior
'The Poor Gentleman'
'Love laughs at locksmiths'
'Bluebeard, or Female curiosity satisfied', a melodrama

William Congreve
'The Mourning Bride', a tragedy

John Cartwright Cross
'Joan of Arc', a ballet-pantomime
'The Purse, or Benevolent Tar', a musical entertainment

Richard Cumberland
'The West Indian', a comedy
'Joanna', a melodrama
'The Jew', a comedy
'The Mysterious Husband', a tragedy

Carlo Antonio Delpini
'Don Juan', a pantomime

T.J. Dibdin
'The Hermione, or Valour's Triumph' music by Attwood, a musical interlude
'Harlequin's Tour, or the Dominion of Fancy', a pantomime
'Harlequin's Almanack', a pantomime
'Harlequin's Habeas'
'The Cabinet'
'The School for Prejudice, or Liberal Opinion', a comedy
'The Jew and the Doctor', a farce
'St David's Day' a musical piece
'The English Fleet in 1342' music by John Braham
'The Volcano, or the Rival Harlequins', a pantomime

John Fawcett
'Perouse'

David Garrick
'Isabella' (after Southern)
'Katherine and Petruchio'

John Gay
'The Beggar's Opera'

W.H. Hamilton, after Greffulhe
'The Portrait of Cervantes'

Prince Hoare
'My Grandmother' music by Stephen Storace, a farce
'Lock and Key' music by Shield, a farce
'No Song, no Supper' music by Shield, a farce
'Chains of the Heart, or the Slave by Choice'

Joseph Holman
'The Votary of Wealth', a comedy

John Home
'Douglas', a tragedy

Thomas Hurlsh
'The British Recruit or Who's Afraid'

Elizabeth Inchbald
'The Wedding Day', a farce

Robert Jephson
'The Count of Narbonne'

Ben Jonson
'Every Man in his Humour', a comedy

Michael Kelly (music)
'Bluebeard'

John Kemble
'Lodoiska'

Nathaniel Lee
'Alexander the Great or the Rival Queen'

Sarah Lee
'The Chapter of Accidents'

T.A. Lloyd
'The Romp', a farce

Charles Macklin
'Love a-la-mode', a farce
'Man of the World', a comedy

Leonard MacNalby
'Robin Hood', a comic opera

Philip Massinger/Middleton
'A New Way to pay old Debts', a comedy

Hannah More
'Percy'

Edward Morris
'The Secret', a comedy

Thomas Morton
'A Cure for the Heartache', a comedy
'The Children in the Wood', a dramatic opera

Arthur Murphy
'The Grecian Daughter', a tragedy
'The Apprentice', a farce
'The Way to keep Him', a comedy with song
'The Citizen', a farce

Kane O'Hara after Henry Fielding
'Tom Thumb', a burletta

John O'Keefe
'Fontainbleu' a comic opera
'Sprigs of Laurel or The Rival Soldiers', a comic opera
'The Prisoner at Large', a farce
'The Lie of the Day'

Thomas Otway
'Venice Preserved', a tragedy

W.C. Oulton
'All in Good Humour', a comic interlude

William Pearce
'Merry Sherwood or Harlequin Forrester', a pantomime

Frederick Pilon
'The Deaf Lover', a farce

Mrs Plowden
'Virginia', an opera

Henry James Pye
'Adelaide', a tragedy

Frederick Reynolds
'The Caravan, or the Driver and his Dog', a historical drama
'Speculation', a comedy
'The Dramatist, or Stop him who can', a comedy
'Life'
'The Rage', a comedy

Nicholas Rowe
'Jane Shore', a tragedy

St John
'Mary Queen of Scots', a tragedy

Richard Brinsley Sheridan
'The School for Scandal', a comedy
'The Critic', a burlesque
'Pizarro' after Kotzebue, a tragedy
'The Duenna' music by Thomas Linley, a comic opera

Sheild/Mrs Brooke
'Rosina', a comic opera

W. Warrington
'Alfonso, King of Castille'

Edward Young
'The Revenge', a tragedy

Other performances seen by PG
– [authors not identified]

Aladdin, or the Wonderful Lamp	Baron Munchaussen
Harlequin's Amulet	The Doctor
An Irishman's Tour through London	John Bull
The Old Grey Mare	Social Harmony

References

Introduction **Philip Godsal, Coachmaker**

1. Flintshire County record office D/IP/1-451, passim & 769
2. Flintshire D/IP/177
3. I am grateful to Professor Bill Rubinstein of the University of Wales, Aberystwth for information and advice.
4. In *North and South*, written in 1854, Mrs Gaskell chose to illustrate the social snobbery of the daughter of a poor clergyman by portraying her as shocked that her mother should treat as social equals a local coachmaker. It was Godsal's evident wealth that secured him from this prejudice.
5. *See* Bibliography for details

Chapter One **Family and Friends**

1. Flintshire D/IP/350
2. However there is evidence in William Pyne's *Costumes of Gt Britain*, 1804 that the tradition of burning Guy Fawkes was well established at that date.
   Philip Godsal himself bought a watercolour by Thomas Stothard, R.A. with the title *The Fifth of November*.
3. P.G. obtained a copy of his Certificate of Baptism from the Curate of St Martin in the Fields on 22 Feb 1796 – Flintshire D/IP/354
4. Flintshire D/IP/221
5. Tewkesbury Library database
6. Details of the history and genealogy of the Webb family are given in a private paper by Mr John Bill.
7. Flintshire D/IP/350
8. This practice has continued to the present day through nine generations.
9. Flintshire D/IP/243
10. *ibid* D/IP/222
11. *ibid* D/IP/350
12. *ibid* D/IP/269 22 Feb & 22 Apr 1799 Berkshire County Record Office has details of the Lake family burials in the parish Church of All Saints, Wokingham – WO/D1/3/5, WO/D1/3/17/4 & WO/D1/3/17/5.
    Although the vault stone of Susannah Godsal can be seen in All Saints there is no sign or record of the Westmacott Memorial.
13. Flintshire D/IP/350 and Tewkesbury Library database. For Anne Webb's death see D/IP/269 1795
14. The vault stone can be seen in Tewkesbury Abbey
15. Bill, Webb Genealogy
16. Flintshire D/IP/269
17. *ibid* D/IP/269
18. *ibid* D/IP/269 1 Oct 1803
19. *ibid* D/IP/269
20. *ibid* D/IP/235 letter of 16 Apr 1816
21. *ibid* D/IP/226
22. *ibid* D/IP/375 letter of 8 Sep 1807
23. *ibid* D/IP/269 31 May 1805
24. *ibid* D/IP/269 21 May 1789
25. *ibid* D/IP/350 11 Aug 1791
26. *ibid* D/IP/269 *passim*
27. See Chapter 11, 101-2 & *passim*
28. See Chapters 11, 104-5 & *passim*
29. See Chapters 10, 91-5; chapter 11, 103-4 & *passim*
30. FlintshireD/IP/212 letter of 21 Aug 1813; see also D/IP/350 22 Nov 1791
31. Flintshire D/IP/269 31 Jan 1804
32. *ibid* D/IP/269 18 & 26 Jun 1806
33. *ibid* D/IP/269 12 Jul 1806
34. *ibid* D/IP/269 30 Apr 1802
35. *ibid* D/IP/269 21 Jun 1804
36. Flintshire D/IP/286
37. *ibid* D/IP/269 12 Jun 1806
38. *ibid* D/IP/269 1 Mar 1826
39. *ibid* D/IP/372 & *see* Chapter 21, 179
40. *ibid* D/IP/269 29 Nov 1805
41. Whitley, Thomas Gainsborough 378
42. Flintshire D/IP/269 29 Nov 1805
43. *ibid* D/IP/269 27 Nov 1811
44. *ibid* D/IP/269 14 Feb 1804
45. *ibid* D/IP/269 25 Oct 1800
46. *ibid* D/IP/269 5 Sep 1802
47. *ibid* D/IP/269
48. *ibid* D/IP/235 letter of 31 Jul 1816
49. *D.N.B.*
50. Flintshire D/IP/269
51. See Chapter 27, 230
52. Gloucester County Record Office, D214 F1/117 dated 2 May 1791

Chapter Two **The Coachmaking Business**

1. *The Times* 6 September 1787
2. e.g. Ann Kavanaugh, *John Fitzgibbon, Earl of Clare: Protestant reaction & English authority in late eighteenth century Ireland*, 98 'Focusing on Fitzgibbon's carriages [Etc] may seem like a descent from serious history into the realm of antiquarian gossip'. As she herself is forced to recognise, Fitzgibbon's coach became a focus of the battle between Irish and English commercial interests and a symbol of the anglophile party in Irish government which drove through the Union between the two countries.

3. See various Street Directories including Lowndes, Andrew's, Kent's, Holden's & Universal British Directory & Appendix 2, 236
4. Rudolph Wackernagel, 'Carlton House Mews: the State Coach of the Prince of Wales & of the King of Hanover: a study of the late eighteenth century "mystery" of coachbuilding' in *Furniture History: the Journal of the Furniture History Society* vol xxxl, 1995 p 60 *& passim*
5. Flintshire D/IP/325
6. *ibid* D/IP/325
7. *ibid* D/IP/354
8. *ibid* D /IP/325
9. *ibid*
10. quoted in A.L. Humphries, 'Long Acre & the Coachbuilders' in *Notes & Queries*, 25 October 1941 228
11. W.B. Adams, *English Pleasure carriages*, 188
12. these descriptions are drawn from Adams, *ibid*, 176-184
13. see Chapter 4, 40
14. *Joseph Farington's Diary*, VI, 2113 & also Henry Angelo's Reminiscences,
15. *The Times* 19 January 1788
16. see Chapter 18,153
17. *Book of English Trades*, 1818, quoted in E.P. Thompson, *The Making of the English Working Class*, 1968, p 261
18. Dorothy M. George, *London Life in the Eighteenth Century* 166-7, 208-9
19. This detail is based on Adams, *ibid*, 68-83 & 176-184 *& passim*
20. Flintshire D/IP/269
21. *ibid* D/IP/365
22. *ibid*
23. I am grateful to Professor Bill Rubinstein of the University of Wales for pointing out this method of assessing relative wealth across historical periods. – see above 'Equivalent Currency Values'
24. Wackernagel, *ibid*, 53
25. Guildhall Library MS 21,438
26. *ibid* & Appendix 1, 235
27. Godsal's membership is recorded in the collection of the Royal Society of Arts
28. Flintshire D/IP/350
   An invoice to P.G. from his solicitors, dated 26 June 1798 includes 'Attending upon you respecting a treaty you had made with Messrs Hassace & Shorter for vending coach springs & for which they are soliciting a patent'
29. Flintshire D/IP/350 and also *see* D.N.B., 'Charles Varlo'
30. Wackernagel, *ibid* 57
31. Mr Barber of 16 Long Acre, *see The Times* 22 May 1795
32. Jenny Uglow, *The Lunar Men*, 131
33. D.N.B. 'Lionel Lukin' & Flintshire D/IP/269 1 Jun 1795
34. Flintshire D/IP/269 12 Jun 1795; also D/IP/350
35. *ibid,*
36. Farington, *ibid*, I, 114
37. Heal's Collection of trade cards, BM
38. quoted in Wackernagel, *ibid* 104 note 37
39. *The Times* 8 Feb 1787
40. *The Times* 18 Feb 1790
41. *The Times* 7 Jan 1790
42. Although P.G. displayed his arms, and indeed paid the tax for

so doing, the College of Arms cannot trace any entitlement to do so – letter of 7 Jun 1966 to Major P.H. Godsal. (private collection)

Chapter Three **Fashionable Carriages**

1. *See* Chapter 8, 75
2. *See* Chapters 6 & 7, 54-70 & Appendices 4 & 5, 238-42
3. Uglow, *ibid*
4. Flintshire D/IP/324, 21 Jun 1777
5. Delaval Papers NT/1251 1787
6. quoted in Wackernagel, *ibid* 60
7. *ibid* 61
8. *ibid* 61
9. *ibid* 52
10. *ibid* 61
11. *The Times*
12. Flintshire D/IP/269 5 Nov 1790
13. *ibid* D/IP/ 350 29 Sep 1790
14. *The Times* 30 September 1790
15. *ibid*
16. *The Globe* 28 Sep 1807
17. *The Times* 29 Mar 1788
18. *The Times* 24 Aug 1790
19. *ibid* 8 Mar 1790
20. *ibid* 16 Mar 1790
21. *ibid* 7 June 1790
22. Flintshire D/IP/269
23. Wackernagel, *ibid* 95
24. Flintshire D/IP/359
25. In collection of Bibliothèque Nationale, Paris, kindly drawn to my attention by Rudolf Wackernagel
26. This first appeared in some copies of Rudolph Ackermann's *Loyal Volunteers* 1798
27. See Chapters 9, 81;10, 89; & 16, 145
28. Wackernagel, 90
29. *ibid* 93
30. suggestion of Michael Snodin of V & A
31. Westminster Archives, Booth Papers, Accesion No 36, Class 39/1
32. L. Hawkins, *Memoirs*, ii, 24
33. Robert Bass, *The Green Dragoon* 192 *& passim*
34. *The Times* 30 September 1790
35. Hickey mentions Hatchett by name elsewhere and therefore knew him
36. *Memoirs of William Hickey*, ed Spencer v 2 333-5
37. *ibid* v 2 334-5
38. *ibid* v 2 333
39. *ibid* v 2 335
40. Flintshire D/IP/325
41. *ibid* D/IP/325 3 Sep 1818
42. *ibid* D/IP/325 9 Sep 1818
43. Hickey, *ibid* v 2 317 321
44. Flintshire D/IP/269 *passim*
45. *ibid*

Chapter Four **The Irish Lord Chancellor's Coach**

1. J.C. Huettner, 'Rudolf Ackermann' in *Zeitgenossen*, IV, 1,

1819.This memoir was written by a distinguished German scholar, resident in England, who had travelled with the Macartney expedition to the Emperor of China (Huettner travelled as tutor to young Staunton, son of Macartney's friend). Huettner was a friend of Ackermann and this memoir, the only one to be written in Ackermann's lifetime, was based on close and long term personal acquaintance. It was published in Leipzig and has not previously been translated or published in English.

2. Flintshire D/IP/350 20 Jul 1789
3. *Faulkner's Journal*, 13 Sep 1790
4. Sophie von la Roche, quoted in Humphries, *ibid* 18 Oct 1941
5. Quoted in W.G. Strickland, 'The State Coach of the Lord Mayor of the City of Dublin & the State Coach of the Earl of Clare, Lord Chancellor of Ireland', *Royal Society of Antiquaries of Ireland,* X 1919, 64-6
6. John Cornforth, 'Coaching forth a masterpiece', *Country Life*, January 1993
7. Anne Kavanaugh, *John Fitzgibbon, Earl of Clare: Protestant reaction & English authority in late eighteenth century Ireland*, Dublin 1998, 108
8. G.E.C., *The Complete Peerage*, III 255-6
9. They would certainly include John Hatchett and Wright & Lukin who, together with Philip Godsal, formed the triumvirate of coachmakers who were the most patronised in the fashionable world – Wackernagel, *ibid* 92 *& passim*
10. Kavanaugh, *ibid* 108
11. Strickland, *ibid* 52-3
12. Flintshire D/IP/269 25 Jan 1799
13. *ibid* D/IP/402
14. *ibid* D/IP/269 26 Jun 1790
15. Flintshire D/IP/269 6 Nov 1800. This appears surprisingly in the Diary ten years after the debt wasincurred. P.G. notes that he paid the publican £20 at the time leaving a balance of £31.10s.0d which he paid ten years late.
16. *The Times* 23 Jul 1790
17. *ibid* 24 Jul 1790
18. *Hibernian Magazine*, Aug 1790, quoted in Strickland, *ibid* 62
19. *The Times* 30 &31 Jul 1790 and 3 Aug 1790
20 *ibid* 30 Jul 1790
21. *ibid* 3 Aug 1790
22. Wackernagel, *ibid* 82
23. *The Dublin Chronicle* 16 Sep 1790, quoted in Strickland, *ibid* 62
24. Flintshire D/IP/269. P.G.'s Diary records that he arrived in Holyhead on 3 Sep and stayed at the Harris Hotel, Capel Street.
25. *ibid* P.G.notes that he dined on 17 Sep with Lord Fitzgibbon and on the following day with John Dwyer, Fitzgibbon's Private Secretary,
26. Fitzgibbon had arrived in Dublin from London on 15 September 1790
27. Quoted in Strickland, *ibid* 63
28. Another newspaper which supported the Government was *Freeman's Journal* which praised the Coach, 'Let Irishmen not grumble when a good example is brought to their doors for profit and improvement'. Quoted in Kavanaugh, *ibid* 109
29. Strickland, *ibid* 63-4
30. *ibid* 54
31. *ibid* 58-9

32. Jim Cooke, *Ireland's Premier Coachbuilder*, nd, 5 & illustrations.
The present author was a Director of Arthur Ackermann & Son Ltd of Bond Street when the Company bought three of these drawings in 1986.
33. W.P. [Wyatt Papworth], 'Rudolph Ackermann of the Strand, Publisher' in *Notes and Queries*, 4th Series, IV, 7 Aug 1869.
34. Strickland, *ibid* 67
35. *ibid*, 66
36 *ibid*, 67
37. *ibid*, 66
38. Letter from Major P.H. Godsal to Faustus Gallery, dated 1979 (in private collection)
39. Wackernagel, *ibid* 112. Lucy Wood believes these panels may not be related to the Fitzgibbon Coach.
40. *ibid*, 112
41. The Whitby Invoice is in Flintshire D/IP/66

Chapter Five **Capital and Creditors**

1. Westminster Archives, Booth Papers No 36, 39/3 31 Jul 1784
2. Flintshire D/IP/351
3. *ibid* D/IP/269 26 Jan 1788.
John Michie's Papers are held in the Westminster Archives
4. Keith Feiling, Warren Hastings 175
5. *Fort William – India House Correspondence* vol IX, 16, 114
6. *ibid*, vol IX , 18 114
7. quoted in Redgrave, A Dictionary of Artists of the English School, 1970 edition, 497
8. *Catalogue of Exhibition at Carlton House Gallery*, 1977 *See also* Fisher (ed), *The Travels of Dean Mohamed*
9. Sydney Grier (ed), *The Letters of Warren Hastings to his Wife* 279
10. *Fort William – India House Correspondence*, vol XV 338 George Forest (ed), Selections from the Letters etc in the Foreign department of the Government of India I, 1055
11. *Fort William – India House Correspondence* vol XV 475
12. *ibid*, vol XIII 48 398
13. Flintshire D/IP/17
14. *ibid* D/IP/269 10 Aug 1795
15. *ibid* 31 Mar 1801
16. *ibid* 5 May 1801
17. *ibid* 19 Feb 1805
18. *ibid* 3 Jan 1793
19. *ibid* 29 Sep 1795 & 4 Jun 1800
20. *ibid* 12 May 1801
21. *ibid* 5 Jan 1799
22. *ibid* 30 May 1814
23. *ibid*, passim
24. *ibid* 27 Mar 1799
25. *ibid*, passim
26. *ibid* 8 Jan 1802
27. *ibid* 21 Dec 1810 & 15 May 1813
28. *ibid* 23 Aug 1806
29. *ibid* 12 Jan 1809
30. *ibid* 9 Jul 1816
31. *ibid*
32. *ibid* Jul 1824
33. *The Times* 24 Oct 1824 & 3 Nov 1824

34. Flintshire D/IP/420
35. *ibid* D/IP/269 19 Feb 1825 & 27 Sep 1825
36. *ibid* 17 Dec 1825
37. *ibid* 20 Dec 1825
38. *ibid* 10 Jan 1826

Chapter Six **Customers and Debtors**

1. Westminster Archives, Booth Papers No 36, 39/1 26 July 1784
2. Humphries, *ibid*, 228
3. See Martin Daunton, 'London & the World' in *London: World City* 24-5. He notes also the rise of provincial banks from other businesses for which see also Uglow, *ibid* 352
4. D.N.B. & Holmes, *Coleridge: darker reflections*
5. Guildhall Library has two caricatures 'A Peep in the City' & 'The City Content'. Details of Eamer's Court Martial are in the Guildhall Collection A.8.3.no 60 and details of his trial for striking the waggoner are in Pam.6541.
6. Flintshire D/IP/361 & D/IP/406
7. *ibid* D/IP/269 21 Feb 1799 & 1 Aug 1812
8. Sir Evan Cotton, *East Indiamen, passim*. Cotton notes that 'Captain Urmston grew his own mustard and cress on a frame stretched with damp flannel' Urmston is also mentioned in the *Fort William Correspondence*, vol IX 169, 583, 599 and vol XIII 130 and in *Hickey, ibid* v 2 313, 322 & v 3 261
9. Flintshire D/IP/361 & D/IP/406
10. Thorne, *ibid* III 415
11. Wackernagel, *ibid* 60
12. *D.N.B.*
13. Flintshire D/IP/355
14. Thorne, *ibid*, V 332-6 and *see also* chapter 4
15. G.E.C., *ibid* XI 238-9; Namier & Brooke, *ibid* III 401; Thorne, *ibid* V 86-7
16. Malcolm Elwin, Lord Byron's Wife; Namier & Brooke, *ibid* III 137-8
17. Westminster Archive, Booth Papers, No 36 39/1
18. Elwin, *ibid* 301; Flintshire D/IP/269 18 Feb 1819
19. G.E.C., *ibid* X11 635; Thorne, *ibid* III 175-8 ;
20. Flintshire D/IP/269 5 Feb 1825
21. *Northumberland County History*, 181; *see also* Namier & Brooke, *ibid* II 311-2
22. *See* extracted Delaval Papers held in Flintshire County Record office, NT/1231
23. Francis Askham, *The Gay Delavals*
24. Flintshire D/IP/358 & D/IP/269 *passim*
25. Askham, *ibid* 188
26. Flintshire D/IP/269 4 & 22 Dec 1802
27. *ibid* D/IP/269 29 Apr 1806
28. *ibid* D/IP/269 26 Apr 1803
29. The case was heard on 16 December 1806
30. Flintshire D/IP/356
31. *ibid* D/IP/269 9 Jun 1800
32. *ibid* D/IP/269 1 Aug 1803
33. G.E.C., *ibid* IV 336
34. Flintshire D/IP/269 10 Oct 1790
35. *ibid* D/IP/359
36. *ibid* D/IP/269
37. *ibid* D/IP/269 12 Mar 1806

38. *ibid* D/IP/356
39. *ibid*

Chapter Seven **The Earl of Egremont**

Quotations are drawn from the Petworth House Archives
PHA 6611, 7530-1, 7534, 7536, 7543, 8079 & 8305

Chapter Eight **The Genealogy of Irish Debtors**

1. Flintshire D /IP/360 & 380
2. *ibid* D/IP/406
3. *ibid* D/IP/406 5 February 1799
4. *ibid* D/IP/380
5. In this section I have made extensive use of G.E.C.*The Complete Peerage*; Thorne, *The History of Parliament*, Kavanaugh, *John Fitzgibbon* & Malcolmson, *John Foster* to clarify the notes in Godsal's Diaries (D/IP/269)
6. Kavanaugh, *ibid* 204
7. *ibid* p 391
8. Flintshire D/IP/269 25 February 1804
9. *ibid* 31 October 1808
10. *ibid* 13 April 1814
11. Kavanaugh, *ibid* 204
12. Flintshire, D/IP/
13. Kavanaugh, *ibid* 204
14. Flintshire D/IP/269 22 June 1790
15. *ibid* 1 January 1800
16. *ibid*
17. G.E.C., *ibid* III 527-8
18. Flintshire D/IP/269 19 October 1821
19. Kavanaugh, *ibid* 209
20. *ibid*, 388
21. Flintshire D/IP/269 9 November 1800
22. *ibid* 18 April 1808
23. Kavanaugh, *ibid* 207, 389
24. Thorne, *ibid* III
25. Flintshire D/IP/269 20 Apr 1815 & 23 Aug 1815 – £1,000 with both Equitable & Pelican
26. *ibid*
27. *ibid* 4 August 1799
28. Kavanaugh, *ibid* 207
29. *ibid*
30. Flintshire D/IP/269 1 May 1799 P.G. records going to Cahir's house in Berkeley Sq & being promised £1,000
31. *ibid*
32. *ibid* D/IP/376
33. *ibid*
34. *ibid* D/IP/269 12 December 1812
35. *ibid*
36. *ibid* 9 April 1817
37. *ibid* 27 May 1819
38. Malcolmson, *John Foster, passim*
39. *ibid* 239
40. *ibid* 323
41. Flintshire D/IP/356
42. Thorne, *ibid* III 795-801
43. *ibid* 798
44. Flintshire D/IP/372

45. Thorne, *ibid* III 147-8
46. Flintshire D/IP/269 8 June 1810
47. Thorne, *ibid* V
48. Flintshire D/IP/370 20 Jun 1796
49. Thorne, *ibid* III 71
50. Flintshire
51. Flintshire D/IP/269
52. *Voyages & Travels in India, Ceylon &c in 1802-6*, 1809
53. Thorne, *ibid* III 72
54. Flintshire D/IP/269 4 January 1815
55. *ibid*, Executors' papers D/IP/227
56. All are given biographical entries in the History of Parliament
57. Flintshire D/IP/269 1789 & 1790

Chapter Nine **Landlord and Tenant**

1. Flintshire D/IP/350
2. *ibid* D/IP/350
3. *ibid* D/IP/354 No 3
4. *ibid* D/IP/350
5. *ibid*
6. *ibid* D/IP/269 16 Jul 1813.
7. *ibid* D/IP/18
8. *ibid* D/IP/354 No 2
9. *ibid* D/IP/269 20 Nov 1789
10. *ibid* D/IP/46
11. *ibid*
12. *ibid* D/IP/325
13. *ibid* D/IP/269 13 Aug 1804 – Assignment dated 27 Apr 1805; D/IP/22
14. *ibid*
15. *ibid* D/IP/269 19 Nov 1808
16. *ibid*
17. Westminster Archive, Booth Papers No 36 3640. P.G. took out a 21 year lease from Mr Guest in 1793 – ref D/IP/269 1 Jan 1794
18. Flintshire D/IP/269 20 Jan & 22 Jun 1801
19. *ibid* D/IP/269 8 Sep 1802
20. *ibid* 7 Jan 1793
21. *ibid* D/IP/350 8 Apr 1788
22. *The London Encyclopaedia* 9
23. Flintshire D/IP/269 22 Jun 1803
24. Ford & Ford, *Images of Brighton*
25. Flintshire D/IP/269 2 Mar 1809
26. *ibid* 17 May 1811
27 P.G. sent his request 'c/o The Duke of Wellington, Paris'
28. Flintshire D/IP/269 4 Feb & 1 Aug 1817
29. *ibid* D/IP/350
    Mrs Abington left the London stage and performed in Dublin for the next decade. When she returned to London in 1798/9 a biographical notice in *Public Characters* (vol 2 186) noted that, whereas earlier the audience believed in the reality of the play, now her face and figure were such that it was obvious that this was indeed a fiction.
30. Flintshire D/IP/17
31. *ibid* D/IP/269
32. Westminster Archives, Microfilm Reels 459 & 462
33. Thorne, *ibid* IV 294-6
34. Flintshire D/IP/269

35. *ibid*
36. Judy Egerton, *George Stubbs 1724-1806* 177
37. Flintshire D/IP/269
38. *ibid* 1817 *passim*
39. *ibid* D/IP/269. A notice of the death of Lady Euphemia Stewart at the age of 89 appears in the *Gentleman's Magazine* of 1818, vol ii 640
40. *See* Chapter 14
41. Thorne, *ibid* IV, 295; *see also* Flintshire D/IP/369
42. Flintshire D/IP/269 21 Jan 1811
42. P.G. bought several of his tenant's publications.
44. Weinreb & Hibbert, *The London Encyclopaedia* 895
45. Flintshire D/IP/269

Chapter Ten **The Hampstead Years**

1. Flintshire D/IP/269; *see also* manuscript pamplet by E.F. Oppé, *Ladywell Court, formerly Holford's House* in Camden Local Studies Library
2. Camden, Manorial Court Baron Records 30 74
3. *ibid*, Court Baron meeting of 7 June 1792
4. *see* Map
5. Flintshire D/IP/269 7 Jan 1793; the Court Baron met on 25 Feb 1793
6. Flintshire D/IP/269 20 Apr, 25 May, 15 Jun & 20 Oct 1795
7. Camden, Court Baron of 29 May 1797
8. *ibid*, Court Baron of 14 May 1804
9. Flintshire D/IP/269 14 Apr 1799
10. Quoted anonymously, but dated 1814 in Peter Thorold, *The London Rich* 161
11. Thorold, *ibid* 161
12. *ibid* 161
    He stood as Parliamentary Candidate for the County of Sussex in 1774 (Poll Record in collection of Henry Smith, Esq)
13. For Holford *see* Felicity McQueen, 'The Holfords of Hampstead' in *Camden Historical Review 6*
14. Camden Local Studies Catalogue card has pasted cutting from un-named newspaper of the sale details of Grove House in the year 1817
15. Farington, *ibid* III 1089; also S.C.M. 'The Barmicides' in *The Hampstead Annual 1798* 128 Also Farington, *ibid* III 1089
16. S.C.M, Hampstead Annual, *ibid* 130
17. E.E. Newton, 'Josiah Boydell and Loyal Hampstead Volunteers' in *Transactions of the Hampstead Antiquarian & Historical Society, 1899* 125; Thomas Barrett, Annals of Hampstead 42
18. *See* Chapters 10 & 16
19. *ibid*
20. Flintshire D/IP/269 21 Jul 1801
21. *ibid* 28 Jul 1801
22. Newton, *ibid* 126; Barrett, *ibid* 44
23. Newton, *ibid* 127
24. *See* Chapter 15
25. Flintshire D/IP/269 2 Nov 1801
26. *ibid* 18 Jun 1802
27. *ibid* 1 Jul 1802
28. Newton, *ibid* 127
29. Flintshire D/IP/269 18 Jun 1804

30. *ibid* 4 Jun 1804
31. Camden 30 74 Deed of Covenant between Philip Godsal and Thomas Cockburn 16 May 1805
32. M.D. George, *Catalogue of Political & Social Satire in B.M.*
33. *Hampstead Annual, ibid* 130
34. Newton, *ibid* 122
35. Flintshire D/IP/269 24 Jan 1805
36. *ibid* 27 Jan 1806
37. *ibid* D/IP/443
38. *ibid*
39. *ibid* D/IP/269 29 Jun 1807
40. *ibid* 9 Jul 1807
41. *ibid* 27 Jul 1808
42. *ibid* 11 May 1809
43. *ibid* 31 Jan 1810
44. *ibid* 13 Feb 1813
45. *ibid* 1 Mar & 20 Apr 1811
46. *ibid*

Chapter Eleven **Nelson's Attorney**

1. Reminiscences of Henry Angelo II 317
2. *See* Chapter five
3. The 'Fly' was pictured in an aquatint by and after Rowlandson and published by Ackermann on 16 May 1798 – *see* page 37
4. Birdcage Walk was knocked down when Trafalgar Square was built
5. A cornet is a 2nd lieutenant in a cavalry regiment. Haslewood's Commission has been preserved in the BL Add Mss 30999 f4. It reads in part 'George the Third, by the Grace of God, King of Great Britain, France [sic] and Ireland, Defender of the Faith &c to our Trusty and Wellbeloved William Haslewood, Gent, Greeting. We do by these Presents constitute and appoint you to be Cornet of that Troop, whereof…, Esq is Captain in the Corps of Light Horse Volunteers of the Cities of London & Westminster commanded by our Trusty and Wellbeloved Colonel Charles Herries, and to serve in the case of invasion or Actual Rebellion in the said Cities and their Environs within the distance of Ten miles only, but not to take rank in the Army except during the time the said Corps being called into Actual Service…
6. *See* Chapter sixteen
7. Flintshire D/IP/269 26 May 1799; *see also* Chapter twenty-one
8. BL Add Mss 34918 ff 233, 9 March 1801; Sir William Nicholas, *Dispatches & Letters of Lord Nelson*, VII, ccx, letter 24 November 1801. For an explanation of Prize Money see *Oxford Companion* to *Ships and the Sea.*
9. This was a later recollection sent to the editor of *Nelson's Letters*, and dated 13 April 1846
10. BL Eg Mss 2,240 f 99, f 106 in response to Haslewood's letter, in which he writes that he had received Nelson's instructions re Merton from Lady Hamilton (BL Add Mss 34918 ff 193)
11. *ibid*, letter dated 31 August 1801. The surveyor was the celebrated Samuel Pepys Cockerel, Surveyor to the East India Company and to St Paul's Cathederal and architect of his brother's fantasy house at Sezincote in Gloucestershire

12. National Maritime Museum Library, Mss 9960, Croker Collection, Phillips Papers
13. Flintshire, D/IP/375, letter of 6 Jan 1802
14. *ibid*, D/IP/269 16 Jan 1802 and *passim*
15. BL Add Mss 34918 ff 334, letter of 16 July 1802 – Nelson's will was signed on 10 May 1803
16. Nicholas, *ibid*, vii,cxcix
17. *See* Chapter eleven
18. Flintshire D/IP/375, letter dated 22 March 1803
19. *ibid*, August 1803
20. Nicholas, *ibid*, vol V 216
21. *ibid* 370, note
22. Flintshire D/IP/269 22 Jan 1804
23. *ibid*, 6 Feb 1804
24. *ibid*, 3 August 1804. In this month the Haslewoods were enjoying a holiday in Tenby, Pembrokeshire (*see* letter from Maria to P.G. dated 3 August 1804 (Flintshire D/IP/375)
25. Sir John Acton was Generalissimo of armies of the Kingdom of Naples. English born he had inherited the family estate of Aldenham Hall in Shropshire in 1791
26. Haslewood is referring grandiloquently to the family farm at Higley, Shropshire
27. The letter to Nelson is in BL Add Ms 34922 f 202
28. Flora Fraser, *Beloved Emma* 28. Nelson bequeathed Horatia £4,000.
29. Nicholas, *ibid*, VI , 441, letter of 16 May 1805 – *see also* Nicholas V, 197 for a previous codicil
30. BL Add Mss 34922 f202
31. BL Add Mss 34931 f dated 16 May 1805. Haslewood signed it 'from the humblest but not the least sincere of your Lordship's friends and well-wishers'.
32. Nicholas, *ibid*, V, 371 note. This was a recollection of Haslewood in 1846.
33. *The Order of Procession Etc Etc* is in Flintshire D/IP/441
34. Dorothy Stuart, *Dearest Bess: the life & times of Lady Elizabeth Foster*
35. Farington, *ibid* VII 2672
36. The altered invitation card is in the private collection of Philip Godsal, Esq
37. BL Add Mss 34992, letter dated 20 May 1806
38. *ibid*, 6 June 1806; *see also* in *Nelsons Letters to his wife* 610-13, six letters of Lady Nelson's attorney Mr Western regarding Haslewood's actions in the administration of the estate. Haslewood had also offended Lady Hamilton, 'I had a very canting letter from Haslewood' quoted in Fraser, *ibid*, 335
39. Flintshire D/IP/269 17 Jan 1808
40. *ibid* D/IP/375, letter dated 8 Sep 1807
41. *ibid* letter 30 Oct 1809
42. *ibid* letter dated 29 Apr 1810
43. *ibid* letter dated 28 Apr 1817
44. The proof sheets of Sir William Nicholas's 'Excursus' on the parentage of Horatia are preserved in BL Add Mss 41492 ff 56-70 with annotations by Haslewood who had provided Nicholas with much of his information. Nicholas records a conversation with Haslewood on 13 April 1846 in which Haslewood said that he did not believe Emma Hamilton to be the mother of Horatia and that she was living with Sir William at the time and could hardly have been *enceinte* without it being noticed. Haslewood said he could not tell

Nicholas 'the name of the mother because it would give great pain to her family but that she was a gentlewoman and the issue of a person of high rank, apparently a nobleman who had seduced the mother. Horatia's mother apparently married into an opulent family. Mr Haslewood spoke positively to these facts. He saw all that was going on when the letters were written by Lady Hamilton to the [?] niece. The mother was a friend of Lady Hamilton. Lord N. always spoke of Horatia as his adopted daughter and professed great affection but Lord N. said he was <u>not</u> the father & his [Haslewood's] only reason for doubting that she was Lord N's daughter was that he knew her mother was at Palermo, though she might havebeen...The mother is either Scots, English or Irish but certainly a <u>gentlewoman</u>.' In a letter which Haslewood gave to Nicholas on the day of their conversation he wrote
Kemp Town, Brighton 13 April 1846
Dear Sir
I was no less surprized than grieved when you told me of a prevailing opinion that Lord Nelson, of his own motion, withdrew from the society of his wife and took up residence altogether with Sir William and Lady Hamilton, and that you have never received from any member of his family any intimation to the contrary. His father, his brother, Dr Nelson (afterwards Earl Nelson), his sisters Mrs Bolton & Mrs Matchem, and their husbands well knew that the separation was unavoidable on Lord Nelson's part; and as I happened to be present when the unhappy rupture took place, I have often talked over with all of them, especially with Mr & Mrs Matchem the particulars which I proceed to relate in justice to the memory of my illustrious friend and in the hope of removing an erroneous impression from your mind.
In the winter of 1800/01 I was breakfasting with Lord and Lady Nelson at their lodgings in Arlington Street and a cheerful conversation was passing on indifferent subjects, when Lord Nelson spoke of something which had been done or said by 'my dear Lady Hamilton, upon which Lady Nelson rose from her chair and exclaimed with much vehemence, 'I am sick of hearing of my dear Lady Hamilton and am resolved you shall give up either her or me'. Lord Nelson, with perfect calmness, said, 'Take care, Fanny, what you say. I love you sincerely; but I cannot forget my obligations to Lady Hamilton and speak of her otherwise than with affection and admiration'. Without one soothing word or gesture, but muttering something about her mind being made up, Lady Nelson left the room and shortly drove from the house. They never lived together afterwards. I believe Lord Nelson took a formal leave of her Ladyship before joining the Fleet under Sir Hyde Parker; but that to the day of her husband's glorious death, she never made any apology for her abrupt and ungentle conduct or any overture towards a reconciliation. I am ,dear sir, your faithful servant,
W. Haslewood.
45. Chichester County Record Office Add Ms 37,545 lease dated 30 September 1823
46. Flintshire, D/IP/375 letter dated 12 January 1824
47. *ibid*, letter dated 17 January 1824
48. *ibid*, letters dated 9 & 10 July
49. *ibid*, letter dated 13 July
50. *ibid*, letter dated 15 July 1824
51. *ibid*, letter dated 15 July 1824
52. *ibid*, letter dated 16 July 1824

Chapter Twelve **Marriage Settlements**

1. Thorne, *ibid*, vol V, 101
2. Flintshire D/IP/365 10 May 1802
3. *ibid* D/IP/269 17 Sep 1802
4. *ibid*
5. *ibid* 17 Sep & 30 Nov 1802
6. *ibid* D/IP/269 18 Sep 1802
7. *ibid* 21 Sep 1802
8. *ibid* 4 Dec 1802
10. *ibid* 22 Dec 1802
11. *ibid* D/IP/269
12. *ibid*
13. Flintshire D/IP/365
14. *ibid* D/IP/269 7 Mar 1803
15. Flintshire D/IP/25 Feb & 7 Mar 1803
16. *ibid*, D/IP/269 8 Mar 1803
17. *ibid*
18. *ibid* 3 Mar 1803
19. *ibid* D/IP/365
20. *ibid* D/IP/177
21. *ibid*

Chapter Thirteen **The Making of a Gentleman**

1. Flintshire D/IP/269 6 Apr 1789
2. *ibid* D/IP/269 14 Dec 1790
3. *ibid*, 21May 1789
4. *ibid*, D/IP/350
5. *ibid*, D/IP/269 24 Oct 1792 & *passim*
6. *ibid*, 1 Mar 1796
7. *ibid*, 16 Jan 1799
8. *ibid*, 20 May 1799 & *passim* to 9 Apr 1801
9. *ibid*, 26 Jul- 8 Aug 1799
10. *ibid*, 23 Oct 1799, 25 Sep 1800 & *passim*
11. *ibid* 25 Jun 1800
12. *ibid* A good description of the Royal Institution at this early period is given in Holmes, *Coleridge: Darker Relections* 116-7 who also notes the curious fact that 'the popularity of the Institution's lectures so often jammed Albermarle Street that it eventually became the first one way street in London'
13. Flintshire D/IP/269
14. Hickey, *ibid* 140
15. Coleridge's first lecture there was in 1807
16 Flintshire D/IP/269 16-31 Jul 1800
17. *ibid* 31 Jan 1801
18. *ibid* 22 Aug 1801
19. *ibid*
20. *ibid* 24 Feb 1802
21. *ibid* D/IP/283
22. Hibbert, *The Encyclopaedia of Oxford* 293
23. Flintshire D/IP/269 13 Aug 1802
24. *ibid* 18 Sep 1802
25. *ibid* 21 Oct 1802
26. *ibid* 23 Oct 1802
27. *ibid* 3 Jan 1803

28. *ibid* 8 Mar 1803
29. *ibid* D/IP/234 [nd]
30. *ibid* 22 Jun 1803
31. *ibid* D/IP/269 17 Aug 1803
32. *ibid* 25 Aug 1802
33. *ibid* 17 Sep 1803
34. *ibid* D/IP/234 12 Jun 1804
35. *ibid* D/IP/269 26 Jul 1804
36. *ibid* 1 Oct 1804
37. *ibid* 6 Apr 1804
38. Flintshire D/IP/269 15 Jun 1805
39. *ibid* 13 Jun & 9 Jul 1805
40. *ibid* 5 Aug 1805
41. *ibid* D/IP/234 2 Jul 1805
42. Flintshire D/IP/269 24 Dec 1805
43. *ibid* D/IP/283
44. Uglow, *ibid* 138-52
45. Fox (ed), London: World City 254
46. Flintshire D/IP/283
47. *See* Thorne, *ibid*, vol V & G.E.C. *ibid* Vol XI
48. Flintshire D/IP/269 27 Jan 1807
49. *ibid* Jan 1807
50. *ibid* 11 & 12 Mar 1807
51. *ibid* 29 Jun 1807
52. *ibid* 28 Nov 1808

Chapter Fourteen **The Marquess of Blandford**

A recollection of the Marquess of Blandford by Captain Gronow, not quoted in the chapter, is of sufficient interest in relation to his dealings with Philip Godsal to be quoted here

> I remember in 1816 going down with him to Whiteknights, which was afterwards sold and is now pulled down. During our journey Lord Blandford opened a sort of cupboard which was fixed on one side of the coach in which we were travelling and which contained a capital luncheon with different kinds of wines and liqueurs. Another part of this roomy vehicle, on a spring being touched, displayed a sort of secretaire with writing materials and a large pocket book; the latter he opened and showed me fifty Bank of England notes for £1,000 each which he told me he had borrowed the day before from a well-known money lender in the City called Levy. He stated that he had given in return a post-obit on his father's death for £150,000 and added, 'You see, Gronow, how the immense fortune of my family will be frittered away: but I can't help it; I must live. My father inherited £500,000 in ready money and £70,000 a year in land; and in all probability, when it comes to my turn to live at Blenheim, I shall have nothing left but the annuity of £5,000 a year on the Post Office.' (Gronow, vol I 315-6)

Godsal's experiences with the Marquess suggest that this apparently far-fetched story was possibly true. If so, then it would be reasonable to speculate that the name of the coachmaker who made Blandford's unique coach was Philip Godsal himself.

1. Flintshire D/IP/403
2. Thorne, *ibid* vol V 236
3. Mary Soames, *The Profligate Duke* (1987) This biography does not mention Philip Godsal
4. Flintshire D/IP/403
5. Undated letter from Blandford's solicitor in University of Reading Archives
6. Flintshire D/IP/403
7. *ibid* D/IP/269
8. BL Add Mss 61677 ff 4-5 & Flintshire D/IP/379
9. Flintshire D/IP/269 & D/IP/403
10. Thorne, *ibid* v V 236; Soames, *ibid* 120
11. Blandford also spent the following totals on coaches with Philip Godsal – see Flintshire D/IP/403 1806=£973.17s.0d; 1807=£767.19s.10d;1808=£482.4s.0d; 1809=£805.8s.0d; 1810=£478.16s.6d
12. Flintshire D/IP/29 & D/IP/403
13. *ibid* D/IP/403
14. BL Add Mss 61677 ff 4-5
15. Boyd Alexander, *Life at Fonthill* 124-5 notes
16. *ibid*, 292-3 & notes
17. Soames, *ibid* 122/3 & *passim*
18. C.A. Wheeler, *Sportsascrapiana*, iv – *see* letter from John Ford of 17 July 1968 in University of Reading Archives
19. Soames, *ibid* 147-8
20. Flintshire D/IP/403 & D/IP/269
21. *ibid* D/IP/269
22. *ibid* D/IP/379 29 Dec 1813
23. *ibid* 31 Dec 1813
24. *ibid* [early Jan 1814]
25. *ibid* 9 Jun 1814
26. *ibid* 14 Jun 1814
27. *ibid*
28. *ibid* D/IP/403 30 Jan 1815
29. *ibid*
30. *ibid* D/IP/369 30 Nov 1815
31. It has not been noticed previously that Farquhar was the man who later bought Fonthill
32. Flintshire D/IP/369 19 Feb 1816 & D/IP364
33. *ibid* D/IP/369 17 Mar 1817
34. *ibid* D/IP/269 29 May 1817
35. A Catalogue of the Sale by Mr Evans of 26 Pall Mall, marked up with the sale prices and buyers' names is held in the University of Reading Archives
36. Flintshire D/IP/379 18 Oct 1821
37. Flintshire D/IP/379 24 Aug 1818 & 21 Dec 1819
38. *ibid* D/IP/379, letter of 21 Dec 1819 ; Soames, *ibid* 203-4
39. *ibid* D/IP/379
40. *ibid* D/IP/269 19 Oct 1820
41. *ibid* 13 Aug 1821 & D/IP/403 9 Aug 1821
42. *ibid* 20 Jun 1823
43. *ibid* D/IP/227 & see D/IP/373 – Legacy Receipt of 1841
44. BL Add Mss 61677 ff 112-18; 61678 f 184
45. Flintshire D/IP/245

Chapter Fifteen **Traveller and Sightseer**

1. Adams, *ibid* 222
2. Flintshire D/IP/269
3. Beresforde, *Woodforde* 228

4. Hickey, *ibid* vol 2 255-6
5. Flintshire D/IP/269
6. *ibid*
7. *ibid*
8. George, *Social & Political Satire in BM* 1803
9. George, *Hogarth to Cruikshank* 149
10. Hickey, *ibid* 289-91; Flintshire D/IP/269 records P.G.'s first visit to Margate in July 1794
11. Flintshire D/IP/269 20 Sep 1800 for P.G. at Mitchiner's
12. *ibid* 17 Sep 1800
13. *ibid* 31 Jul 1800
14. *ibid* 29 Sep 1801; Ford & Ford, *ibid* 136-7
15. Ford & Ford, *ibid* 48-50 & D/IP/269 2 Jun 1820
16. Flintshire D/IP/269 3 Sep 1801
17. *ibid* 9 Sep 1805
18. *D.N.B.*
19. Flintshire D/IP/269 30 Aug 1807
20. *ibid* 9 Sep 1805
21. *ibid* 31 Aug 1807
22. *ibid* 8 Apr 1795
23. *ibid* 4 Jun 1821
24. *ibid* 17 Sep 1795
25. *ibid* 24 Feb 1809
26. *ibid* 31 Dec 1808
27. *ibid*
28. *ibid* 21 Sep 1802

Chapter Sixteen **The Regency Theatre**

1. Iain Macintosh (ed) *The Georgian Playhouse, passim* & George, *Hogarth to Cruikshank* 107-12 & 203-5
2. Flintshire D/IP269
3. *ibid, passim*
4. George, *Hogarth to Cruikshank* 111-2 & George, *Social & Political Satires* vol VIII, *passim*
5. Flintshire D/IP/269
6. *ibid, passim*
7. *ibid* 6 Nov 1812
8. An excellent decription of the life of a touring actor is given in A. Aspinall (ed), *Mrs Jordan & her family – the unpublished letters of Dorothy Jordan to the Duke of Clarence.* She mentions performing in Richmond, Bath, Brighton, Cheltenham, Margate etc.
9. Macintosh, *ibid*, Section X
10. Holmes, *Coleridge: Darker Reflections* 335-38
11. *ibid* 330-2
12. Flintshire D/IP/269
13. George, *Social & Political Satires,* vol VIII Print 10172. A Biography of Carlo appeared in 1804
13a. Harold Rosenthal, *Two Centuries of Opera at Covent Garden* 20
14. *see* Chapter eighteen
15. George, *ibid*
16. Flintshire D/IP/269
17. Farington, *ibid* Vol IV 1341
18. George, *ibid*
19. *see Public Characters*
20. Alexander, *ibid* 271-2
21. Angelo, *ibid* v II 128
22. *D.N.B.*

23. Farington, *ibid,* vol IV 1341
24. George, *Social & Political Satires* vol VIII print 9086
25. Flintshire D/IP/269
26. George, *ibid* vol VIII print 9086
27. Farington, *ibid* vol IV 1522
28. Rosenthal, *ibid*

There are excellent biographical sketches in *Public Characters* 1798-1809 of the following impressarios and performers who appear in Philip Godsal's Diaries – Mrs Abington, Mrs Billington, John Braham, Thomas Harris, Captain Morris, Mrs Robinson & R.B. Sheridan. They and others also appear in the *D.N.B.*
See also Bibliography – Supra

Chapter Seventeen **A Most Clubbable Man**

1. Archives of Royal Society of Arts
2. Fintshire D/IP/269 25 Jun 1800
3. *see* Chapter Ten and Flintshire D/IP/269 21 Feb 1799
4. Flintsire D/IP/269 2 Feb 1796 when P.G. became a member
5. *ibid* 20Apr 1801
6. *ibid* 20 May 1801
7. *ibid* 29 Nov 1808
8. *ibid* 31 Jan 1804
9. *ibid* 11Feb 1805
10. *ibid* 28 Mar 1808
12. *ibid* 7 Apr 1813
13. *ibid* 2 Jan 1813 and attended the Committee meeting with 10 members eight days later when Moira took his formal leave
14. John Wombwell joined the L.H.V. on 13 May 1795
15. Flintshire D/IP/269, *passim*
16. *see* Gillray's print of 16 Jun 1797 *Homer Singing his Verses to the Greeks*
17. Flintshire D/IP/269 17 Aug 1803; Angelo notes (vol 1 207) that the L.H.V. was particularly noted for its horses which could not be surpassed in Europe'
18. *see* Chapter Nine
19. Flintshire D/IP/269 28 Jan 1805
22. *ibid* 12 Jan 1807 *& passim* 1807-8
23. *ibid*

Chapter Eighteen **Gentleman's Dress**

1. Diana Donald, *Followers of Fashion* 13
2. George, *Hogarth to Cruikshank* 138-9
3. *Repository of the Arts etc* April 1810
4. Flintshire D/IP/373, invoice dated '1814'
5. *ibid* D/IP/269 21 Feb 1818
6. Donald, *ibid* 72

Chapter Nineteen **Regency Interiors**

1. *see* Clive Wainwright, *Romantic Interiors; the British Collector at Home, passim.* However, in a private letter to the present author, Lucy Wood of the Victoria and Albert Museum having read this chapter in draft, noted: It would seem that 'Godsal's residences were not decorated as romantic interiors in the sense that this is normally understood. The presence of a few antiquities did not add up to a romantic interior; that was

more to do with the way such pieces were displayed, and usually a strong emphasis on medieval and/or British subjects even if mixed up with classical antiquities. Godsal's interiors sound simply like those of a well educated man of his time – paticularty well educated in the visual arts'.

2. *Carlton House, the Past Glories of George IV's Palace, passim*
3. Flintshire D/IP/269 18 Apr 1792; 8 Nov 1817; 5 Jan 1818 & 4 May 1818
4. Letter from Lucy Wood, dated 16 January 2003
5. Flintshire D/IP/269 22 Mar 1792
6. *ibid* 7 May
7. *ibid*, paid in three instalments – 20 Aug 1805, 20 Nov 1805 & 20 Feb 1806
8. *ibid*
9. *ibid* 29 Jan 1818
10. *ibid* 1803, 1805 & 1806
11. *ibid* 25 Jan & 13 Feb 1819
12. *ibid*
13. *ibid* 14 Jan 1790
14. This painting has only recently come on the market and has been bought by a private collector (2004)
15. In the collection of Philip Godsal, Esq
16. *ibid* & 16a D/IP/269 9 Jun 1802 – P.G. 'paid Mr A. Pope £22.19s.0d for this minature picture & for Sunday's tickets'
17. Flintshire D/IP/269 27 Jan 1813
18. *ibid* D/IP/350 12 Jan & 8 Jun 1791
19. *ibid* D/IP/269
20. *ibid* D/IP/269 16 Aug 1806
21. *ibid* 30 Mar & 2 Dec 1789
22. *ibid* 19 Sep & 7 Dec 1803
23. *ibid* 11 & 20 Nov 1823
24. *ibid* 6 Jul 1825
25. *ibid* 5 Mar 1793
26. *ibid* 21 Mar 1808 – 15 nov 1812
27. *ibid* 1 Jan 1813
28. *ibid* 9 Jun 1806
29. *ibid* 21 nov 1806
30. *ibid* D/IP/373 5 Mar 1806 *& passim* to 1814
31. *ibid* D/IP/269
32. Invoice dated 1 May 1818
33. Flintshire D/IP/269 12 Mar 1802
34. *ibid*
35. *ibid*
36. *ibid*
37. Flintshire D/IP/269 29 Nov 1800
38. *ibid* 5 Nov 1789
39. *ibid* 11 Jan 1805
40. *ibid* 25 Apr 1806
41. *ibid* 14 Jun 1793
42. Carlton House, *ibid* 149-50
43. Many of his books remain in the library at Iscoyd Place
44. Flintshire D/IP/269 15 Apr 1817
45. But *see* reference No 1 in present chapter for *caveat*
46. Flintshire D/IP/269 28 Aug 1823

Chapter Twenty **Investment Portfolio**

1. John Ehrman, *The Younger Pitt* 403. Godsal's investment was made on 30 Apr 1792

2. Uglow, *ibid* 280-86
3. Flintshire D/IP/212, letter of 21 Aug 1813
4. *ibid* 15 Sep 1795
5. *see also* Seymour's son dismissive letter of 10 Sep 1823 (*ibid* D/IP/269 10 Sep 1823)
6. *ibid* D/IIP/212 24 Nov 1823
7. *ibid* 7 Oct 1823
8. *ibid*
9. *ibid* D/IP/211 memorandum of 3 Aug 1797
10. This matter dragged on – *see ibid* D/IP/212 14 Jul 1803
11. *ibid* D/IP/211 12 Oct 1818
12. *ibid* D/IP/269 18 Apr 1804
13. *ibid* 4 Jul 1806
14. *ibid* 4 May 1821
15. *ibid* D/IP/406
16. *ibid* D/IP/227
17. *ibid* D/IP/406 & D/IP/277
18. *ibid* D/IP/269 1st payment 23 May 1823 – 10th payment 14 Mar 1825
19. *ibid* D/IP/406 & D/IP/227
20. *ibid* D/IP/406
21. *ibid* D/IP/269 22 May 1810
22. *ibid* D/IP/269 invested on 23 Jun & 11 Oct 1810; abandoned on 11 Jan 1814
23. *ibid* D/IP/406
24. *ibid*
25, *ibid* D/IP/227
26. *ibid* D/IP/269 23 Mar 1807
27. *ibid* 24 Jan 1805
28, *ibid* D/IP/227

Chapter Twenty-One **Charities and Taxes**

1. Flintshire D/IP/269
2. *see* Chapter Twenty-Five
3. Flintshire D/IP/192 7 Feb 1803
4. Weinreb & Hibbet, *The London Encyclopaedia* 709-10
5. *ibid* 515
6. *ibid*
7. Flintshire D/IP/444
8. *ibid* D/IP/269 10 Jan 1802, P.G. had made his donation of £50 on 1 Oct 1801
9. *ibid* 7 Jul 1817
10. *ibid* 25 mar 1820
11. *ibid* 1818
12. *ibid, passim*
13. *ibid* D/IP/356 3 Feb 1802

Chapter Twenty-Two **Maiden Aunt**

1. Flintshire D/IP/289 receipt of 7 Aug 1790
2. *ibid* D/IP/269 12 Jul 1806
3. *ibis* D/IP/372 12 Aug 1806 & D/IP/2890
4. *ibid* D/IP/269 9 Aug 1812
5. *ibid* D/IP/235 letter of 22 Nov 1813
6. *ibid*
7. *ibid*
8. Flintshire D/IP/235 letter of 21 Apr 1816
9. *ibid* letter of 25 Apr 1816

10. *ibid*
11. *ibid*
12. *ibid* 3 May 1816
13. *ibid* D/IP/384
14. *ibid*
15. *ibid* D/IP/236 letter of 1 Oct 1818
16. *ibid* letter of 3 Jan 1819
17. *ibid* D/IP/384 29 Oct 1819 *et seq*
18. *ibid*
19. *ibid* D/IP/238 letter of 12 Dec 1821
20. *ibid* D/IP/289 Agreement dated 7 Aug 1821
21. *ibid* D/IP/238 letter of 11 Jun 1822
22. *ibid* D/IP/240 letter of 12 Jun 1822
23. *ibid* D/IP/238 letter of 14 Jun 1822
24. *ibid* D/IP/239 letters of 21 & 22 Jun 1822
25. *ibid* D/IP/289
26. *ibid* D/IP/239 letter of 23 Jun 1822
27. *ibid* D/IP/240 letter of 30 Jun 1822
28. *ibid* D/IP/237, *passim*
29. *ibid* D/IP/238 3 Jul 1824

Chapter Twenty-Three **Cheltenham Land and Properties**

1. Flintshire D/IP/269 11 Oct 1806
2. Gloucester County Record Office (G.C.R.O.) D855 M21 189
3. *ibid* D855 M21 189
4. Flintshire D/IP/269 2 Aug 1808
5. *ibid* 19 Sep 1808
6. *ibid* 6 Apr 1809
7. *ibid* 21 & 22 Jun 1809
8. *ibid*
9. G.C.R.O. D855 M23 125
10. *ibid* D855 M23 125
11. G.C.R.O. D855 M24
12. Flintshire D/IP/265 19 oct 1810 & D/IP/269 19 Oct 1810
13. *ibid* D/IP/184 Memorandum to solicitor of Sep 1811 & D/IP/269 20 Sep 1811
14. *ibid* D/IP/183 letter of 13 Nov 1812
15. *ibid* D/IP/269 *passim*
16. *ibid* D/IP/183 letter of 21 Dec 1813
17. *ibid* letter of 23 Dec 1813
18. *ibid* letters of 23 Dec 1813 & 3 Jan 1814
19. *ibid* letter of 10 Jan 1814
20. *ibid* [Feb 1814]
21. *ibid* letter of 26 Apr 1814
22. G.C.R.O. D855 M25 5, 102
23. Flintshire D/IP/183 [nd]
24. *ibid* 7 May 1814
25. *ibid* D/IP/269 19 May 1814
26. G.C.R.O. D855 M25 102; Flintshire D/IP/183 Memorandum of Agreement 12 Sep 1814
27. *see* ground plans Flintshire D/IP/418 & 178
28. *ibid* D/IP/183 20 Jun 1814
29. *ibid* D/IP/269 31 Oct 1816
30. *ibid* 24 Jun 1817
31. *ibid* D/IP/356
32. Flintshire D/IP/356
33. *ibid* D/IP/354
34. *ibid* D/IP/356 9 Seo 1819

35. *ibid* D/IP/178 Gwinnett & Newman bill
36. *ibid* D/IP/356
37. *ibid* D/IP/418
38. *ibid* letter to Seymour [solicitor] 22 Feb 1822
39. *ibid* D/IP/356
40. *ibid* Gwinnett & Newman bill
41. *ibid* D/IP/9
42. *ibid* D/IP/178
43. *ibid* D/IP/269 10 Jun 1825
44. *ibid* D/IP/178
45. *ibid*
46. *ibid* D/IP/269

Chapter Twenty-Four **Life in Regency Cheltenham**

1. Flintshire D/IP/420
2. *ibid* D/IP/269 31 Aug 1814
3. *ibid* 2 Aug 1815
4. *ibid* D/IP/235 letter of 31 July 1816
5. *ibid* D/IP/269 3 Oct 1821
6. *ibid* 19 Jan 1825
7. *ibid* 13 Nov 1820
8. *ibid* 10 Jun 1819
9. *ibid* 4 May 1825
10. *ibid* 7 Jun 1819
11. *ibid* 12 Aug 1823
12. His solicitor Evan Foulkes
13. Flintshire D/IP/269 23 Aug 1821
14. *ibid* 25 Nov 1823
15. *ibid* 11 Feb 1815
16. *ibid* 21 Sep 1815
17. *ibid* 19 Apr 1824 & 7 Jan 1825
18. *ibid* D/IP/194
19. *ibid* D/IP/269 11 Apr 1823
20. *ibid* 9 Dec 1822
21. *ibid* 19 May & 10 Aug 1825
22. *ibid* 4 JUN 1825
23. *ibid* 9 Mar 1826
24. *ibid* D/IP/195

Chapter Twenty-Five **The Making of a Regency Garden**

The principal source of information in this chapter is the Diary of Philip Godsal, Flintshire D/IP/269 *passim* and all details not referenced below are drawn from the Diary

1. Philip Godsal himself used the term 'pleasure ground' to describe his own and other gardens
2. *see* Chapter Ten
3. *see* Chapter Fourteen
4. The copy of this rare and splendid book examined was that in the Lindley Library of the Royal Horticultural Society Library in Vincent Square
5. Brent Elliott, *Flora: an illustrated history of the Garden Flower*, introduction
6. Hill, *Eden* 1
7. Flintshire D/IP/269 13 Dec 1823
8. Hill, *ibid*, Preface
9. Flintshire D/IP/269 1798

10.   *ibid* 1826
11.   *ibid* D/IP/67 letter of 14 January 1826

Chapter Twenty-Six **Food and Drink**

The details quoted of Philip Godsal's purchases of food and drink are all drawn from his Diary, Flintshire D/IP/269

1.   Flintshire D/IP/269 20 Nov 1800 & 23 May 1801 – he bought a new 'kitchen range' for Oxford Street in 1811 at a cost of £35
2.   Reay Tannahill, *The Fine Art of Food*, 110
3.   *D.N.B.*
4.   Holmes, *Coleridge: darker reflections*
5.   Flintshire D/IP/269 22 Sep 1789
6.   *ibid* 15 Feb 1792
7.   *ibid* 1800 *passim*
8.   Holmes, *ibid*
9.   Flintshire D/IP/269 4 June 1804

Chapter Twenty-Seven **Sickness and Health**

1.   Flintshire D/IP/269 8 Feb 1790
2.   *ibid* 29 Oct 1795
3.   *ibid* 15 Feb 1808
4.   *ibid* 2 Apr & 21 Apr 1800
5.   *ibid* 24 Oct 1803
6.   *ibid* 10 Sep 1811
7.   *ibid* 1824
8.   *ibid* 11 Oct 1815
9.   *ibid* 19 May 1814
10.   Sir George Clark, *The Royal College of Physicians* v2 623-4
11.   *D.N.B.*
12.   Blake & Sampson, *A Cheltenham Companion*
13.   Clark, *ibid passim*
14.   Porter, *Doctor of Society*
15.   George, *Hogarth to Cruikshank* 92
16.   Porter, *ibid*
17.   Flintshire D/IP/269
18.   *ibid*
19.   *ibid* D/IP/235 letter of 31 Jul 1816
20.   Flintshire D/IP/269 10 May 1817

21.   *ibid* 24 Jan 1818
22.   *D.N.B.*
23.   Flintshire D/IP/269 22 Apr 1818
24.   *ibid*
25.   *ibid* 29 Jul 1818 & 23 Feb 1819
26.   *ibid* 3 Aug 1818
27.   *D.N.B.*
28.   Flintshire D/IP/269 27 Aug 1818
29.   Claire Tomalin, *Samuel Pepys: the unequalled self* 62
30.   Flintshire D/IP/269 29 Aug 1818
31.   *ibid* 24 Oct 1818
32.   *ibid* D/IP/236 letter of 1 Oct 1818
32a *ibid* D/IP/677
33.   *ibid* D/IP/269 22 Dec 1818
34.   *ibid* D/IP/236 3 Jan 1819
35.   *ibid* D/IP/269 14 Jan 1819
36.   *ibid* D/IP/287
37.   *ibid* D/IP/269
38.   *ibid* D/IP/384

Chapter Twenty-Eight **Death and Legacy**

1.   Flinthire D/IP/269 27 Jul 1803
2.   *ibid* D/IP/286 letter of 2 Aug 1818
3.   undated letter [Jan 1819] and letter of 24 Jan 1819
4.   *ibid* letter of 31 May 1819
5.   *ibid* D/IP/269
6.   *ibid* D/IP/286 letter of 4 Feb 1819
7.   *ibid*
8.   *ibid* D/IP/272
9.   ibid D/IP/388 The four page itemised bill is dated 20 April and provides the detail used in this chapter
10.   *ibid*
11.   *ibid* D/IP/226 14 Apr 1818
12.   *ibid* D/IP/365 3 Jun 1826
13.   *ibid* D/IP/375 letter of 10 July 1824
14.   *ibid* D/IP/227
15.   *ibid*
16.   *see* Chapter Twelve & Flintshire D/IIP/365 for Susannah's marriage settlement
17.   *ibid* D/IP/375 letter of 9 July 1824
18.   *ibid* D/IP/373 Legacy Receipt dated 5 July 1841

coaches which were Godsal's concern.

The various London Directories of the period – Lowndes, Andrew's, Kent's, Holden's and the Universal British Directory have listings of coachmakers.

Much the most important modern work of scholarship is the article by Rudolf Wackernagel in *Furniture History' the Journal of the Furniture History Society*, vol xxxi 1995 'Carlton house Mews: The State Coach of the Prince of Wales & of the King of Hanover: a study of the late eighteenth century 'mystery' of coach building'.

The records of the Honorable Company of Coachmakers and Loriners were destroyed in a direct hit on their Livery Hall during the second World War. The Guildhall Library however has records of Masters and Apprentices (MS 5643) and these records have provided some information on Godsal's business.

A history of the Worshipful Company of Coachmakers & Coach harness makers 1677-1977, edited by Harold Nockolds (1977) is a useful livery company history but of limited value to the student of the business of coachmaking.

The Irish Lord Chancellor's Coach, designed by Ackermann and built by Godsal is housed in the National Museum of Ireland, Newbridge House, Dublin and an excellent article on it, and the Irish coachmaking industry, by W.G. Strickland was published in *The Royal Society of Antiquaries of Ireland, X 1919*. There is also a description with photographs in John Cornforth, 'Coaching forth a masterpiece' in *Country Life* on 21 January 1993.

There is a model of the coach in the Lady Lever Gallery, Port Sunlight and a published catalogue of the model by Lucy Wood.

The most informative sources are W.B. Adams, *English Pleasure Carriages* (1837), reprinted 1971. Wm Felton, *A Treatise on Carriages* (1794-8), reprinted Rudolph Ackermann, Fourteen Books of *Fashionable Carriages* (1791- 1820).

Other books etc consulted include
Two articles by A.L. Humphries in *Notes & Queries* on 18/10/1941 and 25/10 /1941.
Marilyn Watney, *The Elegant Carriage* (1961)
John Ford, *Ackermann; the business of Art* (1983)
Michael Snodin, 'Charles & Edward Crace & Rococo Coach Painting' in *The Craces: Royal Decorators 1768-1899* ed Megan Aldrich (1990).
John Copeland, *Roads & their Traffic* (1968).
Ian McNeil, *Joseph Bramah: a century of invention 1749-1851*, (1968) (chapter on 'Coaching Comforts').
Tom Ryder, 'Carriage Designers, a review of the part played by

a few talented individuals in the evolution of carriages' in *Carriage Journal* XXVII, No 4 (1990).
George Athelstan Krupp, *History of Coaches* (1877).
Ralph Strauss, *Carriages and Coaches* (1912).
H. Reader Lack (ed), *Patents for Inventions, Abridgements or Specifications relating to Carriages & other vehicles for common roads 1625-1866* (1880).
W.C. Blews, *Brighton Coaches* (1894). The most scholarly of the many coaching books and less restricted in subject matter than its title suggests.

The Honorable East India Company

Godsal's business was financed by two major loans by members of the East India Company, John Michie, a London wine merchant and one of the Directors of the Honorable East India Company and John Wombwell, the Accountant for the Company in Oudh and paymaster of the British soldiers serving in that province. Michie's papers are in the Booth Collection in the Westminster Archives office.

Information about Wombwell is in the Records of the East India company which were published as *Fort William – India House Correspondence*, vols IX, XIII & XV, Calcutta 1959.

George Forrest (ed), *Selections from the Letters, Dispatches & other State Papers in the Foreign Department of the Government of India 1772-1785*, vol 3, 1890.
Keith Feiling, *Warren Hastings,* 1954 has interesting information on Wombwell's early career.

Sydney Grier (ed), *The Letters of Warren Hastings to his wife*, 1905 has other information. Wombwell appears in two paintings by Johann Zoffany including the well known, Colonel Mordaunt's Cock Match.

Michael Fisher (ed), *The Travels of Dean Mahomed*, University of California (1997) has fascinating detail of Lucknow and Oude when Wombwell was a resident.

Godsal invested in the trading cargo of at least two East Indiamen under the command of Captain James Urmston. Information about Captain Urmston is in Hickey's Memoirs and in the *Fort William – India House correspondence & the Select Letters* etc edited by Forrest. Sir Evan Cotton, *East Indiamen: the East India Company Maritime Service* (1949) is excellent on Urmston and the trade in general.

There is information in Hickey's *Memoirs* about Richard Sullivan who sponsored Philip Lake Godsal for membership of the Royal Institution.

Interior Decoration

Godsal employed the leading contemporary designer, craftsmen and manufacturers employed by the Prince of Wales

at Carlton House and the Royal Pavilion Brighton, the Craces, Fricker & Henderson, Robson & Hale, Ashlin & Colling, Benjamin Vulliamy. There is excellent detail on all of these in:
Henry Roberts, *A History of the Royal Pavilion* (1939).
John Dinkel, *The Royal Pavilion Brighton* (1983).
Carlton House: the past glories of George IV's palace (1991).
The following works have also been consulted:
Megan Aldrich (ed), *The Craces: Royal Decorators* (1990).
Clive Wainwright, *The Romantic Interior: The British Collector at Home* 1750-1830 (1989).
Charles Saumurez Smith, *Eighteenth Century Decoration & Design: the Domestic Interior in England* (1993).
John Fowler & John Cornforth, *English Decoration in the Eighteenth Century* (1974).
Celina Fox (editor) *London World City 1800-1840* (1992) is, as always, of the greatest use.

Gardens
Thomas Hill, *Eden: or a complete body of gardening* (1757).
Brent Elliott, *Flora: an illustrated history of the garden flower* (2001).

The Theatre
Two American publications proved invaluable in tracing productions witnessed by Godsal and actors seen.
The London Stage 1776-1800 edited by Charles Beecher Hogan (1968).
A Biographical Dictionary of Actors, Actresses, Musicians, Dancers, Managers &c 1660-1800 by Highfill, Burnim & Langhams (1973-).
Also Iain Macintosh (ed), *The Georgian Playhouse: Actors, Artists, Audiences & Architecture*, the Catalogue of an Exhibition (1975).
Harold Rosenthal, *Two Centuries of Opera at Covent Garden* (1958).
Ian Macintosh, 'Departing Glories of the British Theatre' in *London World City* (1992).
Public Characters 1798-1809, 10 vols.
A. Aspinall (ed), *Mrs Jordan & her family: unpublished letters from Dorothy Jordan to the Duke of Clarence* (1951). *D.N.B.*

The Royal Academy
David Solkin (ed), *Art on the line: the Royal Academy exhibitions at Somerset House 1780-1836*, the Catalogue of an Exhibition (2001).

Medical Matters
No fewer than five of the medical men consulted by Godsal merit articles in the *D.N.B.*
Other books providing useful information were:
Roy Porter, *Doctor of Society: Thomas Beddoes and the sick trade in late enlightenment England* (1992).
Roy Porter (ed), *Patients & Practitioners: lay perceptions of medicine in pre-industrial society* (1985).
Roy & Dorothy Porter, *Patients' Progress* (1989).
G.N. Clark, *The Royal College of Physicians*, vol II (1966).
M.D. George, *Hogarth to Cruikshank: Social Change in Graphic Satire* (1967).

Volunteer Regiments
Austin Gee, *The British Volunteer Movement 1794-1814* (2003).

Fashion
Ackermann's *Repository of Arts etc* 1810.
M.D. George, *Hogarth to Cruikshank: Social Change in Graphic Satire* (1967).
London World City 1800-1840 (1992).
Diana Donald (ed), *Followers of Fashion: Graphic Satires from the Georgian period*, the catalogue of an exhibition (2002).

General Histories
The two volumes by J. Steven Watson and L. Woodward in the Oxford History of England series have been consulted; also two old favourites, Halévy's *England in 1815* and *The Liberal Awakening* which always seem to provide the information I seek.

Index

Numbers in italics refer to illustratons. PG refers to Philip Godsal. PLG refers to Philip Lake Godsal.